THE ORIGINS OF AMERICAN PUBLIC FINANCE

Recent Titles in
Contributions in Economics and Economic History

Finance and World Order: Financial Fragility, Systemic Risk, and Transnational Regimes
Adriano Lucatelli

Space and Transport in the World-System
Paul S. Ciccantell and Stephen G. Bunker, editors

Chinese Maritime Activities and Socioeconomic Development, c.2100 B.C.–1900 A.D.
Gang Deng

Sino-American Economic Relations, 1944–1949
C. X. George Wei

Growth and Variability in State Tax Revenue: An Anatomy of State Fiscal Crises
Randall G. Holcombe and Russell S. Sobel

Poverty, Female-Headed Households, and Sustainable Economic Development
Nerina Vecchio and Kartik C. Roy

The Causes of the 1929 Stock Market Crash: The Speculative Orgy or a New Era
Harold Bierman, Jr.

The Role of Precious Metals in European Economic Development: From Roman Times to the Eve of the Industrial Revolution
S.M.H. Bozorgnia

Energy and Organization: Growth and Distribution Reexamined
Bernard C. Beaudreau

Silver and Gold: The Political Economy of International Monetary Conferences, 1867–1892
Steven P. Reti

Inequality and Equity: Economics of Greed, Politics of Envy, Ethics of Equality
Charles T. Stewart, Jr.

Democracy in Desperation: The Depression of 1893
Douglas Steeples and David O. Whitten

THE ORIGINS OF AMERICAN PUBLIC FINANCE

Debates over Money, Debt, and Taxes in the Constitutional Era, 1776–1836

Donald R. Stabile

Contributions in Economics and Economic History, Number 198
David O. Whitten, Series Adviser

GREENWOOD PRESS
Westport, Connecticut • London

Library of Congress Cataloging-in-Publication Data

Stabile, Donald.
     The origins of American public finance : debates over money, debt,
and taxes in the Constitutional era, 1776–1836 / Donald R. Stabile ;
foreword by David O. Whitten.
        p. cm. — (Contributions in economics and economic history,
ISSN 0084–9235 ; no. 198)
     Includes bibliographical references and index.
     ISBN 0–313–30754–7 (alk. paper)
     1. Finance, Public—United States—History—18th century.
2. Finance, Public—United States—History—19th century.
I. Title. II. Series
HJ247.S73 1998
336.73—dc21   98–11163

British Library Cataloguing in Publication Data is available.

Library of Congress Catalog Card Number: 98–11163
ISBN: 0–313–30754–7
ISSN: 0084–9235

First published in 1998

Greenwood Press, 88 Post Road West, Westport, CT 06881
An imprint of Greenwood Publishing Group, Inc.

Printed in the United States of America

CONTENTS

FOREWORD

"Pledging to tame 'an all-powerful, unaccountable and often downright tone-deaf' Internal Revenue Service, President Clinton Friday [October 10, 1997] unveiled a plan to reform the agency . . . 'The IRS should be above reproach. Americans who work hard and pay their taxes, deserve to be treated fairly. . . . Abuse or bullying or callousness by officials of our government are unacceptable whenever and wherever they occur. If they occur once, it's once too many. But especially in connection with the IRS, it is important that they be rooted out.' "[1]

Two centuries before President Bill Clinton addressed the politically sensitive national tax collector's misuse of the taxpaying American public, the first secretary of the treasury, Alexander Hamilton, warned "that those citizens upon whom it [the national tax collection system] is immediately to operate, be secured from every species of injury by the misconduct of the officers to be employed."[2] Hamilton knew his fellow Americans and their distaste for taxes. He had served in the Continental army and as an aide to General Washington and had fought with distinction, especially at Yorktown. Hamilton knew the American War of Independence was a manifestation of the broader, more glorious American revolution rooted in organized rebellion against the British Revenue Act of 1764 (popularly known as the Sugar Act, the law reduced the tax on sugar and molasses imported into Britain's American colonies from non-British sources but tightened enforcement) the Stamp Act of 1765, the Townshend duties, and the Tea Act of 1773—Parliamentary measures that Americans, with their proclivity for truncating broad conflicts into slogans, aggregated into "taxation without representation."

Hamilton was the architect of American public finance. He founded and organized the Treasury Department and launched the federally chartered joint-stock Bank of the United States as the fiscal agent of government. The first secretary was not on hand to defend his financial edifice against those who would demolish it—Hamilton died at the hands of Aaron Burr in a duel fought on the sands of Weehawken, New Jersey, July 11, 1804—but he anticipated a continuation of the opposition he had faced during its construction. American pertinacity that had prevailed in a war for independence waged against a vastly superior foe was directed at the secretary, undermining collection of his taxes to support and retire the public debt incurred by the Confederation government and the states in the course of war. The taxes that spurred the War of Independence had been levied to help pay the large national debt Great Britain had accumulated in the Seven Years' War—the French and Indian War in the colonies. Hamilton's plan of taxes, similarly sparked by war debt, also triggered a clash of arms, the Whiskey Rebellion (1791–94). That rebellion, like Shays' (1786–87) and Fries' (1798–99), served notice that while Americans might endure the yoke of taxes, they would yet toil to fling it off.

How did Americans channel their aversion to taxes, design and ratify a constitution, and create a federal government empowered to levy and collect taxes? How did officials inhibit conflict while establishing the edifice of federal bureaucracy? How has that government prevailed in the face of concerted dissension? These are questions addressed by Donald R. Stabile in *The Origins of American Public Finance: Debates Over Money, Debt, and Taxes in the Constitutional Era, 1776– 1836.* Stabile, professor of economics at St. Mary's College of Maryland, associate editor (economics), *Business Library Review,* author of *Work and Welfare: The Social Costs of Labor in the History of Economic Thought,*[3] and coauthor of *The Public Debt of the United States: An Historical Perspective, 1775–1990,*[4] is exceptionally prepared to set out and examine the people, events, and forces that produced the United States and an operating system to direct it: a federal government born of tension between citizens who esteemed it essential for maintaining the principles that had driven Americans to break from Great Britain and citizens who judged it inimical to those very principles. Stabile brings to bear his intimate acquaintance with the writings of the English classical economists, especially Adam Smith and David Hume, as he explains how England spawned American views of government, fueled the colonists' drive for independence, and influenced U.S. tax and debt policies.

The Origins of American Public Finance extends beyond historical analysis to the underpinnings of contemporary federal issues. The actors have changed, but 1990s political battles are much like their two-centuries-old antecedents. In the 1790s Alexander Hamilton, an appointed official, was the financial wizard feared and despised for his power to influence the financial arena. In the 1990s newspapers report tremors in the New York Stock Exchange (NYSE) after a speech by Federal Reserve chair Alan Greenspan, an appointed official criticized for holding too much power. The Bank of the United States (BUS) was the hated central monetary authority of the 1790s. The BUS is a historical footnote in the 1990s, but the Federal Reserve System has assumed its role as a target of abuse and blame.

Politicians in the 1790s argued over direct and indirect taxation and the constitutionality of each; in the 1990s they debate the merits of a national sales tax over the progressive income tax. Secretary Hamilton assured progress toward paying off the national debt (a surplus in the federal budget), while his political opponents insisted that the debt was not shrinking but growing (a deficit in the federal budget). President Clinton assures that the deficit is falling and that a surplus is in sight, while his political opponents insist that the deficit is not shrinking but increasing. Counting the same numbers for different conclusions is not a contemporary creation but an American diversion. Congressman Newt Gingrich calls for reduced government spending in the 1990s much as Congressman Albert Gallatin called for reduced government spending in the 1790s.

In 1800 John Adams, second president of the United States, lost his bid for a second term to Thomas Jefferson. The Adams presidency had heightened American patriotic fervor with celebrated successes by the U.S. Navy (with the support of the British Royal Navy) during the two-year undeclared naval war with France. Nevertheless, a policy of increased taxes to finance military spending contributed to Adams' election loss. In 1991 George Bush, forty-first president of the United States, lost his bid for a second term to William Clinton. The Bush presidency rekindled American patriotic fervor with a celebrated success by the U.S. armed forces (with the support of international allies) during the Persian Gulf War. Nevertheless, the call for increased taxes after a campaign promise of no new taxes ("read my lips") contributed to Bush's election loss.

Jefferson's victory over Adams reflected voters' discontent with the Federalists' (Washington and Adams were the only Federalist presidents) creation of a large, expensive central government that, at the expense of Congress, vested too much power in the executive. Of greater importance, that government ran on revenue from unpopular taxes. Jefferson reduced spending—the navy all but disappeared under the frugal oversight of Secretary of the Treasury Albert Gallatin—so that tariffs might provide the bulk of federal funding. Not quite two centuries later Democratic president Clinton (Jefferson's vice president was George Clinton) and a Republican Congress are busily dismantling the military machine and social welfare agencies so that taxes can be reduced. Clinton, like Jefferson, can adjust the fiscal machinery but dares not replace it. In Jefferson's words, "[W]e can pay off his [Hamilton's] debts in 15 years, but we can never get rid of his financial system."[5] Forty-two presidents have scratched their names on governmental machinery cast by Hamilton.

Even congressional efforts to draft a constitutional amendment requiring that federal budgets be balanced are reenactments of bipartisan battles waged 200 years ago. Jefferson wrote: "I wish it were possible to obtain a single amendment of our constitution . . . I mean an additional article, taking from the federal government the power of borrowing."[6]

Another contemporary political battle rooted in the constitutional era is protectionism in international trade. Nascent industrialists in the Northeast sought tariffs high enough to protect their factories from foreign, especially British, imports. Southern politicians recognized protectionism as subsidies to northern industry and contested increases in import duties, even threatening to secede from the Union.

International trade is as important to the nation in the 1990s as it was in the 1790s. Lines are drawn over what goods will be admitted to the American market and the reception of U.S. exports abroad. The North American Free Trade Agreement (NAFTA) is the center of conflict in the 1990s. Although states do not threaten to leave the Union, corporations move production facilities to the most accommodating city, state, or nation as trade agreements alter profitability.

The Origins of American Public Finance is not a history book but an explanation of the origins of constitutional debate alive in the United States at the end of the twentieth century. There are more combatants in 1990 than there were in 1790, and the communications media permit instant reporting of contemporary debate, but the underlying issues are the same as argued 200 years ago. Opponents of the Bank of the United States have as counterparts modern-day opponents of the Federal Reserve System. Critics of internal taxes in the 1790s are replaced by critics of the modern-day income tax. Federal spending remains as hotly contested as ever. Stabile's careful analysis of the historical antecedents of conflict over money, debt, and taxes brings modern economic controversy into focus.

David O. Whitten

NOTES

1. Steven Tomma, "Clinton's IRS Reform Doesn't Pacify Congress," *Columbus (Georgia) Ledger-Enquirer* (October 11, 1997): p. A4.

2. Alexander Hamilton, First Report on the Public Credit, reprinted in Samuel McKee, Jr., ed., *Alexander Hamilton's Papers on Public Credit, Commerce, and Finance*, American Heritage Series, ed. Oskar Piest, no. 18 (New York: Liberal Arts Press, 1957), p. 43.

3. Donald R. Stabile, *Work and Welfare: The Social Costs of Labor in the History of Economic Thought* (Westport, CT: Greenwood Press, 1996).

4. Donald R. Stabile and Jeffrey A. Cantor, *The Public Debt of the United States: An Historical Perspective, 1775-1990* (New York: Praeger, 1991).

5. Cited in Sidney Ratner, *Taxation and Democracy in America* (New York: John Wiley and Sons, 1967), p. 12.

6. Cited in James D. Savage, *Balanced Budgets and American Politics* (Ithaca, NY: Cornell University Press, 1988), p. 106.

PREFACE

At the outset I want to acknowledge a bias in this book. Like Justice Oliver Wendell Holmes, Jr., I believe that taxes are the price we pay for civilization. Scoffers might insist that the price has become too high. It seems to me, however, that a society affluent enough to bestow multimillion-dollar incomes on entertainment and sports celebrities can afford to pay its taxes. My bias is to think that since citizens of the United States want government programs, they should be willing to pay for them with taxes.

Yes, I pay my fair share of taxes. As a single person with no home mortgage deduction, I probably pay more than my fair share. Although I wish the process of calculating those taxes were simpler, I do not mind paying them. In my life I have received many benefits from taxes. What is most important, I was educated at public schools and at land grant universities where taxpayers subsidized my tuition. I would not be the person I am, could not write this book, without the help of those taxpayers, and I now acknowledge their support.

In addition, that education has brought me a good job and a comfortable income. As a result I am in sound financial shape, with money flowing into my tax-sheltered retirement plan and a separate investment account. In addition, thanks to the bull market, that plan and account have been increasing in value by more than I get paid for teaching economics. My latest projection is that when I retire, I will have more than enough money to support the modest lifestyle I have adopted.

Will I need to collect Social Security? It does not look like it. My projections have not included Social Security in my retirement plan. Will I take it? Yes, I will. As an economist I recognize how unpredictable events can offset careful planning. To give myself peace of mind, I am going to start collecting Social Security. No matter what happens to my retirement plan, I will have a steady source of income to protect me from the risks of life. To me, Social Security represents an insurance plan against those risks.

Now I know the Social Security system is in trouble and acknowledge that adding to that trouble is selfish of me if I do not need to. Here is what I am going to do in return for the insurance Social Security will give me. Each month in my retirement when my Social Security check comes, if my other income is sufficient for my needs, I will use that check to buy U.S. savings bonds. Those bonds will be placed in a separate place from my other assets, in, let us call it, a personal security account. In my last will and testament there will be a bequest of the contents of that account to the Social Security Trust Fund.

Having had peace of mind granted me by a guarantee of a minimum income, I am willing to give back the Social Security money I have not needed to use. I will do the same for any Medicare payments. After all, why should my estate be preserved and my heirs be enriched at the expense of taxpayers? I have been enriched enough at taxpayer expense, and in this small way I hope to repay taxpayers for the benefits they have provided me. My acknowledgments to them will be in something more than words.

My acknowledgment to others who have helped me on this book must remain in words, however. Andy Kozak read the entire manuscript several times and offered valuable comments and advice. Blu Putnam gave me the use of a laptop computer that came in very handy. Alice Caldwell furnished me a place to stay, food to eat, and good company while I was researching this project at the American Antiquarian Society. Laurie Hudicek compiled the bibliography and helped to prepare the manuscript. Larry Vote, acting provost at St. Mary's College of Maryland, provided funds for page preparation. David Whitten has offered me years of support and encouragement, heartening me with his reminders, through his words and through his example, that the scholar's life is a productive life. The benefits taxpayers have given me, as I hope this book attests, have not been entirely wasted.

Introduction: To Mortgage the Public Revenues

Popular opinion and some schools of legal theory tell us that in trying to understand how our national government and legal system operate, we should look to the original intent of the framers of the Constitution.[1] With public finance, however, constitutional scholars have offered little evidence of that original intent.

In the form with which it left the hands of the framers, the Constitution of the United States placed few restrictions on the taxing power of the federal government. All references to taxation were contained in Article I, dealing with the legislative branch. Section 7 provided that "all bills for raising revenue shall originate in the House of Representatives; but the Senate may propose or concur with amendments as on other bills." Section 8 gave Congress the power "to lay and collect taxes, duties, imposts and excises . . . but all duties, imposts and excises shall be uniform throughout the United States." Section 9 put two limits on Congress' power to tax: "No capitation, or other direct tax shall be laid, unless in proportion to the census or enumeration herein before directed to be taken," and "No tax or duty shall be laid on articles exported from any State."

Why was it necessary to spell out a taxing power for Congress and put its source with the House of Representatives? Of all the possible limits that could be placed on the taxing power of the federal government, why did the framers choose the particular ones that they delineated? Was the taxing power as controversial as other aspects of the Constitution when the framers were debating it? What other forms of public finance were permitted? Were there any methods of public finance that the Constitution banned?

These are a few of the questions about the beginnings of federal taxation that this book addresses by centering on the constitutional questions surrounding federal government financing in the period from 1776 to 1836. It is a study of how the need for a federal taxing power shaped the framing of the Constitution and how the Constitution and its implementation set forth limits on the methods of public finance. The focus of the study is on the efforts of the framers of the Constitution to establish a taxing power for the national government to avoid the use of money and debt that had financed the War of Independence. It examines the debates over the type of taxes the federal government levied during the first crucial years of the nation's history, when, after the passage of the Constitution, Federalists sought a broader tax base. It then describes the Jeffersonians' effort to limit taxes to tariffs, examines the testing of the tax system in the first national crisis of the War of 1812, and ends with Andrew Jackson's triumph of public finance, payment of the public debt in 1836.

The goal of the book is to chronicle the economic and political ideas expressed in the debate over public finance in the new nation. At the center of that debate was the issue of what powers of taxation the national government should have. As noted, the Constitution gave the power to tax to the government it established. The debate over that tax power, however, had been unfolding for most of the decade preceding the Constitutional Convention. Moreover, the debate continued during the convention, the ratification fight, and the next four decades. This book tells the story of that debate. While the original intent behind the Constitution regarding public finance was obscured by that debate, something can be said about the economic and political ideas that motivated the first generation of leaders in the United States when it came to government finance.

ECONOMICS, POLITICS, AND IDEAS

After the Constitution was drafted, its authors agreed in its Preamble that their intent was "to promote the general welfare." In the ensuing two centuries, theories of economic and political behavior developed to the point where the idea of the general welfare is found to be implausible. Instead, economic and political interpretations of human behavior now concentrate on how individuals act in their own interest or how they behave as exemplars of the interest of their socioeconomic class. Both of these explanations of human motivation are limited, however, as they emphasize economic or political gain as the only form of human motivation.

Human behavior can be more complicated than the search for individual or group gain in economics and politics. The story of public finance and the Constitution told in this book is based on a neglected system of political economy, dating from the last century. Practitioners of this political economy regarded humans as complex creatures whose behavior was influenced by a variety of factors in their social environment.[2] Economic and political interests of either an individual or class nature were part of any social environment, to be sure, but ideas that promoted principled behavior and an interest in the common good also had some powerful influences on human behavior.

From this approach, the question for political economy, then, is the extent to which social forces influence human action toward individual interest or whether or not those factors foster a conscious effort to promote the general welfare. In terms of this book, that question for political economy boils down to this: What did the individuals who made up the political leadership of the United States during the period under scrutiny see as the general welfare?

In matters of public finance, there was a clear consensus of what would promote the general welfare: payment of the public debt incurred during the War of Independence. No one suggested that the debt be repudiated; everyone agreed that it was good for the country to have the debt paid. The question was how to do it, and that was where conflict and compromise took place.

When the Founding Fathers formulated the Constitution, after considerable debate, they planned in general how the federal government would finance its spending; when they implemented the new rules in the first five decades of the federal government's existence, they disagreed greatly over what the rules meant. In those debates and disagreements, distinct individuals acted dissimilarly at different times. Sometimes they swapped votes, and other times they voted with vision, but enough of them voted with vision to place the government's finances on a sound basis.

The differing outlooks among American leaders during this period can be ascribed to a variety of influences. There were the economic division of rich versus poor, the geographic differences of big versus small states and North versus South, and the cultural difference of Anglophiles versus Francophiles. This book keys in on the difference between commercial versus agrarian attitudes concerning money, debt, and taxes.

The early debates over public finance took place in a period of rising commercial activity in England and in the United States and many ideas expressed in the debate reflected how commerce was changing social attitudes toward economic activity. Commerce, trade, and the banking and credit system that went with them were not well understood at this time, especially not by agrarians.

To be sure, in the United States where land had to be bought, cleared and put into production, the agrarian sector was always imbued with a commercial side. Still, the agrarian attitude toward debt and credit remained different from the view that prevailed in commerce. Agrarians might go into debt to buy and improve land; then their hope was to pay off the debt by profiting from the sale of the produce of the land or from the sale of the land itself. Debt was something agrarians rid themselves of when possible, for to be in debt was to be beholden to share their income with someone else. Whether or not agrarians got out of debt was not as important as having an ideal of being debt-free. They should be frugal until they reached that ideal. Agrarians, Herbert E. Sloan notes, "both needed and feared credit. Real debt—as opposed to advances intended to bridge the gap between purchases and the receipt of payment for a crop—was clearly to be avoided."[3]

From a commercial perspective, debt was just another tool of business, another way to keep goods circulating. Under a business system of money and banking, debt was simply a line of credit to be used when necessary and paid off when required, even if through additional debt. There was no stigma to being in debt if one was prudent about it. To be sure, it was better to be debt-free or at least able to keep up payments. The important point about borrowing was what was done with funds.

In the formulation of policies for public finance in the new government, each side would get a turn. The Federalist period would see the ascendancy of the commercial perspective championed by Alexander Hamilton, while the agrarian viewpoint would hold forth under Thomas Jefferson. The problem of public finance that both sides confronted, as this book's title suggests, was one of money, debt, and taxes and which of these was the system of public finance on which the nation's future would depend. By studying the ideas advanced and the actions taken by political and intellectual leaders in the United States during its first half century, this book shows how an intelligent body of public figures grappled with the issue of how to handle the federal government's basic need for revenue.

Since they were not unified in their approach to this basic need, the debates that they had over how to fund government spending give a picture of how they viewed the constitutional powers of the new government. In these debates, policies for establishing public credit and collecting taxes were at the center of a variety of issues regarding the overall philosophy of government. An activist government will have considerable financial requirements. Those with a commercial attitude, favoring an active government, were not troubled by relatively high taxes or a large government debt; they had to find ways to explain and justify higher taxes to voters or else rely on money or debt. As advocates of limited government action, agrarians wanted to keep the debt small and taxes low; they stressed the need to cut government budgets.

Given these differing views of government and finance, the debates over the Constitution were many, for more than a few contentious issues had to be resolved over the type of central government it proposed, how that government would relate to the states, and with what rights it would provide its citizens. Constitutional historians have studied the choices made on these issues and what compromises took place for those choices to be made. Regarding public finance, the key decision to be made related to the type of revenue system the new government would have. The Revolutionary War had been funded by paper money and debt; now the issue was whether or not there would be taxes. Those were the three options they saw themselves confronting, and it is to a consideration of the relative merits of each that we now turn.

PUBLIC FINANCE

Democratic governments in market economies face a subtle problem in managing their finances. As their economies develop and become more complex, the need for government programs grows greater. No matter how much we may decry the growth of wasteful spending in Washington, some of it, and more than in the past, is necessary. We all want the government to do more for us, even if we do not admit it.

Although this increase in government spending is popular, higher taxes to pay for it is not, because taxes impose a direct cost on voters. Taxes are not the only policy option for financing spending programs, however. Government can also finance its spending by printing money or by borrowing it, and, while these measures also exact a cost on voters, those costs are indirect.

When the government borrows money in financial markets, it sells bonds. This sale increases the supply of bonds in those markets. If the amount of money available for the purchase of bonds stays constant, the extra supply of bonds causes the price of bonds to decrease, inducing interest rates to rise. The rise of interest rates may be large or small, depending on how large an increase the extra bonds amount to and whether or not the money available to purchase bonds stays constant. Instead of paying taxes, individuals experience a cost from higher interest rates.

If the government chooses to print money and spend it, the persons selling directly to the government face an increased demand for their goods. If additional production is not possible, this extra demand might cause them to raise prices to the government and to their other customers. When they collect that additional money and then spend it, that will increase demand elsewhere in the economy, causing further price increases. This ripple of spending, especially if the government keeps adding to it, can continue to spread throughout the economy as the generalized form of price increases known as inflation. Inflation also inflicts costs on the general population.

Since these interest rate and inflation costs are more subtle than the direct impact of taxation, policies that resort to the printing press or to borrowing are often more popular than taxes due to their being less noticed. Thus, they make it easier to expand government programs. "Print and spend" and "borrow and spend" are as effective in funding new programs as "tax and spend" and probably more palatable to the public. Those who are adamantly opposed to government-induced inflation need to compare its effects not simply with steady prices but with higher taxes or more government debt.

Each of these methods of government finance—money, debt, and taxes— has costs and benefits. The problem is choosing the least of the evils or, more accurately, a balanced mix of them. There is a modern bias against printing money due to a fear of inflation, but that bias has not always been as strong as the distaste for taxes. For the last two decades, the United States has seemingly favored debt over taxes, although it is questionable how long that can last. Which policy to choose is arguable, and that is why there have been debates on this issue, with never a definitive answer.

Modern-day efforts to pass a balanced budget amendment to the Constitution, the latest turn in the debate over money, debt, and taxes, suggest that the linkage between government finance and the role of government remains a concern. To show how far the debate has come, when the country first declared its independence, the national government was totally dependent on the state governments for its revenues. Now the situation has reversed, with federal block grants, highway construction funds, disaster relief, aid to education, and welfare assistance making the states rely on the central government for financial support, and the states are always asking for more.

This book explores the first phase of that transformation through an investigation of what political and economic thinkers had to say about the need for a federal tax system and the constitutional issues involved in instituting and changing it. Moreover, taxes formed only one of the trinity of policies for how to fund government programs, for there were also money and debt. An important question in this study is why taxes became favored over borrowing or printing money. Just as important is a subsidiary question: Did early leaders in the United States know that these were the options they faced? In providing some answers to both questions, this book looks at three sources of knowledge available to leaders in that era: the ideas of public finance they could have found in the economic literature, the experience they had with public finance in the colonial and Revolutionary eras, and their own attitudes toward money and credit. It takes as a starting point the economic theories of money, debt, and taxes that influenced the Founding Fathers, for in formulating their plans they did not start from scratch. They were familiar with the English system of government finance and, just as important, had knowledge of the economic analysis of that system. They were all avid readers and not shy about borrowing from the theorists they studied.

There can be no doubt as to the credentials of the two economic thinkers on whom the Founding Fathers relied most. David Hume and Adam Smith were renowned sages in their time.[4] Repeatedly, as this book shows, political leaders and writers used them and their ideas as authorities on public finance. Their ideas will form a background for the rest of this book. As the next sections explain, they understood very well the relative merits of money, debt and taxes as methods of public finance.

HUME AND SMITH ON TAXES

There were any number of writers on government and taxation upon whom the framers could have drawn for inspiration in devising a tax policy. The French school of economists called the Physiocrats had already set forth a theory in support of taxing land, but in the main, the framers relied heavily on their English intellectual heritage as represented by Hume and Smith.

Hume was the earlier of the two, and his note on taxes dates to 1752. In it Hume had three important points to make. First, he argued in favor of taxes on commodities. Among commodities to be taxed, he believed that a tax on necessities would be effective in raising money without hurting the economy. Some might think, as Smith later did, that taxing necessities would cause wages to rise. Hume asserted that the poor could "encrease their industry, perform more work, and live as well as before, without demanding more for their labor." A consumption tax was a supply-side tax that increased human effort. Hume's treatment of this issue shows the difficulty of estimating the impact of a tax; his view, not much accepted by economists, was that the heavier the tax burden on them, the harder individuals, especially the working poor, would work to maintain their standard of living. Few thinkers since Hume have had the audacity to propose such a dire view of taxes.

Despite this view Hume's second and telling point was that "the best taxes are such as are levied on consumptions, especially those of luxury; for such taxes are least felt by the people." Consumption taxes on luxuries were voluntary, since they could be avoided by not purchasing the taxed item. As a result, if the tax were too high, purchases would decline, and less tax revenue would come in, serving as a check on the rapacity of the government.

Finding ways to check the greed of the government led to Hume's third point. Here he looked directly at the issue with which the founders of the United States would later grapple, tax collection by a central government. How can a central government be restrained from overtaxing its citizens, many of whom would be far removed from direct contact with it? At first glance it would appear that limits on the taxing powers of a central government might be effective in prohibiting tax oppression. A better strategy might be to have local government collect taxes and send them on to the central government. Hume said no. Using Turkey as an example, he argued that the central government would merely put pressure on its subunits for a larger share of their collections as an indirect tax. Giving the central government direct powers of taxing would make its leaders feel more strongly the problems of tax collection.[5] Putting central government officials directly in charge of taxes would make them feel the heat of public disapproval of high taxes.

Hume's brief essay on taxes had little more to say on what type of tax to employ, beyond a tax on commodities. The major statement on taxes at the time was in Smith's classic book *An Inquiry into the Nature and Causes of the Wealth of Nations* (1776). This book is usually considered a blueprint for a laissez-faire economy, but about 200 of its pages are devoted to public finance, and Smith listed as second of the two main objectives of political economy "to supply the state or commonwealth with a revenue sufficient for the public services."[6]

As a prelude to his study of taxes, Smith identified the key areas on which a government must spend: defense, justice, public works and public institutions, public works and public institutions in support of commerce, the education of youth, the instruction of people of all ages, and the support of the dignity of the sovereign, and he devoted a lengthy chapter to discussion of them.[7] What government spends its money on is a complicated issue that is not a concern in this book, except as a sidelight. The important point for Smith was that as society became commercialized, government found more things to spend on—hence, it had a rising need for revenue.

Smith clearly understood that a growing private sector required more spending by the government and that this spending had to be financed with taxes. With taxes a necessity, Smith set down four conditions that would make them more palatable to the public.

First, he touched on the issue of fairness. For a tax to be acceptable, taxpayers must feel that it was fair. For Smith, fairness meant that "the subjects of every state ought to contribute toward the support of the government, as nearly as possible, in proportion to their respective abilities; that is, in proportion to the revenue which they respectively enjoy under the protection of the state." At this stage of his writing, Smith left it unclear whether the phrase "in proportion to their respective abilities" indicated a progressive tax or a flat tax.

His second condition was that "the tax which each individual is bound to pay ought to be certain, and not arbitrary." All people should know what was expected of them and not be subjected to the "power of the tax-gatherer, who can aggravate the tax upon any obnoxious contributor." Uncertainty gave too much play to tax collectors and "encourages the insolence . . . of men who are naturally unpopular." Tax rates should be clear and simple.

Smith's third point is relatively minor today, but it was more an issue in his time. He stated, "Every tax ought to be levied at the time, or in the manner, in which it is most likely to be convenient for the contributor to pay it." Today most federal income taxes are collected through withholding from wages or by quarterly payments, both in predictable ways that reduce their inconvenience, but this was not always the case in the United States, especially in its predominantly agrarian period, when there was not always cash to be had.

Finally, Smith set forth, a tax should achieve efficiency in its collection. It should take the smallest number possible of tax collectors, to reduce administrative costs. It should have a minimal impact on the productiveness of taxpayers and not "discourage them from applying to certain branches of business which give maintenance and employment to great multitudes." It should not encourage tax cheating, which ruins the business of cheaters when they are caught. It should not subject "people to the frequent visits and the odious examination of the taxgatherers." This could result in "much unnecessary trouble, vexation, and oppression," which, while not an expense, was still a burden.[8]

Smith's four principles of taxes—equality, certainty, convenience of payment, and efficiency of collection—remained vague in their general form, so Smith took care to examine different forms of tax and how they might work. He spent a good deal of his effort on taxes related to land, for that was a very common tax used by the English government, but in the United States, with a few exceptions, property taxes have been reserved for local governments. Smith's views on income taxes and commodity taxes are more germane to this book.

The first form of income Smith took up was profit on capital. If the profits of business were taxed, he argued, the businessman, to retain his income, "could raise the rate of his profit only by raising the price of his goods; in which case the final payment of the tax would fall upon the consumers of those goods." If that were not possible, he would have to pay lower interest on his capital. A tax on interest was also not effective, for the owner of capital "would remove his stock (i.e., capital) to another country where he could carry on his business, or enjoy his fortune more at his ease." This, too, could cause unemployment and reduce tax collection from those other sources.

Efforts to place a tax on capital, similar to the tax on land, had difficulties in determining how much capital a person had. Land was visible, but calculating a value for a person's capital required a "severe inquisition," which would violate the maxim of efficiency in collection, and most countries avoided that type of examination by using "some very loose, and, therefore, more or less arbitrary estimation." This led to inequality, with landowners paying a higher portion of their wealth in taxes than capital owners, and uncertainty.

Taxes on wages were also ineffective. Smith had earlier argued that wages were determined by the demand for labor in an industry and the cost of necessities. He also believed that the wage tended to a subsistence level, even though that did include something more than biological subsistence. A tax on wages, when they were at subsistence, would necessitate an increase in wages. Smith disagreed with Hume on this issue because he felt that workers usually worked at their maximum effectiveness and that higher wages would encourage greater work effort. The increase of wages would have to be greater than the tax rate. A person making $100 a week taxed at 20% would have to earn $125 to keep take-home pay at $100. Either prices must rise, or some workers must be laid off until demand put wages at the higher rate. In England at Smith's time, as well as in the United States for a long period, no taxes on income were instituted.

With taxes on income not being effective as revenue raisers, Smith turned his attention to taxes on commodities, otherwise called excise taxes. On the same principle by which he would exempt a tax on subsistence wages, Smith argued that no tax should fall on the items of that subsistence. These would result only in higher wages and higher prices. The poor should pay no tax, because their after-tax wage would have to reflect a tax either on wages or on necessities, both of which would be shifted to others. As a result, Smith advised, "The middling and superior ranks of people, if they understood their own interest, ought always to oppose all taxes upon the necessities of life, as well as all direct taxes upon the wages of labor. The final payment of both the one and the other falls altogether upon themselves, and always with a considerable overcharge." Necessities should be exempt from taxation.

"It is otherwise," he continued, "with taxes upon what I call luxuries. The rise in the price of the taxed commodities, will not necessarily occasion any rise in the wages of labor. A tax upon tobacco, for example, though a luxury of the poor as well as of the rich, will not raise wages." The same principle held for beer or wine. Any payment of tax on luxuries was voluntary. This view could be considered as support of progressive taxation, as a luxury tax hits the rich more heavily than the poor. Further support for Smith's approval of a progressive tax can be found in his discussion of property taxes. He had no problem with placing a higher rate on the sumptuous homes of the wealthy. In this case, he wrote, "It is not very unreasonable that the rich should contribute to the public expense, not only in proportion to their revenue, but something more than in that proportion."[9]

The key to Smith was whether or not a tax had an impact on economic growth. Since investment and high wages were crucial to growth in his system, Smith wanted to avoid taxing incomes from profits and wages. To avoid taxing incomes intended for reinvestment, the best tax for Smith was a tax on luxury items, as a tax either on consumption or on large homes. Spending on these represented money that would not be reinvested, so taxes on them would not impede growth. He found that with the exception of salt, soap, leather, and candles, that was the policy of England regarding excise taxes.

Smith next considered one other type of tax on commodities, a customs tax on imported goods. These were the oldest taxes, and "they seem to have been called customs, as denoting customary payments which have been in use from time immemorial." Their original popularity resulted from their being imposed on merchants, thought of as inferior, especially when they were foreigners. As a result, however, they were often allowed to become excessively high, leading, Smith observed, to "the saying of Dr. Swift, that in the arithmetic of the customs two and two, instead of making four, make some times only one."

The point Smith was making here with customs became very crucial to the federal tax system. For its first century, the United States government relied on tariffs for the bulk of its revenues. At the same time there was pressure to use tariffs to protect manufacturing in the United States. These two goals were contradictory, however, as Smith knew. A tariff aimed at revenue requires many imported goods to be successful and will not be very protective, while a protective tariff will eliminate imports along with the revenue they bring in. Although he approved of tariffs for raising revenue, Smith believed it to be a mistake "to employ taxation as an instrument, not of revenue, but of monopoly." (Smith's analysis of protective tariffs is presented in Chapter 10.)

The same trade-off between revenue and reduced consumption from higher taxes applied to items of home production. If individuals reduced their consumption of taxed items, the tax collections would decline. It all depended on what economists call price elasticity of demand, that is, the degree to which sales of a product are sensitive to price changes. Whether or not tax policy "wonks" of earlier times appreciated this problem is described later. Smith certainly did, writing, "When the diminution of revenue is the effect of the diminution of consumption, there can be but one remedy, and that is the lowering of the tax."

Besides their impact on demand, excise taxes had efficiency problems. They required a large body of tax collectors, especially the large numbers of customs collectors (Smith served a time as a commissioner of customs). In addition, taxes on commodities either discouraged the industry that produced them, in the case of taxes on domestic products, or over encouraged industries that produced articles in competition with imported items on which a tariff has been laid.

Given these problems, Smith deemed taxes on luxuries to be best. Indeed, he found that taxes on luxuries were "as agreeable to the three first of the four general maxims concerning taxation, as any other." Since most imported items were luxuries, Smith had few objections to customs duties, except for the tariff on food items, as in the infamous Corn Laws, which divided England for half a century. These duties on imported wheat were designed to protect English agriculture from foreign competition, however, and not to raise revenues.[10]

Despite protectionist policies, Smith generally approved of the English tax system. As he wrote, with regard to this point, "Our state is not perfect, and might be mended, but it is as good as or better than that of most of our neighbors."[11] Smith, who argued against most of England's commercial policies, approved of its tax policy.

This approval is also significant for understanding the tax policies of the United States. In addition to reading about taxation, early government officials had the example of England's tax system, with which they were all too familiar. Smith's approval of that system in words and through his use of examples aided those who wished to follow or adapt the English system in the United States.

HUME AND SMITH ON DEBT

Hume and Smith also had some useful observations about the government's going into debt. Hume took a very sober view that debt was to be avoided by government as much as possible. In ancient times, wealth was accumulated before wars so as to pay for them when they came. Only in modern times did nations borrow. Borrowing set off a vicious cycle, however. Hume wrote: "Our modern expedient, which has become very general, is to mortgage the public revenues, and to trust that posterity will pay off the incumberances contracted by their ancestors. And they, having before their eyes, so good an example of their wise fathers, have the same prudent reliance on their posterity." So the cycle would continue, leading Hume to conclude "that the ancient maxims are, in this respect, more prudent than the modern."[12]

There were some advantages to having a public debt. Hume pointed out that "public securities are with us become a kind of money." Any merchant or trader holding government securities could use them to finance new undertakings. While they were waiting for new business to arise, they could gain from the interest on their public securities. They thus required less profit on their business, which "renders the commodity cheaper, causes a greater consumption, quickens the labor of the common people, and helps to spread art and industry throughout the whole society."[13] Public debt could foster economic growth.

Against this advantage, Hume found several costs to having public debt. Wealth would accumulate in concentrated form, especially in cities. Government securities, when they operated like paper money, would make precious metals less available. Public debt would lead to higher taxes. The portion of public debt owned by foreigners would make the public "tributary to them." To the extent that wealthy idlers lived off their interest payments on the debt, it would "give great encouragement to an useless and unactive life."[14]

On balance, Hume found that the costs of a public debt outweighed the advantages. He especially worried that a growing debt would lead to increasing taxes "until the whole income of every individual in the state must lie entirely at the mercy of the sovereign." As a result he did not think that the governments of Europe, even England, could survive additional increases of their public debt, for that must lead to circumstances where "the whole fabric, already tottering, falls to the ground, and buries thousands in its ruins. And this, I think, may be called the natural death of public credit."[15]

Smith took a more sanguine view of a nation's ability to support public credit. In the past when there was slight commerce, sovereigns had little to spend on and set aside a stock of wealth. As commerce grew, so did the sovereign's need for spending money. The same process held true for the state that replaced the sovereign. As commerce grew, so did the wherewithal of taxation. In times of war, however, the need to spend rose faster than the ability to tax. Citizens resented a sudden increase in taxes, and even if they did not, collections lagged behind needed spending. Fortunately, commercial society also created large stocks of capital to be borrowed, at the right interest rate, of course.

After a war, it was not possible to keep taxes high enough to pay off the war debt. In fact, Smith wrote of "the progress of the enormous debts which at present oppress, and will in the long run probably ruin, all the great nations of Europe."[16] Smith made many fine forecasts about the future of capitalism, so we need not criticize him for this erroneous prediction, although it should cause skepticism concerning the dire forecasts currently being made regarding the size of the United States public debt. Prediction aside, Smith wanted to warn against artificial schemes to reduce the debt. Two are germane to this study.

The first one, prevalent in his day as a funding system in England, was a sinking fund, whereby an annual amount of taxes was to be set aside to eliminate the government's debt. Smith did not think this likely, as any excess of tax collections above normal operating expenses would be needed to pay for interest on the debt. Only when interest rates declined would there be an increase in the sinking fund and any reduction in debt.[17] Since the sinking fund would become one of Alexander Hamilton's pet remedies for paying off the United States public debt, Smith's comments were important.

Second, Smith warned against a tendency governments had of paying off their debts through a debasement of money. The methods Smith used as examples were the changing of the denomination of coins or mixing in alloys with the precious metal content of coins.[18] Monetary devaluation may help a state pay off its debts, but the effect was ruinous on creditors. The same idea held for the issuance of paper money. As described later, several of the American colonies used paper money as a temporary way to pay their expenses. Smith was well aware of this usage and the negative effect it had when the colony redeemed its debt "at the depreciated value to which it gradually falls."[19] Smith was not against the use of paper money, however. To see how he thought it should be used, it is necessary to look more closely at what he and Hume had to say about money, banking, and credit.

HUME AND SMITH ON MONEY

Hume characterized money as a medium of exchange. He wrote, "It is none of the wheels of trade. It is the oil which renders the motion of the wheels more smooth and easy." It followed from this perspective that the more money that existed, the smoother trade would be. In particular, there was a direct relationship between the amount of money and prices: "It is the proportion between the circulating money, and the commodities on the market, which determines the prices."[20]

Some rise in prices was not damaging to the economy. In the national economy, a rise in prices was a stimulus to commerce and industry, as long as the rise in prices came slowly and with a suitable lag after the increase in money. As Hume put it, "It is easy to trace the money in its progress through the whole commonwealth; where we shall find, that it must first quicken the diligence of every individual, before it encrease the price of labor."[21]

Two points in Hume's analysis need to be highlighted. First, when he talked about money, he meant precious metals, that is, specie. Second, like many thinkers of his day, Hume was concerned about the cost of labor regarding its wages. High wages were seen by many in his time as detrimental to the industry of the masses. In addition they were thought to bring disadvantages in international trade, allowing "the poorer states to undersell the richer in all foreign markets." This latter disadvantage made Hume doubtful of "the benefit of banks and paper-credit." True, paper money had utility in making it easy to carry around large sums, but that ease was countered by the impact of "encreasing money beyond its natural proportion to labor and commodities" and causing their prices to rise too rapidly.

Since private banks often issued excessive amounts of paper money, there needed to be a public bank to keep that issuance in check, a bank that "locked up all the money it received." Such a public bank, although it would cost the government the salaries of its employees, would be worth it when it led to "the destruction of paper-credit." In addition, the funds kept in the public bank "would be a convenience in times of great public danger and distress; and what part of it was used might be replaced at leisure, when peace and tranquility were restored to the nation."[22] In other words, a public bank would be a ready source of public credit.

Smith characterized money as the "great wheel of circulation," the commodity that enabled individuals to trade by serving as a unit of exchange. Many commodities had served this function, with precious metals being the most common.[23] Precious metals had a disadvantage, however, in that they were often expensive to obtain. As a result, commercial societies were finding it efficient to employ paper money in transactions. Smith wrote, "The substitution of paper in the room of gold and silver money, replaces a very expensive instrument of commerce with one much less costly, and sometimes equally convenient. Circulation comes to be carried out by a new wheel, which costs less both to erect and to maintain than the old one."[24] The tricky part was in how the supply of paper money was managed.

The best type of paper money was that produced as circulating notes by banks. Whenever members of a community had confidence in its local banks, bankers could issue notes backed by gold, and these would circulate as readily as gold. For the nation as a whole, however, there was a limit as to how much paper was needed to circulate in comparison to the total of goods bought and sold, although Smith recognized that such a limit could not be calculated very easily, nor did it have to be. As long as banks had to pay their notes in gold on demand, if too much paper money was issued in comparison to how much was needed for goods to circulate, individuals would take their excess paper money to a bank to redeem it for gold. The threat of such bank runs in the case of too much paper money being issued would serve as a check on banks.[25] With banks in charge of paper money, the common view that "the increase of paper money . . . necessarily augments the money price of commodities" was not always true. In England and Scotland, banks had issued paper money with no impact on prices.[26]

It was different when government issued the paper money. Here Smith drew on the experiences of the American colonies, which issued paper money "not in bank notes payable to the bearer on demand, but in a government paper, of which the payment was not exigible till several years after it was issued." Only if a government limited its issuance of paper money to the amount of taxes needed to be paid would this paper money keep its value. That had not always been the case in the colonies, and the purchasing power of their paper money declined through the inflation that was caused by its issuance.[27]

Smith's message was clear. Paper money was useful to society when it was issued by banks. Prudent banking methods, brought about by competition among banks, would keep the issuance of paper money within bounds. When governments issued paper money, there was no such check, and the potential for too much to be issued with the result of inflation was obvious.

THE AMERICAN EXPERIENCE

The writings of Hume and, as shown in this book, especially Smith were reference points for American leaders. Smith was used as an authority or as an antagonist an impressive number of times by thinkers and doers in the early United States, but how they used his ideas varied, because these leaders were also guided by their own experiences, both personal and political.

The leaders of political life in the early United States came from a variety of economic classes and professions, including the law. They followed Hume and Smith in wanting to see the government out of debt but differed in the lengths to which they would go to realize that goal. Agrarians like Jefferson and Madison would see debt as something to be eliminated as soon as possible and would adopt taxing and spending policies that would ensure that this happened; they sought the weakest possible national government. Commercially minded persons such as Hamilton and Robert Morris would see the debt as something to be managed; whether or not they ever eliminated it was a matter of indifference to them. They thought it more important to have a strong central government to serve the needs of commerce.

These differences would all be played out in the political arena and would influence the choices political leaders of the new nation made regarding public finance. In this broad experience those leaders took what they had read in Hume and Smith, placed it in a context of their personal attitude toward money, debt, and taxes, and proceeded to manage the government's finances.

That is the story this book tells. Chapter 1 looks at the Continental Congress during the Revolutionary War and describes why it persisted in the error Smith warned of, issuing excessive paper money. Chapter 2 tells of the efforts to make the Articles of Confederation workable in a period when the government had no taxing power. Chapter 3 examines the role money, debt, and taxes played in the debates at the Constitutional Convention. Chapter 4 continues that examination by looking at taxes in the debate over the ratification of the Constitution. With the Constitution ratified, the government had to be made operational, which is the story of Chapter 5. Once the government was in place, a tax and debt plan was installed by Hamilton, as Chapter 6 relates. Chapter 7 continues the story of the Federalist Party's tax system during the Adams administration. A major change in tax and debt policy took place with the Jefferson era, with taxes, spending, and the debt all reduced, as detailed in Chapter 8. The Jefferson system failed to survive the crisis of the War of 1812, however, and Chapter 9 recounts a revival of Hamiltonianism. Finally, Chapter 10 ends the story with the intensification of the use of tariffs for protectionism and the payment of the public debt by Andrew Jackson.

When looked at from the vantage point of public finance, the spirit of American history becomes muted. As Hamilton suspected, there is more glory in a single battle than in a thirty-year plan to eliminate the public debt. George Washington had three budgets with deficits, but he remains the father of our country, enshrined on Mount Rushmore and on the one-dollar bill. Still, the history of public finance in the early republic is a story worth telling, for the battle of the budget is a battle that never ends.

CONCLUSION

When a government needs to pay for the resources it uses, it has three basic options: money, debt, and taxes. The standard economic analysis of the day, as exemplified by Hume and Smith, stressed the need to use taxes as the major source of revenue; money and debt were felt to have too many negative consequences. When taxes were used to pay for government programs, they should be imposed in ways that made them more agreeable to taxpayers and that had a minimal disruption on the economy. These two early tax specialists, Hume and Smith, thought a tax on luxuries satisfied both these conditions very well. In Smith's case a luxury tax met three of his four criteria for a good tax—it was fair, certain, and convenient. He was troubled only by its impact on efficiency in influencing the survival of particular industries. Equally important, Smith had no problems with tariffs, as long as they were intended simply to raise revenue. Perhaps his favorite tax, if that word could ever apply to a tax, was a tariff on luxuries.

If there were one maxim to be derived from Smith's views on taxes, it would be that the purpose of the tax system was to raise revenue for the government while yielding a minimal disruption of the economy. The idea that the tax system would be tinkered with to promote the growth of any industry or of the economy was alien to Smith. That was why he felt that the rich and frivolous should contribute the most toward the revenue needs of the government. A curtailment of spending on luxury items would have minimal impact on the economy.

We see in the following chapters how closely thinking on public finance in the United States followed the advice of Hume and Smith regarding money, debt, and taxes. Certainly, Smith thought it was advice that was sorely needed in the new country. At the time he was writing, English colonies, at least the ones that later became the United States, were resisting efforts to place taxes on them. Smith felt those taxes were fair, because England spent money protecting the colonies from England's and their enemies. If those taxes could not be collected, then perhaps a separation was in order. As he put it, in his usual, ironic way, "The rulers of Great Britain have, for more than a century past, amused the people with the imagination that they possessed a great empire on the west side of the Atlantic." Instead of an empire, however, it was "but the project of an empire," and an immensely expensive project at that.

It was time to make or break. "If the project cannot be completed," he concluded, "it ought to be given up." If those colonies could not be made to pay their fair share of their own governance, let them go and see if they can pay for it by themselves.[28] Here Smith's prediction was on the mark, at least in terms of separation of the colonies from England. Just as important, it was a challenge: could those former colonies be more successful than England at wresting taxes from their citizens? That is the topic to which we turn.

NOTES

1. Jack N. Rakove, *Original Meanings: Politics and Ideas in the Making of the Constitution* (New York: Alfred A. Knopf, 1996), pp. xiii–xvi, 1–24 and 338–42.

2. Practitioners of this older political economy would include Adam Smith, John Stuart Mill, and Thorstein Veblen. See Donald R. Stabile, *Work and Welfare: The Social Costs of Labor in the History of Economic Thought* (Westport, CT: Greenwood Press, 1996).

3. Herbert E. Sloan, *Principle and Interest: Thomas Jefferson and the Problem of Debt* (New York: Oxford University Press, 1995), p. 30.

4. For a discussion of eighteenth-century English writing on taxes and debt, see Sloan, *Principle and Interest*, pp. 94–100.

5. David Hume, "Of Taxes," in Ernest C. Mossner, ed., *An Enquiry concerning Human Understanding and Other Essays* (New York: Washington Square Press, 1963), pp. 280–84.

6. Adam Smith, *An Inquiry into the Nature and Causes of the Wealth of Nations*, 2 vol. (Chicago: University of Chicago Press, 1976), vol. 1, p. 449.

7. Ibid., pp. 213–340.

8. Ibid., pp. 350–52.

9. Ibid., p. 368.

10. Ibid., pp. 374–418.

11. Ibid., pp. 427–31.

12. David Hume, "Of Public Credit," in Eugene F. Miller, ed., *Essays: Moral, Political and Literary* (Indianapolis: Liberty Classics, 1987), p. 350.

13. Ibid., p. 353.

14. Ibid., p. 355.

15. Ibid., pp. 361–63.

16. Smith, *Wealth*, vol. 2, pp. 440–47 (quotation on p. 446).

17. Ibid., pp. 444–57.

18. Ibid., pp. 467–70.

19. Smith, Wealth, vol 2, p. 479.

20. Hume, "Of Money," in *Essays*, pp. 281 and 291.

21. Ibid., p. 267.

22. Ibid., pp. 284–85.

23. Smith, *Wealth*, vol. 1, pp 26–32.

24. Ibid., vol. 2, p. 309.

25. Ibid., pp. 315–20.

26. Ibid., p. 345.

27. Ibid., pp. 347–50.

28. Ibid., p. 486.

Chapter 1

TOO FREQUENT EMISSIONS

Taxation in a new nation can never be easy. Political leaders must consolidate support for their programs among a population that has not yet shown its loyalty to the new regime. When, as was the case with the United States, the new government was really something new under the sun, an experiment in democracy, efforts to win popular support were essential. The difficulty faced by leaders at the time was compounded by their having to marshal sufficient forces to fight a war against an unrelenting opponent, well armed and committed to maintaining its hold on its colonies. To resolve this dilemma regarding taxes, leaders of the fledgling nation stuck with what was familiar, to them and to their constituents. They adopted the financing system to which they were accustomed and that had worked tolerably well for them, if not for their former rulers in London.

That financing system stressed money over debt and taxes, however. As a result, most of the Revolutionary War was paid for with paper money. This use of paper money was not as irresponsible as we might think today. Rather, it represented a continuation of tried-and-true methods of government finance that had been generally accepted in the colonies.

COLONIAL FINANCE

During the colonial period, each colony followed its own policy of taxation. Because the colonial governments did little in the way of governing, their needs for revenue were modest. In general they relied on property taxes, poll taxes (a per capita tax on individuals), faculty taxes (taxes on income due to gains in capital or based on the value of personal abilities), excise taxes, and taxes on imports from overseas and from other colonies.[1] With Pennsylvania, for example, in 1765 Ben

Franklin outlined its taxes to the English Parliament as follows: "There are taxes on all estates, real and personal; a poll tax; a tax on all offices, professions, trades and businesses, according to their profits; an excise on all wine, rum and other spirits; and a duty of ten pounds per head on all Negroes imported, with some other duties."[2]

Regional differences might alter the mix. In the South the planter aristocracy avoided taxes on land and, as slavery became important, kept poll taxes to a minimum. The emphasis was on tariffs on imports and exports. In New England the poll tax fitted in more with an egalitarian view of every person's having the same value, even though there were differences in the ability to pay. Tariffs were minor but common, especially on exports.[3] There was no system of national taxation.

There were collection problems, though, due to the time it took to collect the taxes and to the difficulty taxpayers had in finding gold and silver coins to pay their taxes. To get around this problem, the colonies printed bills of credit (paper money) to pay their accounts directly. This paper money would be redeemed with gold or silver coins collected through the later payment of taxes, and the legislation authorizing the printing of the bills of credit specified the taxes that would be used to redeem them and the time by which this would be done. In some cases taxes could be paid with the bills of credit, which was another way to reduce the amount of them that circulated. In this ingenious way the colonies really were involved with short-term borrowing (the bills of credit represented a debt of the colony issuing them). With nothing backing them, these bills rested for their value on confidence on the issuing government, bolstered by having them declared acceptable for payment by law.[4]

There were times, however, when colonial legislatures would abuse this system. Bills of credit would not be paid when due, and in some cases unscrupulous legislators would reissue those that had been redeemed. As Paul Studenski and Herman Kroos state the case, "Since the colonists loathed paying taxes, and paper money seemed an easy method of paying government expenses, the levying of taxes was postponed and more and more new bills were issued to retire the old bills, as well as pay new expenses."[5] Overissue of the bills led to their fall in value.

While the impacts of these abuses on the economy were small, they caused concern in England. In 1751 Parliament placed strict regulations on the New England colonies to control their issuing of bills of credit. An effort to extend the rules to the rest of the colonies in 1764 eventually led to the strictures against making the bills legal tender and ordered that they be retired when stipulated. This law was very unpopular and became another source of dispute between the Old and New Worlds.[6]

When the government in England wanted revenues from the colonies, it asked colonial legislatures to pay a direct share in military expenses under a system of requisition, whereby each colony would contribute its quota of the required amount. The colonies were free to impose taxes to meet this requisition as they saw fit. For spending in the Seven Years' War, however, Parliament began imposing specific taxes on the colonies. The Sugar Act of 1764 placed a tariff of threepence per gallon on imports of molasses to the colonies. England had long put tariffs on traded items to regulate their flow under the Navigation Acts. Revenue was not the intent of those tariffs, which cost about four times more to collect than they raised.[7]

With Parliament's recognition that the colonies were costing £300,000 per year, it determined to impose one-third of that cost directly on the colonies with taxes. The Stamp Act of 1765 required payment of a tax to purchase a stamp to be put on all legal documents. It was the first tax Parliament had placed directly on the colonists.

Colonial thinkers, following Ben Franklin, objected to these taxes by making a distinction between an internal tax (the Stamp Act) and an external tax (the Sugar Act), arguing that internal taxes were not legal without representation, while external taxes were acceptable because they regulated trade. The Stamp Act Congress, called to organize a protest against the tax, reminded Parliament of "the undoubted right of Englishmen, that no taxes be imposed on them but with their own consent, given personally or by their representatives."[8] The Stamp Act proved so unpopular that a boycott of English goods was organized until it was repealed in 1766.

Part of its unpopularity was due to its requirement for payment in coin. As Franklin stated the problem, "In my opinion, there is not gold and silver enough in the colonies to pay the stamp act duty for one year."[9] Adam Smith disagreed, maintaining that the colonies had sufficient amounts of paper money to handle their internal trade and were able to find enough gold and silver for trade with England. They could find the gold and silver for taxes.[10]

Besides, per capita taxes in the colonies were very low, about one-fourth of what they were in England.[11] Because England had a very high public debt and was making large annual interest payments on it, there were pressures to impose additional taxes on the Americans. Members of Parliament did not buy the colonists' argument that their consent was needed for taxation, with one member's stating that "enacting laws and laying taxes so intirely go together that if we surrender the one we lose the others."[12]

To placate the colonists, Parliament passed a series of external taxes as duties on imports under the broad name of the Townsend Acts. These taxes were strictly enforced, moreover, and smugglers were severely punished by having their property, especially their ships, confiscated. By this time, the colonists appreciated that the distinction between internal taxes and external taxes was not important in terms of their impact. The point of contention became, as John Dickinson put it in his newspaper series "The Letters of a Pennsylvania Farmer" (1767), that Parliament had no right "to lay on these colonies any tax whatever."[13]

The Townsend Act taxes helped set off the Revolutionary War under the cry of "taxation without representation is tyranny." This cry is misleading, however. The colonists were lightly taxed, and many taxes were imposed by colonial legislatures under which local government prevailed. What may have driven the Revolutionary fervor was the anticipation that England was going to continue to raise taxes. "Once

Parliament lays a tax," Jared Ingersoll proclaimed, "no matter how moderate, who can say what will follow."[14] Perhaps the colonials found taxation a tyranny in any form. Whatever the reasoning, they went to war, and taxes were a key issue in their decision to fight.

CURRENCY FINANCE

When the American colonists took the drastic step of declaring their independence from England and forming their own government, they faced the difficult task of financing a war in a country pervaded by an antigovernment sentiment that included antipathy toward taxes. With a widely dispersed populace consisting mainly of small, subsistence farmers, the American colonies bred a special sense of independence. In the isolated communities where most Americans lived, each family depended on itself and possibly its neighbors for protection from attack or during other emergencies. The government, even of their own commonwealth, was a far-off entity of little concern or value. Why pay taxes to support it?

The ideal of government espoused during the Revolutionary period was that it should serve the public good. "The word republic," Thomas Paine wrote, "means the public good." To achieve this ideal, citizens had to place themselves above their self-interests. Protection against self-interested leaders and definition of the public good were best accomplished at the local level; republics worked best, if at all, in limited geographic areas. These were the commonsense views of the time.

When the colonists made their break with England, it was just as reasonable for them to form separate states as it was to form a national union. While the initial phases of the break were accomplished by a national Continental Congress, most attention was placed on forming state governments. The period just after the Declaration of Independence saw the drafting of state constitutions, which took a priority over the national government. There was a clear intent to keep the locus of governmental power close to home. John Adams stated the case well in 1776: "There is something very unnatural and odious in a Government 1000 leagues off. An whole government of our own Choice, managed by Persons whom We love, revere and can confide in, has charms in it for which Men will fight."[15] Adams, of course, referred to the government in London as being far-off.

A contradiction in this idea soon emerged, however. To fight a war on the American continent against a foe willing to attack on all fronts, the former colonies needed some form of national coordination by a central government. In a large continent such as America, the national government could be as removed from the people as London.

At the time the push for independence took place, the colonies had no national identity; their citizens associated themselves more with regional or class interests than with any larger entity, except for England, of course. Even though England was falling into disrepute, the movement toward independence and revolution was not a certainty. The existence of loyalists toward England and moderates who sought conciliation required that leaders in the Continental Congress had to make compromises to gain widespread support.

The Continental Congress operated on an ad hoc basis for years, with its members having ties to the state legislatures that sent them as delegates. When those members did begin drafting a plan of government that eventually became the Articles of Confederation, it took six drafts to complete it. Finished in 1777, the Articles of Confederation were not ratified by all the states until 1781, despite twelve of the states having approved it by 1779.

Part of the problem of ratification was that it required a unanimous vote of all states, and Maryland held back its approval over the issue of who would control the land in the West, the states laying claim to them or the Continental Congress. This problem of unanimity continued throughout the period of the Articles of Confederation. Although the issue of representation in the Congress on the basis of population had been debated, sheer political necessity dictated that each state be given one vote. It was uncertain how loyal citizens would be to the national government, so its form addressed the widest possible popularity in all of the states.[16]

This pattern of local rule counted heavily in the system of taxes set up by the revolutionary government. The Continental Congress was not given any power to raise taxes. Instead, it had to ask for funds from the separate states, under a system of requisition similar to the one England had used. As a short-term measure set by previous procedure, Congress planned to issue bills of credit and resolved "that each colony provide ways and means to sink its portion of the bills ordered to be emitted." At this time, each colony's portion of the requisition was to be "determined according to the number of inhabitants, of all ages, including negroes and mulattoes." The proceeds from the requisition were to be used to retire the bills of credit. As the bills came in, the treasurers, in the presence of a congressional committee, were to "burn and destroy them."[17]

The person chiefly responsible for planning the use of paper money, Gouverneur Morris, had previously been opposed to currency finance. He had written that such a scheme was "a never failing source of national debt." In a crisis, however, paper money was the only option available to the Congress.[18] Morris stated the general problem of public finance in blunt terms: "America having never been much taxed . . . and the Contest being on the very Question of Taxation the laying of Imposts unless from the last Necessity would have been Madness."[19]

In October 1777, Congress changed the basis for each state's quota to the value of land and buildings and other improvements on it.[20] The states felt no urgency to fulfill the requisition. John Jay, as president of the Congress, appealed to the states in asking for money, "Let it never be said that America had no sooner become independent than she became insolvent."[21] He appealed in vain, for no money came. The Continental Congress followed the colonial precedent of emitting bills of credit—the continental dollar, in hopes that the requisition would eventually bring in enough revenue to call in the bills.

This use of paper money to finance the war represented an effort of the Continental Congress to grapple with a variety of problems, including the unpopularity of taxes. Highly regarded leaders such as Thomas Paine and Alexander Hamilton looked at the issuance of paper money as a necessity and a reasonable substitute for taxes. Besides, the initial issuance set forth the time and amount of redemption by the states. Ben Franklin noted with his usual wisdom that the inflation the printing and spending of money caused was "a kind of imperceptible tax."[22] Franklin elaborated on this wisdom, writing of currency finance, "It performs its office when we issue it, it pays and clothes troops, and provides victuals and ammunition, and when we are obliged to issue a quantity excessive, it pays itself off by depreciation."[23]

Not everyone agreed with the benefits of this inflation tax. George Washington was against it, writing in November 1777, "It is much to be wished that a remedy could be applied to the depreciation of our currency. . . . Long have I been persuaded of the indispensable necessity of a tax for the purpose of sinking the paper money, and why it has been delayed better politicians than I must account for."[24] Washington had reason to complain, as inflation greatly reduced the worth of the debt he was owed and the leases he had negotiated on his land.[25]

In a thorough analysis of the problem of inflation early in the Confederation period, one colonial writer, Petaliah Webster, warned that "payment in promises or bills of credit is a temporary expedient, and will always be dangerous, where the quantity increases too much." The recourse to this rapid expansion of printed money was to raise taxes "equal to the excess of the currency" above what was needed to support commerce. If this were not done, the debt of the Congress, as represented by its printed dollars, would become too large to be repaid. As to tax antipathy, Webster countered, "It is rare that the people refuse burdens or even grumble under them, when, by general conviction, they are necessary for the public good."[26] Political leaders in the Congress agreed and tried to do something about the situation.

TENTATIVE MOVES TO TAXATION

In September 1778, the congressional Committee on Finance made several recommendations to strengthen the system of public finance. First, it proposed that Congress undertake loans, both at home and abroad. Second, it suggested "that it will be proper to call on the several states to pay in their quotas of ten Million Dollars." Third, the states were also to be asked to furnish $2 million a year for ten years as a fund to redeem the paper money and pay other debt. Fourth, the committee, realizing that the system of requisition was flawed, broached the issue of a national tax system, with a plan that requested "that a Poll Tax be laid throughout America of $\frac{1}{2}$ Doll. per Head on all Inhabitants" and "that a Duty of two per cent be laid on Commodities imported." Both taxes would be used to pay off debt and would remain in force "until the final Payment of the Continental debt."

The report of the committee also gave estimates of the total issue of bills of credit and other debt and what needed to be done. It approximated that by January 1780, $120 million in bills would have been issued but that $80 million would have been called in through loans and the state quotas. The total debt at that time was projected to be $60 million, with annual interest payments of $3.2 million. These payments would be covered by $1.5 million from the poll tax, $500,000 from the 2% duty, and $2 million from the states, giving a slight reserve for contingencies.

It was a plan that worked out on paper, but Congress did not accept it. Some of the loans were approved, as was the call for the states to pay their quotas. The request for the annual fund from the states and the new taxes were postponed. Instead, the Congress resolved "that sixty copies of the said report be printed for the use of the members, and that the printer be under an oath not to divulge any part of the said report."[27] Secrecy was in order when the subject of taxation was raised.

Tenaciously, the Committee on Finance advanced another plan in October 1778. This time it prefaced its report with the statements on the evils of currency finance, pointing out "it is indispensably necessary to restore the Value of the Money by reducing the Quantity." It urged that all bills issued before April 1778 ($46.5 million) be called in and destroyed. Since additional bills amounting to $40 million would be issued in the next year, they should be made redeemable within eighteen years. To retire them and other debt, the states would be asked for a $6 million-a-year fund. Meanwhile, the bills were to be taken out of circulation in exchange for loan certificates bearing 6% interest.

This debt-for-dollars swap would raise the debt to nearly $60 million, carrying interest payments of $3.6 million. With the states paying in $6 million a year, the interest could be paid and enough debt retired to eliminate the debt in ten years, leaving $45 million of paper money in circulation. As an alternative, if no bills were called in, and more issued as planned, the total of bills and debt would be $104 million. Payment by the states of $6 million a year for eighteen years would pay off this amount.[28] Here was another thoughtful plan that went nowhere.

Leaders of the Continental Congress also thought the war would be short and that at its early end taxes could be used to redeem the dollars they were issuing. Instead, the war dragged on, and more than $225 million bills had been issued by 1779, with only about $13 million redeemed. One delegate to the Congress saw no reason to "consent to load my constituents with taxes when we can send to our printer and get a wagon load of money, one quire of which will pay for the whole."[29]

For an analysis of the problem, we can again turn to Petaliah Webster. He recognized that the war was being financed by currency depreciation, that is, an inflation tax. In fact, he maintained, the loss of value of the continental dollars had reduced the burden of the previous war debt to less than half its face value. As a result, he concluded, that "all of the expenditures of the war for three years past except for foreign debts and internal loans . . . have been actually paid in depreciation of our currency, which is perhaps the most inconvenient method of levying public taxes that could be invented." The problem with the inflation tax was that it rewarded "the dissipating, slack, lazy, and dilatory sort, who commonly keep themselves in debt."[30]

Webster recommended taxes in place of currency finance. He pointed out that the taxes needed to pay for the war would be less than what Britain would impose on the country if the war were lost; Webster estimated that "the tax demanded will amount to about 4 hard dollars in a year to each person," not an onerous burden.[31] Any increased taxes, however, would fall on the "sort" who gained from the inflation tax, and they apparently formed a vocal pressure group. Webster's espousal of tax increases made economic, but not political, sense. As Jack Rakove observes, "When Congress and the new provincial regimes were anxious to attain maximum popular support, the political liabilities of taxation outweighed its financial benefits."[32] The Revolutionary War may have been as popular as we like to think today, but its popularity was not overwhelming.

CURRENCY FINANCE CONTINUES

In April 1779, the Committee on the Treasury reported that neither loan certificates nor taxes were sufficiently effective to call in the previous emission as planned. It then admitted, "The emission of new money is therefore our principal resource, and it must keep pace with the expenditures, at the same time that those expenditures increase with such rapidity that it is impossible to foresee when they will terminate." The committee proposed "economy in the public expense" and called for payment of past and new quotas by the states.[33] It also believed that since the large amount of paper money in circulation gave most citizens an adequate supply of it, they displayed "the utmost chearfulness in contributing their proportion of the expences by taxes." All that was needed was for the states to have the resolve to collect those taxes.[34]

A month later, Congress acted with an address directed at the states. It admitted that "your representatives in Congress were obliged to emit paper money; an expedient that you knew to have been before generally and successfully practiced on this continent." Moreover, "they were very sensible of the inconveniencies with which too frequent emissions would be attended, and endeavored to avoid them." They had tried debt and taxes as an offset, but "our enemies prosecuting the war by sea and land with implacable fury and with some success, taxation at home and borrowing abroad, in the midst of difficulties and dangers, were alike impracticable. Hence the continued necessity of new emission." Now things were settling down, and the state governments were well formed. As a result, Congress felt it could call on the states for $45 million in addition to the $15 million already requisitioned.[35]

These continuous appeals by Congress to the states for revenues proved futile, as they, too, were strapped for revenue. Taxes contributed less than $6 million to the total costs of the war of about $66 million.[36] Even the confiscations of large land holdings left behind by Tories who sought safety in England or Canada were insufficient. The states were not better at raising revenue than the national government would have been. The states issued more than $200 million of their own bills of credit, with very few redeemed.[37]

The excessive issue of paper money (about 80% of total government spending up to 1780) caused high inflation; in 1777, $1.25 in continental dollars equaled $1 in gold, but by 1781 it took $167.50 in the paper bills to buy $1 in gold. This was a very high inflation tax. Some of the inflation was offset through the issuance of government securities either for sale or in exchange for commodities. At one point, Congress considered making citizens buy government securities in exchange for paper dollars to reduce the number of dollars in circulation but decided that forced loans would be as unpopular as taxes.[38]

Other Americans also took up the subject of public finance. One anonymously written pamphlet dated 1779 started with the admission, "The subject of finance seems to be little understood in America" and proceeded to explain how the inability to raise taxes meant that "bills of credit were issued on the faith of the people." As long as the issuances were reasonable, no problems resulted, as the bills "stole upon us by slow degrees, as it were imperceptibly." As a short-term, stopgap measure, currency finance and a small inflation tax worked tolerably well.

Then the issuances became overdone. The author of the pamphlet calculated that with respect to the quantity of money needed for the commerce of the country, "the generality of opinion fix it at no more than thirty nor less than twenty millions of dollars." He estimated that $150 million had been issued, or six times more than needed. That should have meant a sixfold increase in prices, but the accompanying loss of faith in the government made the inflation worse. As a result of this loss of faith, "[t]he degree of depreciation of money, while it continues increasing, will always exceed the proportion of its excess in quantity." This was why the inflationary tax was underestimated.

To avoid the inflation tax, he continued, "[s]ome are for relying on taxes alone; but this I fear would leave us in the lurch." The use of borrowed funds also was difficult, for the depreciation of money made lending to the government very risky. Indeed, "the idea that the public debt is discharged, or diminished *pro tanto*, by the depreciation of money operating as a tax on the possessors of it," he went on, could not be considered "an equal and just tax." To avoid this tax, he proposed that the states accept responsibility for the emitted bills of credit, promising specific taxes to redeem them when the war was over. This would restore public faith in the bills, which would enable the floating of domestic loans to finance the remainder of the war; the value of the bonds should also be pegged to the French livre to protect bondholders from depreciation of continental currency. As for taxes, he left them a matter for the individual states to determine, given the circumstances of their citizens.[39]

This last stance on taxes would be a key issue with regard to the distribution of the taxing power between the state and national governments. The idea that the state governments had a better fix on how and when to tax their citizens than did the national government underlay the entire system of requisition. Given its quota, each state would raise taxes in its own way.

The Congress also faced an issue of how to allot its revenue requests to individual states. For much of the war, the requests were portioned on the value of land in the state as well as buildings and improvements in each state but did not count the value of slaves.[40] This was a victory for the southern states. Not that it mattered, for the system never worked.

Thomas Paine gave his own analysis of the problem of laying taxes on a reluctant citizenry. By his calculations, the share of Pennsylvania's quota of taxes of residents of Philadelphia amounted to "five pence per head per month," not a very large sum and about one-third the rate in England. If payment of a small tax like this "will remove all these difficulties, make people secure in their homes, leave them to follow the business of their stores and farms unimpeded, and not only keep out, but drive out the enemy from the country: and if the neglect of raising this sum will let them in, and produce the evils that might be prevented, on which side, I ask, does the wisdom, interest and policy lie? Or rather would it not be an insult to reason to put the question?"

Paine admitted that he broached the issue of taxes to show that the amount was not the problem; his advice for Pennsylvania was to put a tax on land, imports, and liquor. In defense of the tariff, he gave a simple explanation that would be used repeatedly in U.S. history:

There are many reasons why a duty on imports is the most convenient duty or tax that can be collected, one of which is, because the whole is payable in a few places in a country, and it likewise operates with the greatest ease and equality, because every one pays in proportion to what he consumes, so people in general consume in proportion to what they can afford, and therefore the tax is regulated by the abilities which every man supposes himself to have, or in other words, every man becomes his own assessor, and pays by a little at a time when it suits him to buy. Besides, it is a tax which people may pay or let alone by not consuming the articles; and though the alternative may have no influence on their conduct, the power of choosing is an agreeable thing to the mind.[41]

Paine's thoughts here, especially with regard to tariffs, followed Adam Smith's notion that a tariff on luxury goods was the best tax, but despite that and despite Paine's showing that the level of taxes needed was low, the tax requisitions on the states by the Continental Congress were not forthcoming.

Members of Congress tried to deal with the problem of inflation in 1780, recognizing that "the present fluctuating state of the Paper Currency, is productive of evils which cannot be effectively remedied, without calling in and sinking the whole." The Congress asked each state to remove part of the paper money from circulation, assigning each state its quota of a total of $200 million to be redeemed. At the same time, the dollars were to be devalued at a rate of forty to one. As the old bills came in, they would be retired and replaced with new ones at one-twentieth of the value of the old bills. About $119 million of the old bills were tendered and eliminated. The states, however, could not play their part in this plan,[42] and the new bills soon depreciated further, making them deserving of the phrase "not worth a continental." The national government abandoned all pretense of making them good.

With this abandonment of currency finance, the Continental Congress lost some of its power. James Madison recognized this loss. In May 1780, he wrote to Jefferson that while Congress "exercised the indefinite power of emitting on the credit of their constituents they had the whole wealth and resources of the continent within their command, and could go on with their affairs independently and as they pleased. Since the resolution passed for shutting the press, this power has been given up and they are now . . . dependent on the states." Madison was not overly concerned by currency finance, having written specifically against Hume's notion that the quantity of money determined its value; equally important to Madison was the credit standing of the issuer of the paper money.[43]

This dependency had disastrous results. On June 26, 1780, the Board of Treasury reported that with respect to a request for "one million forty-five-thousand dollars to make the necessary provisions to enable General Washington to move his army," they had to inform Congress "that it is utterly out of the Power of the Board to make any provision for this demand, the Treasury of the United States at this time being totally exhausted." The report also noted that the states were in arrears by $45 million on their quotas.[44] Timely loans from France, Holland and Spain enabled the colonists to keep on fighting until England was defeated.[45] "Borrow and spend" replaced "print and spend."

ANOTHER PUSH FOR TAXES

In 1781, just before the war ended, the advocates of a stronger central government became a majority of the Congress. To improve the government's finances, the advocates of its stronger role immediately revived a previous recommendation of the Committee of Finance, raising a national tariff, called an impost. The plan was to give Congress the power to impose a 5% duty on imports and dedicate the proceeds to payment of the public debt. The tariff would "continue until such debts are extinguished."[46] This funding of the debt would give foreigners confidence in the government and make them more willing to grant additional loans.

The impost was just part of the overall plan of the new members of Congress. They still pressed the states for their quota under the requisitions and proposed that the states pay a 6% interest rate "where any states shall appear to have been deficient in advancing their proportions."[47]

To support this plan, members of the Board of Treasury reported on the state of the government's finances, admitting that "from the unsettled condition of the publick accounts they can only give a general view of the publick debts." Even that general view was dismal. The total debt, adjusted for inflation, including a devaluation of bills of credit at a 75-to-1 ratio, was $24 million.

The committee members then felt it "necessary to state the measures which Congress have pursued to" finance the war. They traced out the history of issuing of bills of credit starting with the first $2 million on June 22, 1775, and how the states had been asked to provide for the redemption of them. They also allowed that a hope for a reconciliation with England had played a part in the financing plan, only to be dashed. Requests were made to the states for taxes. One statement can sum up what happened throughout the war: "Unfortunately the tax failed, and the sums obtained from loans were greatly inadequate to the expenditure: consequently more money was emitted; and notwithstanding the favourable turn in our affairs in 1778, depreciation increased with amazing rapidity." As a result of "the continual depreciation of the continental currency, the community was suffering great injustice, the public finances were deranged, and the necessary dispositions for the defence of the commonwealth much impeded."

Congress had constantly asked the states for taxes and for the calling in of bills of credit, but "their expectations were again disappointed." As a result, the army went unpaid. The point of the review of finance was not "to criminate, but to show that Congress have done everything in their power to carry on the war, and to prevent the embarrassments under which our affairs now labor." The report also was designed to demonstrate "the absolute necessity of the states immediately granting the duties on imports and prizes as asked by Congress."[48]

The military was also brought into the fray on the issue of back pay owed to soldiers and the funding of pensions granted to officers in 1780. When the army was struggling at Valley Forge, Alexander Hamilton had admonished Congress, "We begin to hate the country for its neglect of us."[49] Deprived of any means of payment for its supplies, the army turned to outright confiscation, issuing loan certificates in the name of Congress in "payment." These certificates became part of the national debt. State governments had also used this seizure of needed supplies as a means of meeting their responsibility for supporting the war.

In February 1781, the reformers made one of their important moves by putting Robert Morris in charge of finances. Morris took more executive control over fiscal operations and tried to get Congress to tell the states that if they did not pay their share of the government's debt, they would be subject to federal taxes levied within their state.[50]

Morris found a capable ally when Hamilton became a member of Congress from New York. To bolster public opinion in favor of the plan of taxation, Hamilton provided his own analysis of the government's financial problems in a series of essays, "The Continentalist," numbers 1-6, appearing in *The New York Packet and the American Advertiser* from July 1781 to July 1782. At the heart of these problems, Hamilton wrote, was "jealousy of power," which limited the authority of the central government. As a result with respect to that government, he feared, "if it is too weak at first, it will continually grow weaker."[51]

This result came from the tendency of each local government to put its interests above those of the national government, being "more disposed to advance its own authority upon the ruins of that of the confederacy." These governments would also "have more empire over the minds of their subjects, than the general one," because they operated closer to home. The people, too, would thus put their local interests above the national interest.[52]

By this means Hamilton explained the poor treatment being accorded to the army, as well as its ineffectiveness in fighting the war. There was no direct national support for its efforts.[53] That lack of support showed clearly in the tax system of the Congress.

Hamilton proposed an overhaul of this tax system, including the right to levy tariffs, put taxes on land, and raise a "modest capitation tax" ("a dollar or even a half dollar per head") from all civilian males above the age of fifteen. These three items were essential, along with less needed taxes on mines and the right of the central government to sell public land. "The great defect of the confederation," he continued, "is, that it gives the United States no property, or in other words, no revenue, nor the means of acquiring it." This defect was especially detrimental toward maintaining the credit rating of the government, he added, linking taxes to the national debt. As he put it, "This credit being secured through Congress, the funds ought to be provided, declared and vested in them." A good credit rating was important, he concluded, in agreement with Adam Smith, because even "nations the most opulent and powerful are obliged to have recourse to loans, in time of war."[54]

Hamilton agreed with Smith and Hume that the best tax was a tariff on luxury items, writing: "It is agreed that imposts on trade, when not immoderate or improperly laid, is one of the most eligible species of taxation. They fall in great measure upon articles not of absolute necessity, and being partly transferred to the price of the commodity, are so far imperceptibly paid by the consumer. It is therefore the mode which may be excersized by the federal government with least exception or disgust."

He further followed Smith by arguing that government could not abuse this power to tax, because a tariff too high would cause a reduction of revenue: "Experience has shown that moderate duties are more productive than high ones." Moreover, the merchant, not the consumer, might pay the taxes, as the ability of the merchant to raise prices to pass the duty onto customers depended on "the quantity of goods at market in proportion on the demand."[55]

Hamilton recognized that the national government would be better able to make use of the tariff than would be the separate states. The states might compete with each other in trade wars, reducing tariffs to bring business to their own ports. To the charge that the tariff fell unequally on the larger importing states, he responded that all of the states had suitable ports and could develop international trade. Besides, he concluded, "it is impossible to devise any specific tax, that will operate equally on the whole community."[56]

Hamilton's was but one voice, however, and the debate over the tariff continued. Rhode Island had not approved it by 1782, remaining the lone holdout. That state relied heavily on maritime trade, so it found a tariff unfair; it also had its own tariff for tax purposes. Its delegate to Congress, David Howell, took a legal high ground. He wrote, "Should our little State have the credit of preventing the 5 p Cent from taking effect it would be to us an additional gem." By this he meant that the tariff "was but an entering wedge, others will follow—a land tax, a poll tax, & an Excise.

Is it not best to oppose the first in such a manner as to discourage application for the others?"[57]

Rhode Island's objections were brought together in a pamphlet printed in Providence in 1782. In the main they rested on the unfairness of the impost, which would hit a commercial state like Rhode Island much more heavily than an agricultural state. Even within the state, different persons would feel the tax differently, regardless of whether the tax was paid by the consumer, merchant, or a combination of the two. Again the issue of national needs for revenue was raised and answered as it had been in the past: "If our safety as a people depends on what is called a permanent Continental fund, which I very much doubt, would it not be a safer, a more equal and just method, after having ascertained the sum that the fund shall consist of, to apportion it to each State, to be paid quarterly or annually; then such a mode of collecting it could be adopted as would be most suitable to the circumstances of each State in particular, known best and perhaps only to the inhabitants themselves."[58]

Efforts were made to negotiate with the Rhode Island legislature, but the Rhode Islanders remained fixed in their opposition, with their legislature maintaining that an indefinite grant of taxing powers to Congress would make its members "independent of their constituents; and so the proposed impost is repugnant to the liberty of the United States."[59] With this attitude, the smallest state was able to block any tax plan proposed by the Congress.

Advocates of a stronger central government took the lesson of Rhode Island to heart. Madison pointed to Rhode Island's hypocrisy when its delegates voted for money to be spent by Congress and approved of government borrowing. "And yet," he lamented, "they absolutely refuse the only fund which could be satisfactory to lenders. The indignation against this perverse sister is increased by her shameful delinquency in the constitutional requisition."[60]

Writing from military headquarters in Newburgh, New York, Major Samuel Shaw placed his finger on the problem: "No money, no funds, and what is worse, no disposition in the people to establish funds. . . . That the smallest State in the union should thus counteract and annul the proceedings of the other twelve argues an awful defect in the Confederation."[61] Madison identified the same problem when he wrote, "A jealousy is already perceived among some States that others will eventually *elude their share of the burden.*"[62]

This was the worst part of the quandary facing Congress. If it looked as if one state would escape paying its share of the requisition, then prudence directed that each state not pay its quota; when all thought that way, none would pay. Madison would learn this all too well, for on the eve of a delegation from Congress setting out to negotiate with leaders in Rhode Island, word came that his own Virginia had canceled its approval of the impost.[63]

Not everyone saw the need for federal taxes. One pamphlet writer, for example, proposed "a method of Supporting Government without taxing or fining the People." This writer identified that "by our daily Experience, we find that the assessing and levying of Taxes, is a difficult, perplexing, troublesome and disagreeable Work; and with all, we can scarcely come to any Equality and Justice among the Community." As a result, the "Dislike of the People . . . attending Taxation" caused him "to think that Nature had been unfriendly to a free Government in this one Thing only: So that a free Government could scarcely be maintained without a general Virtue among the inhabitants to support it freely." Instead of taxes, he would resort to the "promising Advantages which attends the Depreciation of a Paper Currency," especially since "the ill Consequences which attended this Depreciation may be easily remedied."

In the past, he continued, governments issued bills of credit and then called a portion of them in with taxes and destroyed them. Instead of a tax, he conjectured, could not the government have "ordered every Man, by Proclamation, to burn the [unnecessary] Part of the Cash in his Possession? This certainly would have saved the Expence of Collectors of this Tax." The point was not to impose a mandatory burning of money but, what amounted to the same thing, to justify a tax on money.

What the writer intended was for a schedule of taxes to be placed on each paper dollar issued. Say a dollar was issued. An annual tax could be imposed to reduce the value of the dollar by five cents a year, and after twenty years, the dollar would be without value. In this way the government could print money and spend it, but eventually the value of the money issued would fall to zero. Emissions of bills of credit would take care of themselves. As to the fairness of the tax, the author believed that most money would fall into the hands of the "unworking Callings, such as Merchants, Priests, Physicians, Lawyers, Toymakers, &c." Since these groups spent their money on superfluous items, the tax would fall on luxuries.[64] This scheme was not followed up in a serious way.

CONCLUSION

The debates over the impost and the arguments made by Madison, Morris, and Hamilton were evidence of the dissatisfaction political leaders had with the colonial tax system, as adjusted for the war. They had relied on paper money as a temporary system of finance but understood the inflationary pressures caused by excessive emissions of paper dollars. They wanted a shift to debt and taxes as a new system of government finance.

Proponents of that paper money system claimed that it was a necessary evil, crucial for getting the country through the war. Yet when they tried to remedy the evil, they were stymied by the unanimity requirement of the Articles of Confederation and the failure of the states to pay the requisition. Perhaps in the postwar period consolidation of the government's finances could take place.

NOTES

1. Randolph E. Paul, *Taxation in the United States* (Boston: Little, Brown, 1954), pp. 3–4.

2. Thomas Fleming, *The Man Who Dared Lightning* (New York: William Morrow, 1971), p. 153.

3. Davis R. Dewey, *Financial History of the United States* (New York: Longmans, Green, 1934), pp. 10–14.

4. E. James Ferguson, *The Power of the Purse* (Chapel Hill: University of North Carolina Press, 1962), pp. 5–18.

5. Paul Studenski and Herman E. Kroos, *Financial History of the United States*, 2d ed. (New York: McGraw-Hill, 1963), p. 15.

6. Harold U. Faulkner, *American Economic History* (New York: Harper and Brothers, 1929), p. 156; Ferguson, *Power*, pp. 21–22.

7. Studenski and Kroos, *Financial History*, p. 23.

8. Alfred H. Kelly and Winfred A. Harbison, *The American Constitution: Its Origins and Development*, 4th ed. (New York: W. W. Norton, 1970), p. 68.

9. Fleming, *The Man Who Dared Lightning*, p. 154.

10. Smith, *Wealth*, vol. 2, pp. 480–84. Smith used Pennsylvania as an example of the use of paper money for internal trade. Perhaps he had gotten this information from his good friend Dr. Franklin.

11. Gary M. Walton and Hugh Rockoff, *History of the American Economy*, 6th ed. (New York: Harcourt Brace Jovanovich, 1990), p. 110.

12. Kelly and Harbison, *The American Constitution*, p. 72.

13. Ibid., p. 75.

14. Fleming, *The Man Who Dared Lightning*, p. 135.

15. The last two paragraphs rely on Gordon S. Wood, *The Creation of the American Republic, 1776–1787* (Chapel Hill: University of North Carolina Press, 1969), pp. 46–78; Paine quotation from p. 55, and Adams quotation from p. 78.

16. This view of the problems of the Continental Congress follows closely that of Jack N. Rakove, *The Beginnings of National Politics* (Baltimore: Johns Hopkins University Press, 1979), passim.

17. *Journals of the Continental Congress, 1774–1789*, ed. John C. Fitzpatrick (Washington, DC: U.S. Government Printing Office, 1934), vol. 2, pp. 221–22.

18. Joseph Dorfman, *The Economic Mind in American Civilization*, vol. 1 (New York: Viking Press, 1948), p. 212.

19. Cited in Rakove, *The Beginnings of National Politics*, p. 305.

20. *Journals of the Continental Congress*, vol 9, p. 801.

21. Richard B. Morris, *The Forging of the Union: 1781–1789* (New York: Harper and Row, 1987), p. 35.

22. Rakove, *The Beginnings of National Politics*, p. 208.

23. Dorfman, *The Economic Mind*, p. 217.

24. Letter to John Parke Custis, November 14, 1777, in *The Writings of George Washington*, ed. John C. Fitzpatrick, vol. 10 (Westport, CT: Greenwood Press reprint, 1970), p. 60. The same sentiment is expressed in letters to General Joseph Spencer (January 24, 1778, vol. 10, p. 346) and William Fitzhugh (April 10, 1779, vol. 14, p. 365).

25. Sloan, *Principle and Interest*, p. 36.

26. Petaliah Webster, "An Essay on the Danger of Too Much Circulating Cash in a State, the Ill Consequences Thence Arising, and the Necessary Remedies," October 5, 1776, in *Political Essays on the Nature and Operation of Money, Public Finances and Other Subjects* by Petaliah Webster (New York: Burt Franklin, 1969 reprint of 1791 edition), pp. 2–3, 5, 22.

27. Report of the Committee on Finance, September 19, 1776, *Journals of the Continental Congress*, vol.12, pp. 928–33. According to the editor, the report was in the handwriting of Gouverneur Morris.

28. *Journals of the Continental Congress*, vol.12, pp. 1073–75.

29. Cited in Faulkner, *American Economic History*, p. 173.

30. Petaliah Webster, "A Second Essay on Free Trade and Finance" (August 1779), in Webster, *Political Essays*, pp. 29–31.

31. Petaliah Webster, "A Fifth Essay on Free Trade and Finance" (March 30, 1780), in Webster, *Political Essays*, pp. 99, 122.

32. Rakove, *The Beginnings of National Politics*, p. 206.

33. Report from Treasury Office, April 21, 1779, *Journals of the Continental Congress*, vol. 14, p. 519.

34. *Journals of the Continental Congress*, vol.13, p. 493.

35. "To the Inhabitants of the United States of America," *Journals of the Continental Congress*, vol. 14, pp. 649–50.

36. Dewey, *Financial History*, p. 35. For a through analysis of the efforts of the states to levy taxes and pay their portions of the requisitions, see Roger H. Brown, *Redeeming the Republic: Federalists, Taxation, and the Origins of the Constitution*, Baltimore: Johns Hopkins University Press, 1993, especially pp. 32–40.

37. Janet A. Riesman, "Money, Credit and Federalist Political Economy," in Richard Beeman, Stephen Botein and Edward C. Carter II, eds., *Beyond Confederation: Origins of the Constitution and American National Identity* (Chapel Hill: University of North Carolina Press, 1987), p. 129.

38. Ferguson, *Power of the Purse*, p. 45.

39. *Considerations on the Subject of Finance*, 1779, pamphlet in collection of the American Antiquarian Society, pp. 1–15.

40. Rakove, *The Beginnings of National Politics*, p. 179.

41. Thomas Paine, *The Crisis Extraordinary*, 1780, copy in collection of American Antiquarian Society, pp. 7–13.

42. Rakove, *The Beginnings of National Politics*, p. 212; Studenski and Kroos, *Financial History*, p. 29; *Journals of the Continental Congress*, vol. 16, pp. 205–7.

43. James Madison to Thomas Jefferson, May 6, 1780, in *The Papers of Thomas Jefferson*, ed. Julian P. Boyd, vol. 3 (Princeton, NJ: Princeton University Press, 1951), p. 370; James Madison, "Observations written posterior to the circular Address of Congress in Sept. 1779, and prior to their Act of march, 1780," reprinted in *Federal Reserve Bank of Minneapolis Quarterly Review* (Fall 1997), pp. 3–7.

44. *Journals of the Continental Congress*, vol. 17, pp. 563–64.

45. Donald R. Stabile and Jeffrey A. Cantor, *The Public Debt of the United States: An Historical Perspective*, 1775–1990 (New York: Praeger, 1991), pp. 13–14.

46. *Journals of the Continental Congress*, vol. 19, pp. 102–3.

47. "By the United States in Congress Assembled, February 20, 1782," copy in collection of American Antiquarian Society.

48. Treasury Office, April 16, 1781, *Journals of the Continental Congress*, vol. 19, pp. 402–19.

49. E. James Ferguson, "What Were the Sources of the Constitutional Convention?" in Gordon S. Wood, ed., *The Confederation and the Constitution* (Washington, DC: University Press of America, 1979), p.4.

50. Ferguson, *Power of the Purse*, p. 161.

51. Alexander Hamilton, "The Continentalist, No. I," in Harold C. Syrett and Jacob E. Cooke, eds., *The Papers of Alexander Hamilton* (PAH hereafter) (New York: Columbia University Press, 1961), vol. 2, p. 652.

52. Hamilton, "The Continentalist, No. II," PAH, vol. 2, pp. 655–56.

53. Hamilton, "The Continentalist, No. III," PAH, vol. 2, pp. 660–62.

54. Hamilton, "The Continentalist, No. IV," PAH, vol. 2, pp. 670–72.

55. Hamilton, "The Continentalist, No. V," PAH, vol. 3, pp. 78–80.

56. Hamilton, "The Continentalist, No. VI," PAH, vol. 3, pp. 99–104.

57. Cited in Rakove, *The Beginnings of National Politics*, p. 315.

58. "Thoughts on the Five per Cent," Providence, 1792, copy in collection of American Antiquarian Society, pp. 4–10, quotation from p. 10.

59. Merrill Jensen, *The New Nation: A History of the United States during the Confederation, 1781–1789* (Boston: Northeastern University Press (reprint), 1981), p. 65.

60. Letter to Edmund Randolph, November 19, 1782, *The Papers of James Madison*, ed. William T. Hutchinson and William M. E. Rachal, (Chicago: University of Chicago Press, 1962–   ), vol. 5, p. 289.

61. Cited in Morris, *The Forging*, p. 42.

62. Letter to Edmund Randolph, December 24, 1782, *Madison Papers*, vol. 5, p. 449.

63. Letter from Virginia Delegates to Benjamin Harrison, December 31, 1782, *Madison Papers*, vol. 5, p. 477.

64. "Proposals to Amend and Perfect the Policy of the Government of the United States of AMERICA," Philadelphia, 1782, copy in collection of the American Antiquarian Society, pp. 16–23.

Chapter 2

REQUISITIONS SMALL AND SLOW

With the war over, the country began to settle down with a more stable economy. Prices stabilized, crops were planted and the country experienced a degree of prosperity. Despite these settled conditions, problems with the federal government's finances continued. The national government remained burdened with debt it could not pay, and the debate of whether or not and how to change its tax system persisted.

This debate over money, debt, and taxes would form a prelude to the contest that would eventually take place over the drafting and ratification of the Constitution. The period of the postwar government under the Articles of Confederation has a myth as one of drift, where no one knew what to do about the weak government. As this chapter describes, however, persons in and out of the Congress understood what was going wrong and were formulating plans for how to change policies to set things right. Eventually, they would see that they needed a change in the government and its system of finance for those policies to be put in place. Meanwhile, they faced the frustration of working within a system they found ever more inadequate.

That inadequacy had been addressed just as the war was winding down. After his experiences in trying to manage the government's finances, Robert Morris devised a lengthy plan to put those finances on a surer basis. His plan is worth considering in detail, as it presaged policies that would be enacted a decade later.

THE MORRIS PLAN

In July 1782, Morris sent Congress his plan for putting the government's finances in order.[1] The report is noteworthy for its understanding of public finance viewed from a commercial perspective. It advocated that the national government take over all of the war debt, including what the states owed, hoping that this would make it necessary to grant it greater taxing powers. Morris then considered the alternatives of taxing or borrowing as methods of public finance. He took the commercial perspective that debt was not bad in itself.

"The propriety and utility of public Loans," he began, "have been subjects of much controversy. Those who find themselves saddled with the Debts of a preceding Generation, naturally exclaim against Loans." When the debt was due to folly or extravagance, those claims were perhaps merited; the same complaints would be made when taxes were wasted, and in the case of taxes, "it will appear that the eventual evils which Posterity must sustain from heavy Taxes are greater than from Loans." Therefore, sound government would find it advantageous to use loans plus taxes. Taxes might stimulate individuals to produce more, but when they reduced "the subsistence of the People, they become burdensome and oppressive."

The real burden of taxation was that taxes took money away from industrious persons, which could reduce economic growth. As a counter, however, Morris set forth two ways taxes could increase the wealth of the nation: "First they stimulate industry to provide the means of payment. Secondly, they encourage economy so far as to avoid the purchases of unnecessary things, and keep money in readiness for the Tax-gatherer." Taxation need not be detrimental to the economy.

Nevertheless, debt should supplement taxation. With respect to loans, it was true that "money must be diverted from those channels in which it would otherwise have flowed, and therefore either the public must give better terms than Individuals, or there must be money enough to supply the wants of both." If there were enough funds for both public and private borrowing, then if the government did not borrow, interest rates would fall; government borrowing kept interest rates high, and some persons "are deprived of the means of extending their industry. So that no case of a domestic loan can well be supposed where some public loss will not arise to counterbalance the public gain, except where the creditor spares from his consumption to lend to the Government." In short, there were interest rate costs related to government borrowing, depending on the amount borrowed and the funds available to lend.

So far, then, Morris argued that both debt and taxes had costs and benefits. Both could reduce the amount of money available for private investment, and both could be of benefit if they reduced spending on luxury goods.

The advantage of debt over taxes was that different persons were made to pay. Loans came from the wealthy, so borrowing had the advantage of giving "stability in Government by combining together the interests of moneyed men for its support." In addition, taxes fell heavily on the lower classes, so "the relief obtained for them by such loans more than counterbalances the loss sustained by those, who would have borrowed money to extend their commerce or tillage."

In essence, Morris saw the tax versus debt question in terms of its effect on different income groups. Taxes would hit heavily on the industrious farmer, while loans would be made voluntarily by the wealthy. Government borrowing might reduce investment through the crowding out of private investment, but not by as much as taxes would reduce it from lower incomes. Moreover, "since a plenty of money and consequent ease of obtaining it, induce men to engage in speculations Which are often unprofitable," the crowding out that did take place from higher interest rates was not necessarily a loss.

As for foreign loans, Morris found no problems with them, if they were used for good purposes. It might be argued that interest payments on foreign loans drained specie from the country, but for Morris that was "only saying in other words, that it would be more convenient to receive money as a present than as a Loan." Any loan may take specie away from the area where the borrowing took place, so national boundaries created no special problem. If the borrowed money produced benefits, the debt was worthwhile.

For borrowing to take place, however, Morris was "brought back to the necessity of establishing public credit." The continental government had gradually lost its credit rating through the issuance of bills of credit, and the only way to restore it was "that all paper money ought to be absorbed by taxation (or otherwise) and destroyed." In addition, it was necessary to "provide solid funds for the national debt." Many persons might "grumble at the expence," but they were the sort "content to relieve themselves by Loan from the weight of Taxes." Funding of the debt was an issue of income distribution. Morris observed,

If the Debt were to be paid by a single effort of taxation, it could only create a transfer of property from one Individual to another and the aggregate wealth of the community would be precisely the same. But since nothing more is attempted than merely to fund the debt by providing for the interest (at 6 per cent) the question of ability is resolved to this single point, whether it is easier for *a part of the people* to pay one hundred dollars, than for the *whole people* to pay six dollars.

Paying off the debt immediately was not necessary. All that had to be done was pay the interest on it and revive its value.

Restoring the public's faith in the public debt would also be good for the economy. Many who held debt certificates were deprived of the capital needed to allow "the full exercise of their skill and industry." If the debt were funded, the wealthy would purchase debt from those persons. In this way idle funds in the hands of the wealthy would be transferred to the industrious.

Restoring public credit to make future borrowing possible was also important. "When we omit paying by Taxes the interest of Debts already contracted," Morris continued, "and ask to borrow for the purpose, making the same promises to obtain the new loans, which had been already made to obtain the old, we shall surely be disappointed." Efforts to borrow to pay interest on previous loans would not work. Revenue from the states in payment of their requisitions was needed to fund the interest on the existing debt before more borrowing could take place.

Due to the high level of the debt, however, more taxes were needed. Even if the impost of 5% were granted, there would be a need for more revenue. To bring this revenue into the government, Morris proposed a tax on land of one dollar per hundred acres, a poll tax of one dollar on all freemen and male slaves between the ages of sixteen and sixty, and an excise tax.

In defense of the land tax, Morris maintained that it was certain as to the amount to be paid as well as the time of payment—points Smith had made. Calculation of the tax would be easy. It might also have the advantage of breaking up large land holdings, as the speculators in land would be forced to sell some of their holdings to pay their taxes and reduce their future tax bill. This would place idle land into industrious hands and "would have the salutary operation of an agrarian law without the iniquity." To arguments that the tax be based on the value of land, Morris responded that this would be hard to measure, making the tax uncertain and inconvenient. Arguments against a land tax were made "by those men, who can very well bear the expence, but who wish to shift it from themselves to others."

Morris waved aside objections to a poll tax by pointing out that it worked well already in several states. Besides, it was so small that the rich and middle classes could easily pay it, and the poor would be exempted. Wages were high compared to the tax in the United States, so it did not seem a burden "to ask two days out of a year as a contribution to a payment of public Debts."

Excise taxes also existed in the states, so a national excise could not be opposed. The advantage of excise taxes was that "being mingled with the price, they are less sensible to the people." A tax on "ardent spirits" was especially useful "as a means of compelling vice to support the cause of virtue" and of collecting "from the idle and dissolute that contribution to the public service which they will not otherwise make." Sin taxes are as old as sin.

With all these taxes in place, Morris reported, interest payments on the debt could be met. Any surplus funds would be put into a sinking fund to retire debt.

Morris also considered the impact of his plan on holders of the debt, especially speculators who were buying loan certificates at low prices. Human nature being what it was, preventing speculation by law was not possible. Left to themselves, speculators counteracted each other. As for those who sold their debt certificates cheaply, they were "better able to judge" their own affairs than was the government. Then Morris took up an issue that would later vex Alexander Hamilton: "It is not uncommon to hear, that those who have bought the public Debts for small sums, ought only to be paid their purchase money. The reasons given are, that they have taken advantage of the distressed creditors, and shewn a diffidence in the public faith." In response, Morris answered that they had at least given some relief to those distressed creditors, and they showed as much faith in the government as those who sold their debt. Moreover, legal justice required honoring the transfer of the debt and payment to whoever held it. Hamilton would later build on these arguments but would not surpass the gist of them.

Morris also worked out a plan to establish a bank, in which the government would own a share, to issue paper banknotes. The profits from the bank paid out to the government would be used to pay off its debt. The Bank of North America was instituted under Morris' direction, and he deposited government funds in it. It failed to gain enough capital to create a sound money supply based on its banknotes[2] and did not do the job Morris hoped for.

The congressional committee that took up Morris' report judged that his plan was "in general too exceptionable to meet with the approbation of Congress."[3] To gain support for his plans among the government's creditors, Morris stopped paying any claim that existed before his term of office. He also ceased paying salaries to the army. His plan of taxes on land, commodities, and the right to vote, however, breached the terms of the Articles of Confederation. Congress agreed, for in September 1782 it merely renewed its request for an impost with a motion to offer it again for approval by the states, this time with a time limit of "25 years, unless the debts . . . be discharged in the mean time. In which case they shall cease."[4]

POSTWAR FINANCE

By 1783, the year the Revolutionary War finally ended, members of Congress again began looking for ways to place the government's finances in order by setting up a new system of funding. "In devising these funds," their recommendations read,

Congress did not overlook the mode of supplying the common treasury, provided by the articles of confederation; but after the most respectful consideration of that mode, they were constrained to regard it as inadequate and inapplicable to the form into which the public debt must be thrown. The delays and uncertainties incident to a revenue to be established and collected from time to time by thirteen independent authorities, is at first view irreconcilable with the punctuality essential in the discharge of a national debt.

Congress continued with the compromise plan of an impost limited to no longer than twenty-five years; state agents in each state would collect it, and no other national taxes would be proposed. The impost was justified because taxes on items of consumption were the best, and "of all taxes on consumption, those on foreign commerce are most compatible with the genius and policy of free states." The plan for the impost also allowed that the duties collected would not be used for anything but the discharge of the interest or the principal of the debt from the war. In addition to the tariff, the states were requested to contribute $1.5 million per year, apportioned among them. The basis for this request was that the public debt was estimated to be $42 million, with annual interest charges of $2.4 million. Since the impost was expected to raise $915,956, the requisition was aimed at providing a total amount needed to maintain the interest payments on the debt.[5]

Hamilton and Morris continued their efforts to expand the tax system as set forth in Morris' plan. They wanted the impost to carry specific dollar rates imposed on certain items to avoid controversy over the value on which the 5% tax would be levied, with the tariff to be heaviest on items that were difficult to smuggle. They also proposed Morris' program of land and poll taxes.

Most members of the Congress still thought the Morris program went too far, but not James Madison. To counter the objection that the program "contravenes the articles of confederation," he pointed out that the Articles of Confederation took into account "the necessity of alterations in the federal system." He continued, "They moreover authorize Congress to borrow money. Now in order to borrow money permanent & certain provision is necessary, & if this provision cannot be made in any other way as has been shewn, a general revenue is within the spirit of the confederation."[6] The power to borrow included a power to tax. Madison was on the dangerous ground of the doctrine of implied powers, which he would come to oppose.

At this stage, however, he argued that Congress had "a right to fix the quantum of money necessary for the common purpose. The right of the states is limited to the mode of supply." If Congress' legal authority in this case proved futile, it followed "that in order to fulfil the views of the federal constitution, such a change sd. be made as will render it efficient." As an indication of the type of changes needed, Madison supported the impost, land tax, and poll tax.[7] He urged the states to adopt his plan because it was the smallest change possible in the government that was consistent with paying the public debt.[8]

In the same vein, James Wilson of Pennsylvania went on to show that, given a debt of $40 million and interest payments of $2.4 million, the Morris tax package would be just about enough. Although an excise was "tyrannical & justly obnoxious," it had worked in several states.[9]

Other members of Congress, John Rutledge of South Carolina and Oliver Ellsworth of Connecticut, opposed the entire system, thinking "it wrong to couple any other objects with the Impost; that the States would give us this if anything; and that if a land tax or an excise were combined with it, the whole scheme would fail." John F. Mercer of Virginia "applauded the wisdom of the Confederation in leaving the provision of money to the States" and felt they would not comply unless the taxes were coupled with a popular spending program, such as reimbursing soldiers for their back pay. Arthur Lee of Virginia agreed that use of the funds to pay soldiers would make the states more favorable to the impost, but Wilson maintained that this was a violation of sound financial principles.[10]

As the debate continued, Hamilton argued that the real reason for the objection to the impost was that Rhode Island used its own impost to let goods shipped from its ports to Connecticut shift its tax burden to another state, while Vermont had no debt to be repaid so would not gain from the impost at all.[11] Divisions among the states were responsible for the failure of the impost, a perspective Hamilton would carry for the rest of his life.

Madison repeated his argument that since Congress had the power to issue bills of credit and borrow money, it should have the power to tax. There was no "dangerous association of a power over the purse with the power of the sword," as opponents suggested. Lee answered that "the doctrine maintained by [Madison] was pregnant with dangerous consequences to the liberties" of the states.[12] At one point in the debate, it was even moved that the word "levy" be replaced by "collect" as "less obnoxious to the states."[13]

The broad-based Morris plan again failed, and on April 18, 1783, Congress instead passed a restricted plan of tariff duties, limited to twenty-five years, and sent it to the states for approval.[14] To rebut the objections to the tariff made by Rhode Island, the Congress issued a report written by Hamilton, Madison, and Thomas Fitzsimmons (Pennsylvania). To the claim that the tariff would fall on merchants and thus unfairly tax commercial states, the response was, "The most common experience, joined to the concurrent opinions of the ablest commercial and political observers, have established beyond controversy this general principle, 'that every duty on imports is incorporated with the price of the commodity, and ultimately paid by the consumer.'" As to the claim that the length of the tax was indefinite, the committee answered that the tax would last only until the debt was repaid, being "persuaded that it is as remote from the intention of their constituents to perpetuate that debt, as to extinguish it at once by a faithful neglect of providing the means" to pay interest on it.[15]

Hamilton, even as a member of Congress, was willing to use the army as a way to get taxing power for the central government. He hoped to enlist General Washington in support of this plan, for Washington had the authority to keep the army from getting out of hand. Although he agreed that a better system of revenue was needed, Washington told Hamilton that the army was "a dangerous tool to play with."[16] More peaceful measures were needed. While he did not expound on those measures, in his circular letter of resignation, Washington did insist that the war could have been ended sooner and at lower cost "if the resources of the country could have been properly called forth." The obstacle had been the "WANT OF ENERGY IN THE CONTINENTAL GOVERNMENT." This had resulted in "a partial compliance with the requisitions of congress, in some of the states, and from a failure of punctuality in others." Such "notorious facts" indicated "the defects of our federal constitution, particularly in the prosecution of a war."[17] In this way Washington obliquely lent his luster to support the tax plan.

The different states still had to ratify the call for an impost, however, and although all of them did at one time or another, some withdrew their support, and it never received a unanimous vote.[18] The Congress under the Articles of Confederation never gained the power to tax.

Along with the impost, the Congress also asked the states to contribute their quotas toward an annual requisition of $1.5 million. In making this request, Congress debated changing the basis for apportioning the quota from land to population. Madison "thought the value of land could never be justly or satisfactorily obtained," so a shift to population was in order. A favorable view was also expressed by Abraham Clark of New Jersey, who said that when he was in Congress at the time property was made the basis of the quotas, "the Southern States Wd. have agreed to numbers in preference to the value of land if $\frac{1}{2}$ their slaves only sd. be included: but that the Eastern States would not concur in that proportion." The Congress adjourned for the day with an agreement to shift to population, with only the way of counting slaves to be determined.

The question of how to count slaves in terms of taxation and representation would become a major issue at the Constitutional Convention, and the delegates there ultimately settled on the ratio determined by the Congress in 1783. Since there was no debate at the convention over the actual number chosen, the agreement of 1783 was a crucial moment in U.S. history. Madison recorded the debate, making the proceedings sound almost like an auction. Perhaps this was intentional; perhaps, merely unconscious. Anyway, the debate started at the previous day's suggestion "that two blacks be rated as equal to one freeman." Madison chronicled the move to a consensus as follows:

Mr. Wolcott was for rating them as 4 to 3.

Mr. Carrol as 4 to 1.

Mr. Williamson sd he was principled agst slavery: and that he thought slaves an encumbrance to Society instead of increasing its ability to pay taxes.

Mr. Higginson at 4 to 3.

Mr. Rutledge sd for the sake of the object he wd agree to rate slaves as 2 to 1, but he sincerely thought 3 to 1 would be a juster proportion.

Mr. Holton as 4 to 3.

Mr. Osgood sd he cd not go beyond 4 to 3.

A vote to make the rating 3 to 2 failed, with the southern states voting no in a bloc.

They shelved the issue for a time, but after discussion of the general topic the members returned to it. Madison offered a 5 to 3 rating as "a proof of the sincerity of his professions of liberality." Rutledge seconded the motion, and Wilson noted his agreement to the compromise. Lee opposed the compromise, but it passed by a 5 to 3 vote, the Southern states voting as a bloc in favor.

This issue, to say the least, was very unusual. Since the three-fifths rule was later enshrined in the Constitution, it is worth spending a bit more time on the basis for the unequal rating of slaves and freemen. Madison summarized the two sides as follows:

The arguments used by those who were for rating slaves high were, that the expence of feeding & cloathing them was as far below that incident to freemen as their industry & ingenuity were below those of freemen; and that the warm climate within wch the States having slaves lay, compared wth the rigorous climate and inferior fertility of the others, ought to have great weight in the case & that the exports of the former States were greater than of the latter. On the other side it was said that Slaves were not put to labor as young as the children of labouring families—that, having no interest in their labor, they did as little as possible & omitted every exertion of thought required to facilitate & expedite it; that if the exports of the States having slaves exceeded those of the others, their imports were in proportion, slaves being employed wholly in agriculture, not in manufacturing; & that in fact the balance of trade formerly was much more agst the Sn States than the others.[19]

The issue centered on the value added to a state's income by slaves compared to free persons and hence its ability to pay taxes. A rating of equality of slaves with free labor in terms of taxes might have impeded the investment in slaves, as the southern states would have paid more in taxes as slavery increased. Granting such a tax break to the South was necessary to change the basis for requisitions to population, so it had to be done. The tax break worked, in terms of encouraging investment in slaves, which went on unimpeded for another eighty years.

REFORM DIES OUT

The fight for taxes died down soon after, partly because the Articles of Confederation imposed term limits. Article 5 held no one could hold congressional office "for more than three years in any term of six years." Among the first to be sent home under this rule in 1783 was one of the most respectable advocates of fiscal responsibility at the national level, James Madison. Hamilton followed by resigning, to make money practicing law.

In 1784 a new committee, whose membership included Thomas Jefferson, reported the same dismal story about the government's finances, including the information that interest payments were in arrears to the amount of $5.5 million. The report summarized the underlying problem in terse, but telling, terms, "The payments on this requisition have been small and slow." Things had gotten to such a predicament that the report suggested Congress "warmly to encourage the abler states to go as far beyond this proportion as their happier situation will admit." Such a suggestion surely was woebegone, for the report pointed out that separate states did not care to contribute because they thought that when debt accounts were settled with the central government, they would come out ahead.[20]

The new committee could only repeat the request for a granting of the impost to the central government, but the states moved slowly. There would be no strengthening of the powers of the Congress. A further blow to strong government advocates came when Robert Morris resigned as superintendent of finance in October 1784.

Afterward, the balance of power in Congress shifted back to confederationists more comfortable with the lack of a system of taxes accorded to the central government. Congress could still only ask the individual states for revenue. The states continued to protect their sovereign rights by treating these requests as voluntary and rarely subscribed. Of $8 million requested of the states by Congress in 1782, only $400,000 had come in; from 1784 to 1786 the states contributed a total of about $500,000, with less than $200,000 being sent to Congress during its next fiscal year.[21] As Arthur Lee of Virginia, a supporter of Confederation, summed up the case, "The states would never agree to those plans which tended to aggrandize Congress."[22]

Despite the hindrance of no taxing power, Lee and his colleagues, with support from the states, were able to make some progress with the government's finances. Congress' requests for funds brought in enough to pay its daily expenses, and overall the states contributed 37% of the total requisitioned from them. The states were encouraged to pay off their war debts and to fund a portion of the Congress', although the settlement of the accounts was slow and often guesswork. The Congress was able to get loans and some payments from the states to at least keep up interest payments of the foreign-held debt. When interest payments on the domestic-held debt became overdue, Congress began issuing "indents," debt certificates for the owed interest. The states began accepting these for payment of taxes and sent them back to the Congress as payment for what was owed it. In June 1785 the public debt was calculated at $36.5 million.[23]

In modern times the response of the bond market often gauges government policies, with a lower price of bonds being evidence of a lack of support. In the late 1780s this principle held to an even greater degree. The market value of government debt instruments fell to about one-quarter of their face value.

In January 1786 Congress ordered that its secretary "report the number of states which have complied in whole or in part with the revenue system of April 18, 1783." The report found that with respect to the impost, eight states had approved it completely, two had approved subject to conditions, and "Delaware is said to have passed an act conformable to the recommendation above mentioned, but no official information thereof has yet been transmitted to this office." As for the request for $1.5 annually, only three states (New York, Pennsylvania, and North Carolina) had complied completely, and no other states had contributed after 1783.[24] In 1787 only New York and Pennsylvania remained paid in full on the requisition system.

In February 1786 yet another committee, this one containing James Monroe as a member, reported on the finances. It pointed out that the Congress had three choices: requisitions on the states, borrowing, or issuing bills of credit. The requisitions did not work, no borrowing could take place with interest payments in arrears, and no one would accept non-interest bills in exchange for interest-bearing debt. The only hope was passage of the impost, and that would still be insufficient for a sound financial system.

Even among the Confederation's supporters, the effort to manage government finance took its toll. Samuel Osgood of Massachusetts, who had opposed taxing powers for the government, took a different view when he was put in charge of the treasury. He wrote in 1786, "The united states must be entrusted with Monies other than the scanty pittance they obtain from the annual requisition . . . Congress must . . . be vested with coercive Powers as to the Collection of Money."[25] This feeling was becoming widespread in the Congress.

In 1786 the Congress issued a broadside that stated the concern bluntly. Its first sentence read, "Impressed with a sense of the sacred duty committed to them, and with an anxious and affectionate concern for the interest, honor and safety of their constituents, The United States in Congress assembled, have on various occasions, pointed out the dangerous situation of this nation, for want of funds to discharge the engagements which have been constitutionally made for the common benefits of the union." The requisition for the year would be made, and it was incumbent on the states to meet it to pay the heavy burden of debt and interest payments coming due. It was also time for the states to give the Congress permanent taxes different from the states' revenue sources. If not, the states were warned, their own "constitutions cannot long outlive the fate of the general union; and this union cannot exist without adequate funds."[26]

A rising frustration among members of Congress can be detected. On June 22, 1786, the Board of Treasury stated, "If it be asked what expectations there are that the several States will raise by the ordinary mode of Requisition, the Sums required by the proposed Report, the Answer obviously is, That no reasonable hope of this nature can possibly exist." Again they asked that the impost be granted, although, in this case, the lone negative vote was now from New York. An address was then sent to the states warn them of the nation's "danger, and to urge the adoption of such measures as may avert the Calamities with which it is threatened."[27]

This warning would have little impact on the states, which also had problems with finance. With weak tax plans of their own, several states continued to issue paper money in place of raising taxes. What taxes were paid used the paper money, which gained the support of farmers in a quest for a policy of easy money. The haven of antitax fervor, Rhode Island, was a particularly flagrant example. That state went so far as to compel inhabitants to accept its paper money issues as payment at face value.[28] This placed a very high inflation tax on lenders of money. As a result, they stopped making loans, in Robert Morris' words, "by the dread of paper money and tender laws."[29]

States that levied taxes fared no better. By the summer of 1786 Massachusetts had raised a heavy tax (for the time) in hard cash to pay off its paper securities. Protests from farmers in the west of the state had caused the tax to be reduced by permitting payment in depreciated state securities. Ignorant of this change, the farmers set off the outbreak that became known as Shays' Rebellion.[30] This unhappy event also drew more Americans to the idea of a stronger national government.

THE MOVE FOR A NEW SYSTEM

These financial difficulties of the state and national governments formed part of the impetus for revising the Articles of Confederation. To be sure it was not the only factor. Foreign affairs were in turmoil, as Britain and Spain were interfering with trade in the West and the Barbary pirates plagued merchant sea trade with Europe. The states were ignoring the provisions of the peace treaty with England.

With no tax plan in effect, by 1787 the government was technically in default on a loan from France, both interest and principal payments being in arrears, but the French government agreed to take over the payments.[31] Not a surprising record for a Congress that rarely had a quorum and whose membership shifted constantly. Just as important, the fledgling economy of the new nation was mired in economic problems for most of the 1780s, making tax revenues even harder to come by.

Back home in Virginia, Madison began to deplore the lack of fiscal responsibility of that state's legislature. In New York Hamilton had not supported the compromise plan of 1783, because it was too weakened in the effort to placate all the states—he was already urging Americans to "think Continentally" with regard to government.

By 1787 Hamilton, however, supported the 1783 plan in a speech asking the New York assembly to pass it. In his speech he pointed out the advantages of a national perspective by showing how the pursuit of the interests of each state would demolish them all, a viewpoint Madison shared.[32] He gave two examples. The first related to the requisition system whereby it was in the "interest of every state that the general government should be supplied with the revenues necessary for the national purpose; but it will be the particular interest of each state to pay as little as possible." The same argument held for the collection of taxes by each state using a tariff: "It is a clear point that we cannot carry the duties upon imposts to the same extent by separate arrangements as by a general plan; we must regulate ourselves by what we find done in neighboring states." If other states had low tariffs, New York's could not be raised.

Moreover, since New York and Pennsylvania were now the sole supporters of the Congress, if Pennsylvania stopped its aid, what would New York do? He asked, "Are we willing to be the Atlas of the union? or are we willing to see it perish? . . . Is there not a species of political knight errantry in adhering pertinaciously to a system which throws the whole weight of the confederacy upon this state, or upon one or two more?" Apparently there was, for New York refused to support the impost by a vote of 36 to 21.[33]

There was a certain disregard of reality in this decision that gave another example of how the interests of individual states did not add up to the general interest. In 1786 the House of Assembly of New Jersey had voted not "to comply with the requisition of Congress of the 27th. of September [1786] . . . until all states in the union shall comply with the requisition of April 1783, for an impost."[34] New Jersey would not contribute its quota of the requisition unless New York approved the impost. New York would not approve the impost, even though it was one of two states contributing its quota of the requisition. Was it holding off until the other states paid their share of the requisition? Maybe not, but this sort of gridlock prevented sound finance.

Although they are often pictured as letting the government's finances drift on to collapse without doing anything, ultimately leading to a new form of government, members of the Congress recognized that matters were coming to a head. In early 1787 they approved a committee report that read,

After the most solemn deliberation, and under the fullest conviction that the public embarrassments are such as above represented, the committee are of the opinion, that it has become the duty of congress to declare most explicitly, that the CRISIS HAS ARRIVED, when the people of these united states . . . must decide whether they will *support their rank as a nation by maintaining the PUBLIC FAITH at home or abroad*; or whether for *want of a timely exertion* in establishing a GENERAL REVENUE . . . they will hazard . . . the EXISTENCE OF THE UNION.

In support of the report, Congress agreed to it and resolved that it "may remain wholly acquitted from every imputation of want of attention to the interest and welfare of those whom they represent."[35]

CONCLUSION

The problem of taxation during and after the Revolutionary War was part of the whole dilemma of government that existed during this period. Americans were wary of ceding any powers to a central government. The denial to Congress of the power to raise taxes was not due to carelessness. The intent was to make it a creature of the states and answerable to the people. The national government would be a weak confederation of the states.

There were even those who saw the Articles of Confederation as a temporary plan, expedient only for fighting the war. In 1783 Jefferson took its role to be limited by declaring, "The constant sessions of Congress can not be necessary in times of peace." The Continental Congress hesitantly evolved into a strange (to us today) body. It passed laws and then had responsibility for executing them, yet there was no executive branch. Finances, for example, were handled by committees of the Congress under various names such as the Treasury Committee and the Board of Treasury. In addition, the Congress relied heavily on the states to implement its policies. As Gordon Wood describes it, "What is truly remarkable about the Confederation is the degree of union that was achieved."[36]

In opposition were advocates of a stronger role for the national government, even in those days. They were also among the delegates to the Congress but formed a minority for much of the war and were a majority for only a brief period after it. They tried to place the government's finances on a sound basis and failed. The obstacle was not one of effort and ability on their part but of an unwieldy system of taxation. As Hamilton and Madison understood, the pursuit of individual interest by the separate states did not add up to a smooth movement toward the national interest. To put the nation's finances in order, a stronger government with power over the purse was needed.

The force behind the accomplishment of that objective continued. After a decade of faltering efforts and growing frustration, many political leaders in the United States were ready for change. Since their efforts at reforming the Articles of Confederation had failed, they transformed their activities into a total overhaul of the government through the writing of the United States Constitution. A second revolution was in the making.

NOTES

1. The plan, to be summarized over the next several pages, is located in the *Journals of the Continental Congress*, vol. 22, pp. 429–47.

2. Riesman, "Money, Credit and Federalist Political Economy," pp. 144–48.

3. Letter, Office of Finance, July 29, 1782, *Journals of the Continental Congress*, vol. 22, pp. 429–47.

4. *Journals of the Continental Congress*, vol. 23, p. 546.

5. "Address and Recommendations to the States by the United States in Congress Assembled," Richmond, 1783, copy in collection of American Antiquarian Society, pp. 4–5, estimate of public debt on p. 15 and estimate of receipts of impost on p. 26.

6. Notes of Debates in the Continental Congress by James Madison, *Journals of the Continental Congress*, vol. 25, pp. 872–74.

7. Madison, *Notes*, pp. 874–75.

8. Lance Banning, *The Sacred Fire of Liberty: James Madison and the Founding of the Federal Republic* (Ithaca, NY: Cornell University Press, 1995), p. 38.

9. Madison, *Notes*, pp. 880–81.

10. Ibid., pp. 882, 900 and 903–4.

11. Ibid., p. 902.

12. Ibid., pp. 907–9.

13. Ibid., pp. 945–46.

14. *Journals of the Continental Congress*, vol. 24, pp. 188–92, 195–201, 256–61.

15. *Addresses and Recommendations to the States by the United States in Congress Assembled*, copy in the collection of the American Antiquarian Society, paper number 2.

16. John C. Miller, *Alexander Hamilton: Portrait in Paradox* (New York: Harper and Row, 1959), pp. 93–94.

17. "A Circular Letter from His Excellency General Washington, etc.," June 18, 1783, reprinted in *The American Museum or Repository of Ancient and Modern Fugitive Pieces* (subsequently named *The American Museum, or, Universal Magazine*), Philadelphia, May 1787, pp. 195–97.

18. Rakove, *The Beginnings of National Politics*, pp. 321–22 and 338.

19. Madison, *Notes*, pp. 948–49.

20. *Journals of the Continental Congress*, vol. 26, pp. 185–97.

21. Miller, *Alexander Hamilton*, pp. 84, 149.

22. Cited in Rakove, *The Beginnings of National Politics*, p. 320.

23. Brown, *Redeeming the Republic*, p. 13; *Journals of the Continental Congress*, vol. 28, p. 448.

24. "By the United States in Congress Assembled, January 2, 1786," copy in collection of American Antiquarian Society, no page numbers; *Journals of the Continental Congress*, vol. 31, pp. 7–11.

25. Cited in Rakove, *The Beginnings on National Politics*, p. 341.

26. Broadside, Continental Congress, 1786, copy in collection of American Antiquarian Society, 2 pages.

27. *Journals of the Continental Congress*, vol. 31, pp. 358, 534, 613.

28. Riesman, "Money, Credit and Federalist Political Economy," p. 150.

29. Gordon S. Wood, "Interests and Disinterestedness in the Making of the Constitution," in Richard Beeman, Stephen Botein and Edward C. Carter II, eds., *Beyond Confederation: Origins of the Constitution and American National Identity* (Chapel Hill: University of North Carolina Press), 1987, p. 106.

30. Forest McDonald, *The Presidency of George Washington* (Lawrence: University of Kansas Press, 1974), pp. 244–46.

31. Jensen, *The New Nation*, pp. 382–84.

32. Banning, *The Sacred Fire*, p. 55.

33. "Col. Hamilton's Speech on the Impost," February 18, 1787, *The American Museum, or, Universal Magazine*, Philadelphia, May 1787, pp. 517, 519, 523, 524.

34. Reported in *The New Haven Gazette and Connecticut Magazine*, March 16, 1786.

35. "Extract from the Proceedings of Congress," *The American Museum, or, Universal Magazine*, Philadelphia, April 1787, p. 319. The quoted statement was lifted from a report

of the Board of Treasury, February 8, 1786, *Journals of the Continental Congress*, vol. 31, p. 57.

36. Wood, *Creation*, p. 359; the Jefferson quotation in this paragraph is from the same page.

Chapter 3

To Levy Money Directly

"To extinguish a Debt which exists and to avoid contracting more," Alexander Hamilton wrote in one of his reports as secretary of the treasury, "are ideas always favored by public feeling and opinion; but to pay Taxes for the one or the other purpose, which are the only means of avoiding the evil, is always more or less unpopular."[1] Hamilton wrote these words in 1795, when the fledgling federal government was grappling with how to raise the revenue it needed to operate and to pay off its debts.

As he often did, Hamilton raised an ongoing issue for any democracy: how can a popularly elected government use unpopular means to secure the revenue vital to its functioning? If the debt of the government was to be paid, what system of finance would the government employ, money or taxes? If taxes, which ones would it use? Public finance was one of the many problems facing the men who met in Philadelphia to overhaul the governmental system of the Articles of Confederation, and it has been given scant attention in histories of the Constitutional Convention.

As shown in this chapter, the framers had no problem deciding on taxes over money as the basis for financing the government they were proposing. The sides on the issue of a lack of a centralized taxing power that plagued the Confederation period had shifted. The framers of the Constitution were willing to grant taxing power to the new government they were creating. The question was how much power to give.

The manner in which they answered that question, however, was not through a straightforward analysis of which taxes would be most effective for raising revenue. Although the starting point for taxation would surely be the failed plan of imposts proposed throughout the 1780s, the types of taxation approved by the convention became embroiled in the debates over representation and slavery that took up much of that long, hot summer. Delegates still found it difficult to get beyond the system of requisitions from the states based on a quota system.

THE CONSTITUTIONAL DEBATE OVER TAXES

The steps taken to bring about a change in the governmental system in the United States are clear. A meeting of all the states to discuss their economic problems was called in Annapolis in September 1786. When only five states sent delegates to that meeting, Madison and Hamilton called for a Constitutional Convention, to be held in Philadelphia during the summer of 1787.

To be sure, the delegates to that convention had been pushing for a stronger national government with a taxing power throughout the 1780s. Nearly all who attended the Constitutional Convention had long believed that the central government needed to be strengthened, although they had differed over how strong it should be made. By 1787, however, they agreed that the central government needed the ability to raise its own revenues. A chief issue at the Constitutional Convention was the power of a few small states to block the wishes of a majority to take national action, especially with regard to taxes.

Nowhere had this obstructionism been more evident than with the actions of Rhode Island in preventing the Continental Congress from passing a national tariff. Had that tariff passed, the system of government under the Articles of Confederation might have been rescued. Any effort to strengthen the central government had to include giving it the power to tax.

So recalcitrant was Rhode Island, however, that it did not bother to send delegates to the Constitutional Convention. New York, another reluctant supporter of national taxes, sent a delegation of two opponents of national government who could outvote Hamilton, the other member. When these two opponents left the convention, Hamilton was disfranchised in the deliberations over the Constitution. He, too, withdrew after making a speech in favor of a strong government but returned in time to help with the final draft. Outside the convention were opponents who would have their say in the debates over the ratification of the document. Samuel Adams and Patrick Henry, for example, wanting no part of a stronger national government, stayed home.

The debate over the Constitution–and it is important to remember that there was a long debate over its features and many compromises in settling it–is usually portrayed as between large states and small states or North versus South or debtors versus creditors. There were also representatives of both the agrarian and commercial viewpoints present. The starting point in the debate was the Virginia plan with two houses in the legislature, a judiciary and an executive branch. While the Virginia plan did not succeed in all its particulars, it did set the theme of the convention when the delegates agreed, "A national government ought to be established."[2]

TAXATION AND REPRESENTATION

The Virginia plan was a clear step away from the principle of giving each state one vote that existed under the Articles of Confederation. In setting up the two houses of the legislative branch, the main issue was over the distribution of their membership and the geographical area from which the members of the houses would be elected. The Virginia plan proposed that both houses have representation based on the size of the state, with the larger states having more representation.

Proponents of the Virginia plan used the relationship between taxation and representation to support their position. Edmund Randolph, for example, argued "that the rights of suffrage in the National Legislature ought to be proportioned to the quotas of contributions, or to the number of free inhabitants, as the one or the other rule may seem best in different cases."[3] The idea that representation be in proportion to taxes paid by a state may seem far-fetched. To some extent, however, it reflected an inability of the delegates to break free of the requisition system of the Articles of Confederation.

The idea was that since larger states were supposed to have paid a bigger quota of the requisition, they should have more votes. Whatever the basis for a state's payments of taxes to the new central government, voting in the national Congress should conform to it. Wealthy states could then exercise influence proportionate to their economic strength. During the debates the idea of representation in proportion to wealth was often substituted for representation in proportion to taxes or population, all of which measured relative economic power.

After Randolph offered his plan for representation, Madison moved that the words "or to the numbers of free inhabitants" be removed; through leaving the question of population aside, he wanted to avoid distracting the delegates from the main issue of whether representation was to be by states or by some form of proportion. Nevertheless, Rufus King immediately pointed out that using taxes as a basis for representation might not work, as the proportions would change frequently when tax collections within a state changed. Hamilton then moved that the representation be based on population, at which point the entire issue was postponed.[4]

The first step in reaching a compromise to assure small states that they would not be outvoted by the more populous states in the new Congress was the New Jersey plan for having different rules in each house of the legislature for apportioning representation. The idea of using taxes as the basis for choosing representatives in at least one of the houses continued. John Dickinson, for example, "hoped that each State would retain an equal voice in at least one branch of the National Legislature, and supposed that the sums paid within each state would form a better ratio for the other branch than either the number of inhabitants or the quantum of property."[5]

The first attack on the linkage between taxation and representation came from William Paterson, initiator of the New Jersey plan for protecting the small states. He was afraid that under such a system of representation the large states could outvote the small. That would be unfair, he continued, for "there was no reason that a great individual State contributing much, should have more votes than a small one contributing little, than that a rich individual should have more votes than an indigent one." If a rich person pays more in taxes than a poor one, he continued, since he "has more to be protected . . . so he ought to pay more for the common protection. The same may be said of a large State, wch. has more to be protected than a small one."[6] This justification of higher taxes for the wealthy was in accord with Smith's views, although it is often lost sight of today.

The answer to Paterson by James Wilson was that since, as Paterson agreed, in different states "the number of people was the best measure of their comparative wealth," it was just as sensible that representation be based on population. Paterson's argument for giving each state an equal vote in congress meant that it would take 150 voters in Pennsylvania to match 50 in New Jersey.[7] By Wilson's logic, this outcome was the same as giving citizens of New Jersey three votes for every one vote to a resident of Pennsylvania, just as unfair as letting the wealthy have more votes. Representation had to be based on population.

As the debate continued, the idea of basing representation on taxes would not go away. John Rutledge believed that "the justice of this rule . . . could not be contested." Pierce Butler agreed, "adding that money was power; and that the States ought to have weight in the Govt. in proportion to their wealth." King countered by pointing out that it was uncertain what form of taxes the new government would use, but tariffs seemed very likely. If that were the case, "the non-importing States, as Cont. & N. Jersey, wd. be in a very bad situation indeed. It might so happen that they wd. have no representation."[8]

Ben Franklin then tried a different approach. He proposed that the smaller states say how much they could contribute toward the general revenue. Then the larger states would "oblige themselves to furnish each an equal proportion," with the total then being "absolutely in the disposition of Congress." Each state would have one vote, but with each contributing the same amount, voting would be in proportion to its contributions. If not enough revenue was forthcoming, Congress could ask for more from the larger states, which then might determine the merits "of giving more or less as it should be found proper."[9] Franklin's idea went nowhere.

In later discussions over representation, Madison pointed out, "According to the views of every member, the Genl. Govt. will have powers far beyond those exercised by the British Parliament, when the States were part of the British Empire. It will in particular have the power, without the consent of the State legislatures, to levy money directly on the people themselves." As a result, the people needed to have an equal vote in the national legislation to avoid the "evils which have resulted from the vicious representation in G[reat] B[ritain]."[10] National taxation meant that in the new government representation had to be based on population.

Eventually, the compromise was reached that the Senate would retain membership by state, as had the Continental Congress, whereas membership of the House of Representatives would be based on population. As part of that compromise, all power of raising taxes was given to the House of Representatives, the part of the

Congress most responsible to the people, being elected by them directly and in proportion to population.

The rule stipulating the initiation of taxes in the House of Representatives was also the subject of debate. The initial formulation of the two houses thought of the upper house, the Senate, as being a body composed of a wise elite, chosen indirectly by the people, who would serve long terms and protect the nation from too much democracy. Given this view, some delegates felt that the Senate should have the power to initiate "money bills" because it was smaller and wiser and could take unpopular measures for the good of the country. This limited democracy would protect the wealthy from excessive taxes favored by the general population to keep incomes equal. The smaller states would also be able to keep larger states from imposing taxes on them. When this measure failed, the supporters of national government changed their argument and saw the source of their plans, especially their tax plans, as rising from the people.[11]

In addition, the populous states could feel a little better that taxes had to be initiated in the House of Representatives, although that security was tempered by approval of taxes by the Senate, which smaller states could dominate. Taxation with representation would be maintained, if barely. After all, the Senate still had to approve revenue laws and could amend them. A coalition of small states could block tax programs, but at least no single state could.

The initial proposal for making the House of Representatives more reliant on the people had some difficulties, however. The delegates were still not certain whether to base its membership on population or wealth or a combination of the two. A sticking point was what to do about slaves.

TAXATION AND SLAVERY

The problem of slavery formed a backdrop for the legal and moral issues that entered into the framing of the Constitution. With respect to taxation and representation, the question was easy to pose, if tricky to resolve. Wilson pointed out the dilemma of slavery for the delegates, asking, "Are they admitted as Citizens? then why are they not admitted on an equality with White Citizens? are they admitted as property? then why is not other property admitted into the computation?"[12] Slaves were both people and property, population and wealth. How, then, should slaves be counted in a system whose proponents wanted to link taxpaying ability to representation, however tenuously?

Southerners would want slaves counted as persons or as wealth to get as many representatives as possible for their region depending on how representation was to be apportioned. They would be leery of having antislavery advocates use taxation to put a stiff burden on their wealth to eliminate slavery. A head tax or tax on property could fall heavily on slave owners, however it was levied, but to exclude slaves as persons or property would reduce the representation of the southern states in the House of Representatives.

To make an agreement, the delegates started with the three-fifths rule used under the Articles of Confederation when population replaced wealth as a basis for revenue quotas in 1783. In using population as the basis for representation, each slave would count as three-fifths of a person. The steps to that result were extremely convoluted, however, for the convention had become stuck and an initial vote on the rule to count slaves under the three-fifths rule failed by a 6-to-4 vote.

To break the deadlock, Gouverneur Morris proposed an amendment to the clause pertaining to representation in the House of Representatives by population and wealth, a "proviso that taxation should be in proportion to representation." Each state should pay taxes based on its share of membership in the House of Representatives. George Mason feared that this rule would drive the new government back to the requisition system of the Articles of Confederation. Morris agreed, so he changed the amendment to apply only to "direct taxes. With regard to indirect taxes on *exports* & imports & on consumption, the rule would be inapplicable."[13]

To foster a consensus for Morris' amendment, delegates harked back to the amicable adoption of the three-fifths rule during the Articles of Confederation. King reminded the convention, "As the Southern states are the richest, they would not league themselves with the Northn. unless some respect were paid to their superior wealth. . . . Eleven of the 13 states have agreed to consider Slaves in the apportionment of taxation; and taxation and Representation ought to go together."[14] The compromise established under the Articles of Confederation should be continued in the Constitution.

That compromise, however, reminded the delegates that the Articles of Confederation had permitted a change in the basis or representation from wealth to population. Should the new Congress be granted a similar power? Could the direct tax rule be changed with it? The debate then shifted to whether or not Congress should have the power to establish the rules of representation.

General Charles Cotesworth Pinkney asserted that any form of representation by wealth had to be included in the Constitution and not left to a legislature so "that property in slaves should not be exposed to danger" from being heavily taxed. In opposition, Oliver Ellsworth argued "that the rule of contribution by direct taxation . . . shall be the number of white inhabitants, and three fifths of every other description in the several States, until some other rule that shall more accurately ascertain the wealth of the several States can be devised and adopted by the Legislature."

Randolph objected to giving this power to change the basis for direct taxation and representation to the new Congress and offered, as a substitute, that representation be based on population "according to the ratio recommended by Congress in their resolution of the 18th. day of Apl. 1783" (the three-fifths rule for revenue quotas) to keep slaves as part of the basis for representation. Madison's notes characterized Randolph's concerns as, "He lamented that such a species of property existed, but as it did exist the holders of it would require this security." The rest of the House of Representatives should not be able to outvote the South on slavery, at least not if slaves were part of the basis for representation.

Nevertheless, northerners were still concerned about counting noncitizens toward the population basis for representation. Wilson "observed that less umbrage would perhaps be taken agst. an admission of slaves into the Rule of representation, if it should be so expressed as to make them indirectly only an ingredient into the rule, by saying that they should enter into the rule of taxation: and as representation was to be according to taxation, the end would be equally attained." He proposed that representation be based on taxation, with direct taxes being derived from a population census, as had been done under the Articles of Confederation.

Charles Pinkney tried an amendment making "blacks equal to whites in the ratio of representation." Since they produced wealth as much as any form of labor, and wealth was the basis of taxation, they should be weighted equally as other labor. The amendment failed. Elbridge Gerry then argued that using direct taxes as the basis for representation unfairly hurt states that consumed high levels of imports, for their tax payments would not count toward their number of representatives. The Randolph proposal for basing representation on population with slaves counting as three-fifths of a person then was passed by a vote of 6 for, 2 against and 2 divided.[15]

On the next day, Gerry tried to amend the Randolph proposal by having all direct taxes "assessed on the inhabitants of the several States according to the number of their Representatives respectively in the 1st. branch." Taxation would be linked to representation based on population. George Reed disagreed, arguing that in discussions over the representation issue some states were declining to accept their full representation "to avoid their full share of taxation."

Would states really give up representation in the House of Representatives to avoid paying taxes? That was doubtful, Madison maintained. The real conflict over the Constitution's form was between the North and the South, and the South needed to be protected from being outvoted by the North. He liked the proposal for basing representation on population, including the three-fifths rule, "because it tended to moderate the views both of the opponents & advocates for rating very high, the negroes." Population was selected as the basis for representation, and a motion to eliminate wealth as a basis for representation was passed.[16]

Regarding taxation, the compromise of using population for representation still had an impact in that it resulted in Article 1, Sections 2 and 9, which made direct taxes assessable only in proportion to population. The delegates never intended that direct taxes would be a major source of revenue so did not see this as a big concession. As Luther Martin put it, "Direct taxation should not be used but in case of absolute necessity." He went further, however, and proposed an amendment that when the Congress felt it needed a direct tax, it would calculate the quota for each state as a requisition and "in the case of any of the States failing to comply with such requisitions, then and then only to devise and pass acts directing the mode, and authorizing the collection of the same." The motion was defeated without debate, 8 no, 1 yes, and 1 divided.[17] There would be no return to the system of requisitions by the delegates.

The only problem was that they never clearly defined the term, except implicitly through examples. They always used direct taxes in the context of a system of requisitions to be made upon the states by the central government. This obscurity would cause a series of constitutional dilemmas until a century later, when the direct tax clause would be used by the Supreme Court to invalidate a federal income tax. None of this was within the intent of the delegates.

The idea behind the direct tax article was to count slaves as population for purposes of representation, but not fully, to allay the fears of the North that the South would have too many votes. In return, a limit was placed on the amount of direct taxes that could be imposed on slaves when they were considered property. Any direct tax on slaves as property would have to be levied on property in other states, based on population, and slaves would be undercounted in calculating population.

Madison reported Gouverneur Morris' intentions with regard to his proposals relating to direct taxation and representation as follows, "He had meant it only as a bridge to assist us over a certain gulph; having passed over the gulph, the bridge may be removed."[18] The gulf he referred to was the strong disagreement over the counting of slaves in representation. By first making slaves a property susceptible to direct taxation and having representation based on taxation, they put in slaves as part of the basis for representation. By having direct taxes limited in proportion to population, any direct tax levied on slave states would be placed equally on free states. The unpopularity of direct taxes would prevent their being used to diminish slavery. In the end, the North gave in partially on the issue of representation, and the South sacrificed its extreme position on taxation.

After the compromise was reached, Morris tried to have direct taxes removed from the wording of the article but failed.[19] It would be over a century before the Sixteenth Amendment finally made sure that this clause would not apply to income taxes.

Fearful that the more populous northern states would try to sap the vitality of their peculiar institution by taxing its products, southerners also obtained the limitation that no taxes would be put on exports. Tobacco, rice, and indigo were the chief exports of the United States at the time, and cotton soon would be. As Langdon observed, "It seems to be feared that the Northern States will oppose the trade of the South." Gerry also worried that the federal government could use export taxes to run roughshod over all the states. George Mason agreed, indicating that "if he were for reducing the States to mere corporations as seemed to be the tendency of some arguments, he should be for subjecting their exports as well as imports to a power of general taxation." He also suggested that, given the population and the way voting in Congress was to be apportioned, southerners "had good ground for their suspicion."

The power to tax exports would give the central government too much power over the states and could be used to oppress them. Others agreed, and Madison's effort to allow a tax on exports only with a two-thirds vote of both houses failed.[20]

Morris recognized that these deals were chipping away at the sources of revenue for the new government. He had argued, "Taxes on exports are a necessary source of revenue. For a long time the people of America will not have money to pay direct taxes. Seize and sell their effects and you push them into Revolts."[21] His argument won few votes, and the ban on taxing exports passed. These limits on the taxing power, both legal and social, meant that tariffs would have to be a major source of tax revenues for the new nation.

Even with tariffs, an exception had to be made for slavery. After all, at this time slaves were still being imported from Africa. Many delegates wanted to end this trade, and high tariffs on slaves would be a way to do it. Roger Sherman, on the other hand, "said it was better to let the S. States import slaves than to part with them, if they made that a sine qua non. He was opposed to a tax on slaves imported as making the matter worse, because it implied that they were *property*."[22] Madison continued in this vein, thinking "it wrong to admit in the Constitution the idea that there could be property in men." Nor was it reasonable to tax slaves, for they were not consumable merchandise.

Opponents regretted the exemption of an important article of revenue from the tax base. They also felt, with Mason, that "not to tax, will be the equivalent to a bounty on the importation of slaves." Nathaniel Ghourum agreed that the tariff on slaves would act "as a discouragement to the importation of them." The debate over whether the tariffs should discourage slavery or raise revenue also ended in a compromise. Article 1, Section 9 placed a ban on any laws limiting the importation of slaves until 1808 but added that "a tax or duty may be imposed on such importation not exceeding ten dollars for each person."

The delegates had no doubt over the purpose of the tariff on slaves. Sherman "observed that the smallness of the duty shewed revenue to be the object, not the discouragement of their importation."[23] However little slavery added up in moral terms, it did follow the arithmetic of the customhouse that Adam Smith had pointed out.

Despite the restrictions on taxation written into the Constitution, the new system gave more power to the government than it had under the Articles of Confederation. If the states ratified the new document, Congress could impose tariffs, collect excises, and levy direct taxes. To be sure, it would take a great deal of effort—and this the framers understood—to convince United States citizens to accept that much power. Some restrictions in the taxing power of the new government might have helped sway the citizenry, but the restrictions in the Constitution were not intended for the common good. They were there to protect a special interest in slavery. The change to taxation itself, however, was readily viewed by the framers as being in the common good that they sought to attain.

PROSCRIBING PAPER MONEY

Along with the issue of taxation, the convention took up the question of paper money. They all had experienced the inflation caused by the issuance of the continental currency and had seen the problems caused by continued use of bills of credit by the states. They would have none of that in the new system they were proposing.

The first step concerned the power of the federal government to issue bills of credit. With a draft of the Constitution at hand, Morris made a motion to eliminate a pesky clause "and emit bills on the credit of the U. States." He argued that if the new country had good credit, such emissions were unnecessary. If its credit were bad, they were "unjust & useless." Madison asked whether or not prohibiting the new government from making bills of credit legal tender would be sufficient, in case of an emergency. Morris replied that the rule would still let it be possible to issue notes (debt securities) if they were issued responsibly. He added, "The Monied interest will oppose the plan of Government, if paper emissions be not prohibited."

Mason disagreed that notes could be issued unless Congress was given an express power to do so. He opposed the motion because he did not want to bind the Congress too greatly in case of an emergency, reminding delegates that "the late war would not have been carried on, had such a prohibition existed." Ghourum felt that a power to borrow was sufficient. Mercer seconded Mason, saying he was "a friend to paper money, though in the present state & temper of America" he would not approve of emissions. Still, he did not want to prohibit the government from using it, arguing:

It will stamp suspicion on the Government to deny it a discretion on this point. It was also impolitic to excite the opposition of all those who were friends to paper money. The people of property would be sure to be on the side of the plan, and it was impolitic to purchase their further attachment with the loss of the opposite class of Citizens.

In response, Ellsworth "thought this a favorable moment to shut and bar the door against paper money" while its bad effects were "fresh in the public mind and had excited the disgust of all the respectable part of America." More support would be gained for the Constitution than lost through such a ban. Giving the government the power to borrow would be sufficient for its finance. Wilson went further and suggested that a ban on paper money would "have a most salutary influence of the credit of the U. States." Butler added that no country in Europe used paper money as legal tender. Although Mason, Madison, and Randolph still wanted to enable Congress to issue paper money in case of an emergency, the motion passed by a 9-to-2 vote. Apparently the delegates agreed with Langdon, who said he would "rather reject the whole plan than retain the three words '(and emit bills).' "[24]

The debate on the issue of prohibiting states from emitting paper money was so brief it can be reported verbatim:

Art: XII being taken up.

Mr. Wilson & Mr. Sherman moved to insert after the words "coin money" the words "nor emit bills of credit, nor make any thing but gold & silver coin a tender for payment of debts" making these prohibitions absolute, instead of making them measures allowable (as in the XIII art:) *with the consent of the Legislature of the U.S.*

Mr. Ghourum thought the purpose would be as well served by the provision of art: XIII which makes the consent of the Genl. Legislature necessary, and that in that mode no opposition would be excited; whereas an absolute prohibition of paper money would rouse the most desperate opposition from its partisans.

Mr. Sherman thought this a favorable crisis for crushing paper money. If the consent of the Legislature could authorize emissions of it, the friends of paper money, would make every exertion to get into the Legislature in order to license it.

Debate ended, and the wording was approved, with 8 aye, 1 no, and 1 divided vote.[25]

This vote aimed at ending the system of public finance of using paper money that had been used in the colonies and the states since the earliest times. What the British Parliament had tried to do but failed, the Constitution would attempt to do—ban the emissions of paper money as a system of public finance. Debt and taxes would have to do the job; at least that was the hope.

ASSUMPTION OF THE PUBLIC DEBT

One final question of public finance had to be answered: what to do with the public debt? The debt of the Continental Congress was almost automatically assumed as part of the new government, but a new committee was formed to consider assumption of debt owed by the states. The committee reported back that all debts, those incurred by the old government, by the militia, and by the states, be paid by the new government. There was debate over whether or not the Constitution needed to confer such a power on the new Congress, as it was already a power of the existing Congress. It was also argued that settling the debts of the states would be complicated, as some states had already paid some of their debts, yet all states were still in arrears in payment of the quota.[26]

Another difficulty with the settlement of the debt was over to whom payment should be made. Mason saw "a great distinction between original creditors & those who purchased fraudulently of the ignorant and distressed." The distinction would be hard to make, but he thought the effort should be made. Later purchasers at low prices from original holders should not "stand on the same footing as first Holders," as "the interest they receive even in paper is equal to their purchase money." Here was an agrarian perspective on credit as something to be honorable about.

Gerry responded by saying that he was indifferent to assumption of the debt, as he was "not possessed of more securities than would, by the interest, pay his taxes." Since the government had received value for its debt, "it ought to pay that value to some body." He added, "The frauds on *the soldiers* ought to have been foreseen. These poor & ignorant people could not but part with their securities." He had no objection to revising the debt and paying full value to those who had sold their debt. As for purchasers of the debt securities, Gerry "saw no reason for the censures thrown on them. They keep up the value of the paper. Without them there would be no market."[27]

Members of the convention also debated linkages between the debt and taxes, suggesting that an expiration date be put on all taxes not intended to pay the debt.[28] This plan failed of support. The final document did provide for assumption of all debts incurred "before the adoption of this Constitution" in Article 6. Article 1, section 8 empowered the new government "to borrow money on the credit of the United States." The issue of assuming state debts and discriminating between initial and later holders was left to the new Congress.

CONCLUSION

As this discussion over the taxing powers to be granted to the new government make clear, the debates over the formation of the Constitution resulted in a number of compromises between large states and small states and between the North and South. The compromises negotiated with the defenders of slavery meant that the federal government would rely heavily on tariffs and excise taxes for its revenue. Special interest tax loopholes were thus built into the Constitution.

Yet, the supporters of slavery had not used their bargaining power to avoid taxes. As the wealthiest persons in the country and the ones most likely to import the luxury goods that would bear the brunt of tariffs, slave holders would pay their fair share of taxes. They just wanted to ensure that the tax system would not be used to destroy their peculiar institution.

The compromises over taxes made in the Constitution would make it unclear just what taxing power the federal government would have. To be sure, everyone understood that the new government would have a power to collect a tariff throughout the country. Regarding internal taxes, the document was murky. Were all internal taxes direct, or were some of them indirect? How were direct taxes defined? However these questions were answered, there was some assurance that, since they would be answered in the House of Representatives, they would at least be dealt with in the legislature of the people.

Often overlooked in studying the debates over the type of public finance to be approved by the Constitution was the one ruled out, the printing of paper money. Here there was hardly any debate at all, even though the subject was highly controversial. There was no question of the federal government's printing money; the Constitution gave Congress the power to coin money and regulate its value but not to print money. It also prevented the states from printing money. Members of the convention might be construed as protecting themselves and their property from further issues of debased currency. More important, however, they avoided a potentially critical constitutional crisis, for what would have happened if states had printed paper money and declared it legal tender. Could it have been used to pay federal taxes?

The delegates had faced a difficult task of producing a document on which they could agree among themselves and that would also be agreeable to the electorate. This task they completed, but they could not know when they finished that they had done so. They could not begin to contemplate whether their own agreements would help or hinder the public approval of the Constitution.

NOTES

1. Alexander Hamilton, "Report on a Plan for the Further Support of Public Credit," January 16, 1795, PAH, vol. 18, p. 102.

2. Kelly and Harbison, *The American Constitution*, p. 124.

3. James McClellan and M. E. Bradford, eds., *Jonathan Elliot's Debates in the Several State Conventions on the Adoption of the Federal Constitution*, vol. 3, *Debates in the Federal Convention of 1787 as Reported by James Madison* (Madison Notes hereafter) (Richmond, VA: James River Press, 1989), p. 37, for May 30.

4. Ibid., p. 37, for May 30.

5. Ibid., p. 57, for June 2.

6. Ibid., p. 94, for June 9.

7. Ibid., p. 95, for June 9.

8. Ibid., pp. 96–97, for June 11.

9. Ibid., pp. 99–100, for June 11.

10. Ibid., p. 207, for June 29.

11. Wood, *Creation*, pp. 556–60.

12. Ibid., p. 265, for July 11.

13. Ibid., pp. 266–67, for July 12.

14. Ibid., p. 251, for July 10.

15. Ibid., pp. 268–71, for July 12.

16. Ibid., pp. 272–76.

17. Ibid., p. 473, for August 21.

18. Ibid., p. 345, for July 24.

19. Ibid., p. 600–601, for September 13.

20. Ibid., pp. 476–77, for August 21.

21. Ibid., p. 444, for August 16.

22. Ibid., p. 482, for August 22.

23. Ibid., p. 505, for August 25.

24. James Madison, *The Debates in the Federal Convention of 1787 which Framed the Constitution of the United States of America*, ed. Gaillard Hunt and James Brown Scott (New York: Oxford University Press, 1920), pp. 413–14.

25. Ibid., pp. 477–78.

26. Ibid., pp. 421, 435 and 466.

27. Ibid., pp. 465–66.

28. Ibid., pp. 448 and 467.

Chapter 4

WE THE PEOPLE

James Madison maintained that the place to find the intent behind the Constitution was not in "the opinions or intentions of the body which planned and prepared it" but in the ratifying conventions held in each state.[1] At those conventions, the key defect in the Constitution was considered to be its lack of a bill of rights. There was a common view among delegates at those conventions that the rights to be granted to the people should be listed. No one proposed a right to be free of taxes, but concern over the taxing power being granted to the new government was expressed by participants at the ratifying conventions.

Proponents of the Constitution showed great tactical skill during the ratification process. First, they determined that ratification would be by the people's voice in special state conventions and not by state legislatures. Second, they avoided the problem that had existed in changing the Articles of Confederation by making ratification of the new document depend on a two-thirds majority of those conventions, not unanimity. Third, they called themselves Federalists and not nationalists and pinned the label Anti-Federalist on their opponents; in this way they made a subtle shift in the grounds of the debate by making their opponents appear to be against something important.

This subtle shift in the terms of the debate can be seen in the area of government finance. Of the trinity of methods of public finance—money, debt, and taxes—assumption of debt was taken for granted, and the use of paper money to pay it was eliminated. Taxation remained a key issue, but the issue became what kind of taxes and not whether or not they would be collected by the federal government. Even with the advantages this shift in the debate gave proponents of the Constitution, however, they barely won in their efforts to get the document ratified.

OPPONENTS OF NATIONAL TAXATION

The debate over the Constitution and the tax powers it granted to the federal government took place in two forums, the ratifying conventions and the press. Both sides were well represented, and although the arguments of the opponents to the Constitution have suffered the fate of most losing sides of having become obscured by history, it will be instructive to look at them to see how much they had changed in the period since the Revolutionary War.

Fears about taxes and the Constitution were expressed in newspapers throughout the states almost immediately after the Constitutional Convention. One of the earliest notes of disapproval came in the *Philadelphia Freeman's Journal* of September 26, 1787, almost immediately after adjournment of the convention. The paper gave an article by article appraisal of the Constitution. With regard to the clause on capitation and direct taxes, it was especially vehement: "I confess here a great disappointment . . . For a capitation tax is *impolitic* and *unjust*; it is a tax upon population and falls indiscriminately upon the poor and the rich."[2]

Another Philadelphia paper, the *Independent Gazetteer,* also reported opposition to the Constitution, especially with its taxing powers. It printed a letter attacking the new document in a sarcastic tone: "Among the *blessings* of the new-proposed government our correspondent enumerates the following: . . . 5. Five-fold taxes. . . . 8. Excise laws, custom-house officers, tide and land waiters, cellar rats &c. . . . 12. Poll taxes for our heads, if we chuse to wear them. 13. And death if we dare complain." The item proved popular enough to be reprinted twelve times in papers in eight states.[3]

Perhaps the most vitriolic opposition to the taxing powers was stated in the "Essays of Brutus" in the *New York Journal* in 1787–88. The power of taxation was unlimited, he noted, and would "introduce itself into every corner of the city, and the country—It will wait upon the ladies at their toilet . . . it will enter into the house of every gentleman . . . it will watch the merchant in the counting house . . . it will follow the mechanic to his shop . . . it will be a constant companion of the industrious farmer. . . . To all these different classes of people, and in all these circumstances, in which it will attend them, the language in which it will address them, will be GIVE! GIVE!"[4]

In Maryland, meanwhile, another essayist writing as "A Farmer and Planter" smelled a ruling class conspiracy. He feared that the federal tax system would use the poll tax as a direct tax, because the wealthy would influence it to tax them lightly. His assessment was also disparaging toward the new government. He wrote,

If you should, at any time, think you are imposed upon by Congress and your great Lords and Masters, and refuse or delay to pay your taxes . . . I have not a doubt but that they will, send the militia of Pennsylvania, Boston, or any other state or place, to cut your throats, ravage and destroy your plantation, drive away your cattle and horses, abuse your wives, kill your infants, and ravish your daughters, and live in free quarters, until you get into a good humor, and pay all that they may think proper to ask of you, and you become good and faithful servants and slaves.[5]

Perhaps this writer was being melodramatic. Still there were fears that giving the power to tax to the federal government would lead to oppression.

Patrick Henry, for example, told the Virginia ratification convention that "the oppression arising from taxation, is not from the amount but, from the mode—a thorough acquaintance with the condition of the people, is necessary to a just distribution of taxes. The whole wisdom of the science of Government, with respect to taxation, consists in selecting the mode of collection which will best accommodate to the convenience of the people." Henry wanted the direct taxing power to remain with the states in continuance of the requisition system. He also feared that Virginia's ten representatives would be outvoted in Congress in their efforts to oppose taxes inconvenient to their constituents.

In Maryland Luther Martin also "thought that the States were much better judges of the circumstances of their citizens, and what sum of money could be collected from them by direct taxation."[6] In far-off Paris Thomas Jefferson agreed, asking, "Would it not have been better to assign to Congress exclusively the articles of impost for federal purposes, and to have left direct taxation exclusively to the states? I should suppose the former sufficient for all probable events, aided by the land office."[7]

Another fear was that taxes might be very high. A New York essayist, "Cato," complained that high taxes would ruin the industriousness of New Yorkers: "For, what can inspire you with industry, if the greatest measures of your labours are to be swallowed up in taxes?"[8] Cato identified the supply-side argument that would later be made in the 1980s, and it was an idea he could have inferred from Hume or Smith. Although couched in terms of the oppressiveness of taxes, the argument of the opponents of the Constitution, such as Cato, reflected the fear of having too much power granted to the central government. With this perspective, they found little to favor with the federal system being proposed.

STATE VERSUS FEDERAL TAXES

"We the people," reads the opening line of the Preamble to the Constitution. From our vantage point of more than two centuries later, this hardly seems a controversial phrase, but at the time, it surely was.

The question of a national government was immediately raised by opponents, who were not misled by such populist rhetoric. At the opening of the Virginia ratification convention, Patrick Henry maintained that the issue rested "on that poor little thing—the expression, We, the *people*, instead of the *states*, of America." George Mason agreed, telling the Virginia delegates, "The assumption of this power of laying direct taxes, does of itself, entirely change the confederation of the States into one consolidated government. . . . This power is calculated to annihilate entirely the State Governments." The same issue was raised at the Massachusetts convention by Samuel Adams and put in blunt form by another delegate, who also believed that the phrase "we the people" would "go to an annihilation of the state governments."[9] All efforts to establish a national government would be at the cost of the states.

This opinion was held especially with regard to taxes. Opponents had no solace in being told that the House of Representatives would initiate tax legislation; it was still the House of a national government that they distrusted. Even with its greater numbers than the Senate, the House of Representatives still lacked close contact with the general population. As George Mason argued, in opposing the taxing power of the proposed government, "To make representation real and actual, the number of representatives ought to be adequate; they ought to mix with the people."[10] In Massachusetts John DeWitt raised the same issue, wondering if a member of the House of Representatives could be "presumed knowing your different, peculiar situations—your abilities to pay public taxes, when they ought to be abated, and when encreased."[11] A national government could not give this type of representation.

The answer the Federalists gave was that members of the House of Representatives could be controlled by their need to be reelected every two years; that would make them "mix with the people." Patrick Henry was not impressed. He stated, "I shall be told in this place that those who are to tax us are our representatives. To this I shall answer, that there is no real check to prevent their ruining us. . . . The only semblance of a check is the negative power of not re-electing them. This, sir, is a feeble check."[12] Taxation without enough representation remained a tyranny.

The key to understanding these differences rests with the fear the advocates of state sovereignty had of national usurpation of states' rights. During the ratification debate, proponents of state sovereignty believed that national taxes would supersede state taxes and limit revenue collections at the local level. One cogent opposition statement came from Brutus. On the issue of granting taxing powers to the new government, Brutus put forth a conspiracy theory. He pointed out that there was no limit to the taxing power, since taxes were to be used for defense and general welfare. This meant that members of Congress "only are to determine what is for the general welfare; this power therefore is neither more nor less, than a power to lay and collect taxes, imposts and excises, at their pleasure." In addition, "no state legislature, or any power in state government, have any more to do in carrying this into effect, than the authority of one state has to do with another. In the business of laying and collecting taxes, the idea of confederation is lost."

Even worse, the Constitution took away from the states many of their sources of revenue, such as tariffs on imports. They were left with fewer taxes, but the federal government would also use these taxes for its revenue. Both state and national governments would be competing over a very small tax base. In that case, the national government would win. Brutus continued, "When the federal government begins to exercise the right of taxation in all its parts, the legislatures of the several states will find it impossible to raise monies to support their governments. Without money they cannot be supported, and they must dwindle away, and . . . their powers absorbed in that of the central government." Since the Constitution contained the "necessary and proper clause," it might even be possible for Congress to repeal a state tax law that conflicted with a federal law.[13]

The same fears were expressed by another staunch opponent of the Constitution, "Centinel." He tied his fears to the powers inherent in a standing army. Congress could levy taxes as it saw fit, and "the collection would be enforced by the standing army." This power of taxation must ultimately "absorb the state legislatures and judicatories; and that such was in the contemplation of the framers of it."[14] A population heavily burdened with taxes, he later added, "would directly tend to annihilate the particular governments; for the people fatigued with the operations of two masters would be apt to rid themselves of the weaker."[15]

This fear was not without grounds. The Constitution eliminated the ability of the states to use tariffs for revenue, meaning they would have to use other taxes. In addition, Section 10 of Article 1 kept the states from using one popular method of finance by taking away their powers to "coin money; emit bills of credit; make anything but gold and silver coin a tender in payment of debts." The excessive issuance of paper money by states during the 1780s would be stopped. It would not be hard to interpret this limitation as the first salvo in an attack on state survival. Had not Parliament put limits on the issuance of paper money just before it levied taxes?

To avoid giving a power to levy direct taxes to the central government, Anti-Federalists sought a return to the requisition system. George Mason argued that the requisition system had failed during the war because it tried to do the impossible: "[r]equisitions for more gold and silver than were in the United States." Centinel agreed that "the history of mankind does not furnish a similar instance of an attempt to levy such enormous taxes at once, of a people so wholly unprepared and uninured to them."[16] Given time to get the states and their people on a prosperous footing, they would be able to make the requisition system work.

To do otherwise would be dangerous. It was James Monroe's view "that the exercise of direct taxation and excise, by one body, over the very extensive territory contained within the bounds of the United States, will terminate either in anarchy and a dissolution of the government, or a subversion of liberty." Retention of state control over direct taxes was vital. In Massachusetts, William Symmes analyzed the motives of the Federalists and issued a challenge to them. As he told that state's ratifying convention:

May we not suppose, that the members of the great Convention, had severely felt the impotency of Congress, while they were in it. . . . That the difficulties they had encountered, in obtaining decent requisitions, had wrought in them a degree of impatience, which prompted them to demand the purse-strings of the nation . . . ? I shall not deny these gentlemen the praise of inventing a system completely consistent with itself, and pretty free from contradiction—but I would ask, I shall expect to be answered, how a system can be necessary for us, of which this is a consistent and necessary part?[17]

THE FEDERALIST RESPONSE: TAXATION AND REPRESENTATION

Advocates for the Constitution were not silent in the face of these attacks, and delegates from the Constitutional Convention defended themselves and their plan in speeches at the state ratifying conventions. On the issue of the general power of taxation, perhaps the best defense was that offered by Oliver Ellsworth at the Connecticut ratifying convention. Ellsworth aimed to counter three objections: that the tax power was too broad, that it was biased, and that it should not be granted. He granted that the first objection was correct in substance, that the tax power "extends to all objects of taxation." But that should constitute no basis for fear by the states over losing their own objects of taxation, as the Congress would be considerate of their needs.

With regard to the second objection, that reliance on tariffs was biased toward the South, he responded that direct taxation was ineffective as a revenue raiser. It required that taxpayers have money set aside for taxes, and that was not likely. As an indirect tax, the tariff was more effective; residents of Connecticut were paying a tax to New York when they purchased goods that came in from that state, and few noticed it. A national tariff would be equally hidden, and its collection would "interfere less with the internal police of the states than any other species of taxation. It does not fill the country with revenue officers." It would raise large sums, especially as the country grew, and imports increased. As for the notion that the South would pay fewer taxes under a tariff, Ellsworth felt that they were large importers of luxury goods and would pay a very high tax.

The chief objection, however, was whether or not Congress should even have a tax power. Ellsworth characterized persons making this objection as arguing that such a power should not be granted "because they have the power of the sword; and if we give them the power of the purse, they are despotic." A granting of both powers might become despotic, he agreed, if they were "in the hands of one man, who claims an authority independent of the people." The Congress was a body dependent on the people, so no despotism would take place.[18]

Still it was not clear just how representative that body would be. Opponents could argue that the three-fifths rule would give another bias toward the South, as it gave the South greater voting power than the North.

To defend the Constitution on the issue of the three-fifths rule, Rufus King told the Massachusetts convention, that "by this rule are taxation and representation to be apportioned." Moreover, the rule had been in existence since 1783, but it had not been enforceable. The Constitution would make it so. James Wilson expressed a similar view in Pennsylvania on the principle of "direct taxation and representation." In New York, Hamilton was more specific:

The first thing objected to is that clause which allows a representation for three fifths of the negroes. Much has been said of the impropriety of representing men who have no will of their own. . . . It is the unfortunate situation of the Southern States to have a great part of their population as well as property in blacks. The regulation complained of was one result of the spirit of accommodation which governed the Convention; and without this indulgence no union could possibly have been formed.

Most authorities on government, he continued, believed that representation should be based on population and property, and that was the rule under the New York Constitution. Slaves were more than property; "they are men, though degraded to the condition of slavery." Even in that condition, they were subject to laws as persons. Then he posed the vexing problem in simple terms: "Representation and taxation go together, and one uniform rule ought to apply to both. Would it be just to compute these slaves in the assessment of taxation, and discard them from the estimate in the apportionment of representatives?"[19]

Hamilton raised a telling point on this issue. At this time, states often had a property ownership requirement attached to the right to vote. While it is unclear how restrictive this requirement was, there were persons not allowed to vote because of it (and this does not begin to consider the status of women as voters). These disfranchised individuals also counted for representation. In short, Anti-Federalist concerns over how well the House of Representatives would represent the people could be offset by reminding them that many persons had no voice in government at all, not just slaves.

HAMILTON AND MADISON

The clearest answer to these Anti-Federalist complaints was given by Hamilton and Madison in their contributions to *The Federalist Papers*. Despite the question of whether or not these essays by Hamilton, Madison, and Jay had any influence on the outcome of the ratification, the arguments given by them must have been repeated in other places.

Whatever their influence, this group of position papers in defense of the Constitution is worthy of Clinton Rossiter's claim, "*The Federalist* is the most important work in political science that has ever been written, or is likely ever to be written, in the United States."[20] The many political arguments provided in support of a stronger national government seem fairly obvious now. The notion that a confederation of all states or of several groups of states might lead to wars between them[21] seems unreal, until we recall that even with a national union such a war took place.

More to the point here, Hamilton devoted eight of the papers to questions of the taxing power of the newly proposed government, in an effort to respond to the Anti-Federalists. To begin with, he pointed out the obvious reliance of the federal government on tariffs for its revenue: "It is evident from the state of the country, from the habits of the people, from the experience we have had on the point itself that it is impractical to raise very considerable funds by direct taxation."[22] Hamilton understood that there was much tax resistance in the country.

Tariffs would be a reasonable way to avoid this resistance. As a tax on business, they were placed where money was present, making them convenient to pay. As all goods came in through the Atlantic Coast, there would be efficiency in their collection; few avenues for avoiding them existed. They were also simpler to collect than direct taxes, since most imports came in through a few ports. These advantages were in line with what Adam Smith and Thomas Paine had proposed, and Hamilton felt that the federal government could triple the amount of tariff revenue being collected by the individual states. He even followed Smith by recommending a tariff on "ardent spirits," which would raise substantial revenue, and "if it should tend to diminish the consumption of it, such an effect would be equally favorable to the agriculture, to the economy, to the morals and to the health of the society."[23]

To enhance the appeal of a national tax policy, Hamilton reviewed the defects of tax policy under the Articles of Confederation. The imposition of quotas on states, whether by population or property, had no "pretension of being a just representation," for neither measured the ability to pay of the inhabitants of a state. Some states might be taxed more heavily than others. Taxes on consumption items could not be heavily laid, as they were voluntary. Too high a tax, and consumption would decline, "defeating the end proposed—that is, an extension of the revenue. When applied to this object, the saying is as just as it is witty, that, 'in political arithmetic, two and two do not always make four.' "[24] The resemblance of this statement with Smith's attribution to Swift could not have been accidental.

In terms of the balance of power between the national and state governments, Hamilton believed, "It will always be far more easy for the State governments to encroach upon the national authorities than for the national authorities to encroach upon the State authorities."[25] There need be no fear of a conflict between them over taxes. Relying on Hume's example of Turkey, he pointed out that having the central government rely on others to collect its taxes was ineffective.[26] There had to be a division of labor on taxes between the two sovereignties.

Opponents to the Constitution wanted to limit further the taxing powers of Congress to import duties alone, using the old distinction between internal and external taxes. Hamilton countered that there could be no limits placed on the federal government's taxing powers, save what the Constitution already disallowed, because there was always the chance that national emergencies would call for more spending than the tariff would produce.[27] Throughout the essays, Hamilton played the national security card for all he could.

If the taxing powers of the government were limited to tariffs, then in a time of heavy revenue requirements it would need to raise them very high. This would be ruinous to trade, encourage smuggling, and serve to give protection to domestic monopolies, much as Adam Smith had warned. Moreover, as he had argued earlier in the "Continentalist," Hamilton understood that the burden of the tariff could fall on the consumer or the merchant. Either way, the result would be to cause an unequal tax burden among the states, with those relying on imports paying more than their share. Remembering that citizens could avoid the tariff by not purchasing the taxed items, Hamilton now pointed out that this would just result in greater efforts to clamp down on smugglers and extend the tariff to as many goods as possible,[28] that is, unless the federal government had the power to tax other items.

Having established that "the federal government must of necessity be invested with an unqualified power of taxation in the ordinary modes," Hamilton considered whether or not that power would reduce the power of the states to raise taxes.

To the claim that the national government would usurp through legislation the taxing power of the states, Hamilton waxed polemically, "The moment we launch into conjectures about the usurpations of the federal government, we get into an unfathomable abyss and fairly put ourselves out of reach of all reasoning. Imagination may range at pleasure till it gets bewildered amidst the labyrinths of an enchanted castle, and know not on which side to turn to escape from the apparitions which itself has raised." One could imagine many dangers coming from the powers of the federal government, but that did not make them real. More important, final power rested with the people. Since the states had more influence over them than would the national government, it was the federal government that had to be worried.[29]

Hamilton also reminded his foes that the Constitution gave the Congress no power to limit state taxes, except for the limit that they could not use import duties. The taxing power gave no exclusive power to tax to the national government, except for tariffs, implying "that as to all other taxes, the authority of the States remains undiminished." It was possible that if one level of government put a tax on an item, it might not be wise for the other to tax that same item, but that had nothing to do with the legality of the tax.[30]

Such conflicts would be unlikely to arise, he continued, "because in a short course of time the wants of the states will naturally reduce themselves within *a very narrow compass.*" With the federal government's taking over the wartime debt and the responsibility for maintaining the military, the states would have little need for revenue, beyond paying a few officials.[31]

Even then, however, double taxation might occur, with both jurisdictions putting a tax on the same item. In Hamilton's view this might happen no matter what governmental system was in place. Had the states been faithful to their tax quotas under the Articles of Confederation, they would have increased the taxes they were already imposing on their citizens, giving the same effect as double taxation. The need for revenue of the national government had to be met, no matter who did the collecting. There was no more difficulty concerning the overlapping of the national and state governments than there was between the state and county governments. Taxes would be neither high nor low based on who levied them.[32]

In line with this issue, Hamilton also considered the argument that the House of Representatives was still not numerous enough to have its members move among all their constituents and represent all interests. It was impractical to have all interests represented, and Hamilton left it to Madison to explain why. In relation to taxes, Madison felt that "there will be no peculiar local interests . . . which will not be within the interest of the representative of the district."[33] As active politicians in an area, members of the House of Representatives would be in touch with their constituents, as well as members of the state legislatures. They would be in touch with the problems taxes caused for the people of their districts.

Moreover, to return to Hamilton, there was no need for all groups to be represented. Members of some groups were happy to rely on the wisdom of others to represent them. Mechanics were happy with leadership by merchants, and large and small land owners would have their interests take care of by the middling land owners who formed the backbone of legislatures. "Every landowner will therefore have a common interest to keep the taxes on land as low as possible; and common interest may always be reckoned on as the surest bond of sympathy."[34]

In legislatures dominated by landowners, it was not likely that land or property taxes would be used; there was also a problem of assessing value, a task best performed at the local level, although Hamilton did see that the federal government could use the information gathered by local officials in its own collections. More important, however, he saw that "the pockets of farmers . . . will reluctantly yield but scanty supplies in the unwelcome shape of impositions on their houses and lands; and personal property is too precarious and invisible a fund to be laid hold of."[35] He also disapproved of poll taxes for the national government, even though some states used them.[36]

As a result, the chief tax to be employed by the federal government, according to Hamilton, was a tax on items of consumption, especially imported items. Madison agreed, writing that "taxes on articles imported from other countries . . . will always be a valuable source of revenue; that for a considerable time it must be a principal source; that at this moment it is an essential one."[37] In this agreement Hamilton and Madison followed the tax plans of Adam Smith. Whether or not they did so directly is difficult to ascertain, but they certainly used phrases that could have been taken from *The Wealth of Nations*.

In addition to his contributions to *The Federalist Papers*, Madison made several speeches at the Virginia Ratification Convention in support of a system of national taxation, telling the delegates of "the necessity of a radical change of our system." He told them that the granting of the power to tax to the central government was "necessary for the preservation of the union." To calm their fears, however, he avowed that except for times of war, direct taxes would not be necessary—the tariff would bring in enough revenue for the government's needs.

As to suggestions that requisitions be used in place of those direct taxes, with taxes to be levied only if the requisitions failed, Madison wondered why anyone wanted to bother with this immediate step. He was "convinced, that whenever requisitions shall be made, they will disappoint those who put their trust in them." When the individual state legislatures began deliberating over payment of the requisition, they would worry that other states would not pay up. When all had this worry, none would pay.

When none paid, the central government would be empowered to impose a penalty on them; that was how the requisition system would be altered by opponents to the Constitution. Madison, however, thought this would incite abhorrence of the central government and undermine its authority.

As to the national government's potential tendency to run roughshod over the states with taxes, Madison reminded the Virginia convention that the Continental

Congress could have done so when it was emitting bills of credit. At that time it had no need to rely on the states for resources, yet it did not abuse this freedom. The same would hold for the new system of taxes. Then he concluded by repeating his opinion that the tax power granted to the new government merely added to the powers of the old government "for the purpose of giving efficacy to those which were vested in it before." The old government had the power to raise taxes but not to collect them. The power to tax existed, he went on,

in the confederation as fully as in this constitution. The only difference is this, that now they tax the states, and by this plan they will tax individuals. There is no theoretic difference between the two. But in practice there will be an infinite difference between them. The one is an ineffectual power: The other is adequate to the purpose for which it is given. This change was necessary for the public safety.[38]

Hamilton offered the same point to the ratifying convention of New York state. He reminded delegates that when the Continental Congress had requested the impost, "though it was a very small addition of power to the federal government, it was apposed in this state, without any reasons being offered." At that time, all that had been sought was reform, not "a fundamental change in government."[39] Since reform had been rejected, it was time for a new government. This time, it would be a government equipped with powers to impose taxes and pay off the public debt.

TAXATION AND DEBT

To be sure, Hamilton and Madison were not the only defenders of the taxing powers the Constitution gave to the new government. Petaliah Webster agreed that the power of taxation was "absolutely necessary and unavoidable." It was up to Congress to determine what spending was needed and how to pay for it. This might give Congress a great deal of power, he continued, but "would any man choose a lame horse lest a sound one should run away with him?" Congress might go too far in raising taxes, but that risk could be corrected for at election time.

The upshot of the new system, Webster maintained, was that taxes would be levied and collected from everyone. He then put his finger on part of the problem, saying that "this must look disagreeable, I suppose, to people who, by one shift or another, have avoided paying taxes all their lives."[40] Long an advocate of taxes as the soundest form of public finance, Webster could believe that the Constitution would finally bring about the truth of his ideas that paper money was no substitute for taxation as a source of revenue or for paying debt.

At the Pennsylvania ratifying convention, James Wilson also linked taxation to debt. To opponents who opposed granting a tax power to the federal government, he asked, "Shall it have the power to borrow, and no power to pay the principle or interest? . . . Must we again compel those in Europe, who lent us money in our distress, to advance the money to pay themselves interest on the certificates of the debts due to them?" The same point was made in Pennsylvania by M'Kean.[41] Here was another telling point. By making the federal government reliant on the states for its revenues, the states had really made it reliant on European bankers and governments. Independence was illusory under those conditions.

Wilson also informed the Pennsylvanians of what he thought was the greatest accomplishment of the Constitution, the ending of paper emissions by the states, saying that if that were all the document did, "it would be worth our adoption." To bring home the consequences of paper money and what experience with it had taught, he reminded them: "It is true, we have no tender law in Pennsylvania; but the moment you are conveyed across the Delaware, you find it haunt your journey, and follow close upon your heels. The paper passes commonly at twenty-five or thirty percent discount. How insecure is property?"[42] Struggles over paper money would haunt the United States again after the Civil War. At this time, it was not to be trusted.

THE RATIFICATION VOTE

The issue of paper money played no part in the ratification of the Constitution, so Wilson's viewpoint must have been widely accepted. When the states began holding their own conventions to vote on the Constitution, to encourage passage of the document, Federalists in the state conventions promised to amend it with a bill of rights. In several state conventions, however, a long list of amendments was offered as conditions for approval. As Edward Dumbauld reckons, as many as 216 proposals for amendments were made in eight state conventions. Since there were duplicates, eighty separate amendments were sent forth by eight states. All of these eight states wanted restrictions on Congress' power to tax.[43]

Not all states were troubled by the powers granted the federal government by the Constitution. Delaware ratified quickly by unanimous vote on December 7, 1787. Pennsylvania followed shortly after, giving its approval on December 12 by 46 to 23.[44] The minority in Pennsylvania proposed fifteen amendments, including a provision "that no law shall be passed to restrain the legislatures of the several States from enacting laws for imposing taxes, except imposts and duties on goods exported and imported, and that no taxes, except imposts and duties upon goods imported and exported and postage on letters, shall be levied by the authority of Congress."[45]

New Jersey gave its unanimous approval on December 18, followed by a similar result in Georgia on January 2, 1788. Connecticut approved by 128 to 40 on January 9.[46] None of these states attached any amendments to their votes.

The first sign of trouble came in Massachusetts. A majority of the delegates to its ratifying convention were opposed to the Constitution. Lobbying efforts by Federalists, including getting John Hancock and Sam Adams to support approval, brought enough vote changes to accept the new document by 187 to 168 on February 16.[47] Nine amendments were suggested, including "That Congress do not lay direct Taxes but when Monies arising from the Impost & Excise are insufficient for the publick exigencies nor then until Congress shall have first made requisition upon the States to assess, levy & pay their proportions of such Requisition agreeably to the Census fixed in the said Constitution; in such way and manner as the Legislature of the States shall think best." If states failed in meeting the requisition, Congress could levy a direct tax until the requisition plus 6% interest had been paid.[48] An old policy proposed by Congress under the Articles of Confederation but never approved was finally being assented to. William Symmes told the delegates, "I humbly submit, Sir, whether, if each State had its proportion of some certain gross assigned, according to its numbers, and a power was given to Congress, to collect the same, in case of default in the State, this would not have been a safer Constitution."[49]

Maryland approved by 63 to 11 on April 21.[50] The majority suggested thirteen amendments, while the minority sought fifteen. The minority wanted to deny Congress the right to impose a poll tax and proposed "that all imposts and duties laid by Congress shall be placed to the credit of the state in which the same shall be collected, and be deducted out of each state's quota of the common or general expenses of the government."[51] Marylanders apparently wanted tariff collections to count as part of a system of quotas, even though there was no mention of quotas in the Constitution.

South Carolina passed by a large majority of 149 to 73 on May 23; the efforts of the Pinkneys and Rutledge to protect slavery had worked.[52] A body of amendments was resolved, including one on taxes that repeated the Massachusetts proposal.[53]

On June 21 New Hampshire gave its assent, closely, by 57 to 47.[54] Twelve amendments were proposed, including one on taxes that copied that of Massachusetts.[55] As the ninth state to ratify the Constitution, New Hampshire assured its passage. Nevertheless, debate continued in the remaining states.

Virginia's proved to be a contentious convention, as some of the statements quoted earlier indicate. There was talent on both sides of the debate. After more than three weeks of debate, ratification passed by only 89 to 79.[56] Even to get this slim majority, the Federalists agreed to a proposed bill of rights with twenty clauses and suggested twenty amendments to the body of the Constitution. With regard to taxes, Virginia recommended that "when Congress shall lay direct taxes or excises, they shall immediately inform the Executive power of each State of the quota of such State. . . . And if the Legislature of any State shall pass a law which shall be effectual for raising such quota at the time required by Congress, the taxes and excises laid by Congress shall not be collected, in such State."[57]

The story in New York was even harder for the Constitution. The Anti-Federalists had a clear and solid majority. The problem was that ten states had already approved, making the outcome in New York meaningless. Hamilton threatened that New York City would leave the state and join the new union no matter what the vote was. As a result, seven Anti-Federalists abstained, allowing the document to pass by 30 to 27 on July 26.[58] New York's ratifying convention requested fifty-eight changes to the Constitution. In addition to seeking a ban on a capitation tax and following

Massachusetts on direct taxes, the delegates also asked "that Congress do not impose any Excise on any Article (except Ardent Spirits) of the Growth, Production or Manufacture of the United States, or any of them."[59] Here there was an effort to exempt manufactured goods from any excise tax that might be levied, which passed, despite the objection of Chancellor Robert Livingstone that as domestic manufactures increased, imports must decline and, with them, so would tax receipts.[60]

North Carolina was even less excited about the Constitution than was New York. On their return, the delegates to the Constitutional Convention had reported favorably of the deal they had made on taxes: "The Chief thing we had to fear from such a [national] Government was the Risque of unequal or heavy Taxation." That risk had been avoided by the direct tax rule. As a result, "if a land Tax is laid we are to Pay at the Same Rate, for Example, fifty Citizens of North Carolina can be taxed no more for all their Lands than fifty Citizens in one of the eastern States. This must be greatly in our favour for as Most of their Farms are small . . . we certainly have, one with another, land of twice the Value that they Possess." The same argument held with a poll tax, whereby the three-fifths rule gave another tax break to North Carolinians. In return, "North Carolina does not Appear to us to have given *any thing*."[61]

The North Carolina ratification convention was not impressed. On July 24 by a vote of 184 to 83 it refused to ratify until a list of amendments was guaranteed. When that appeared unlikely, on November 21, ratification passed by 194 to 77.[62] The long list included twenty items in a bill of rights and twenty-six amendments to the document itself. Among those amendments was one on taxes that repeated Virginia's proposal.

Rhode Island proved the wisdom of the framers of the Constitution in not requiring a unanimous vote. That state kept to its implacable stance that had sunk the Articles of Confederation. It did not even call for a ratifying convention until 1790, after the new government had been formed. Even then it took pressure from the federal government to force ratification, by vote of 43 to 32 on May 29, 1790.[63]

In this manner the Constitution was ratified. The next step would be to implement it by organizing the new government and making it work. One of the key obstacles to be overcome was how to raise taxes and to satisfy the states that their fears of the federal government's taxing powers were unwarranted.

CONCLUSION

"Without revenues," Alexander Hamilton had warned in 1780, "a government can have no power. That power which holds the purse-strings absolutely, must rule." While this statement does not sum up all of the debate over the Constitution, it goes to the heart of the matter with regard to taxes. For any state to perform its duties, it must have revenue under its own control. A central government without taxing power was not a government at all.

To be sure, that was what many Americans wanted at the end of the Revolutionary War—no central government. There were few governmental duties needed at the national level. Those duties turned out to be more than these Americans thought, however. The lack of taxing power led to fractioned wrangling among the states over their contributions. As a result, the Congress, as one critic later put it, "may DECLARE every thing, but can DO nothing."[64]

Others, quick to condemn failure, sought greater powers for the central government. They came up with a new form of government that they embedded in the Constitution. Paramount among the powers of that new government was the power to tax. They knew their steps were unprecedented in this area but went ahead nonetheless. If reform would not work, a new system of government was necessary.

Their opponents recognized that new steps were being taken and fought them. Americans had gone to war to dispute a strong government's policy of taxing them. They had won. Passage of the Constitution would snatch their victory from them. The proposed amendments to the Constitution related to taxes indicated that the idea of the states' responding to requisitions from the central government remained important. As Patrick Henry put it, with his usual flair for drama, "I will never give up that *darling* word requisitions—My country may give it up—A majority may wrest it from me, but I will never give it up till my grave."[65] Those who had opposed reform were willing to grant it now, to try to make the system of requisitions work.

Hamilton disagreed. In his view, "The principle of regulating the contributions of the States to the common treasury by QUOTAS is another fundamental error in the Confederation. Its repugnancy to an adequate supply of the national exigencies has been already pointed out, and has sufficiently appeared from the trial which has been made of it."[66] The requisition system had not worked, and politicians like Henry were using it as a mask for avoiding taxes for as long as possible.

The only alternative to taxes was the printing of money with its resulting inflation tax. This was the policy several states followed. From a national perspective it was a bad policy, for inflation in the different states impeded economic advance. The Federalists were against this policy, either for the states or for the federal government.

Years later in his autobiography, Jefferson agreed with Hamilton's assessment on the need for taxes. He wrote, "Among the debilities of the government of the Confederation, no one was more distinguished or more distressing than the utter impossibility of obtaining, from the states, the money necessary for the payment of debts, or even for the necessary expenses of government. Some contributed a little, some less, & some nothing, and the last furnished at length an excuse for the first to do nothing also."[67] The idea of the requisition had a long standing even before the revolution and had never worked. The Constitution ended it.

At first glance, the division over the Constitution seems to have been between advocates of state versus national sovereignty. Certainly, Madison, Jefferson, Hamilton, and Washington agreed that the central government needed more power, especially the power to tax. In truth, there were three sides to the Federalist/Anti-Federalist debate. Between the two extremes were moderates who sought balance between the two spheres of power. During the ratification period they allied with the Federalists to get the Constitution passed. As the Federalists took charge of the new government, these moderates began setting out their own position. But that is the concern of the rest of this book.

NOTES

1. Banning, *The Sacred Fire*, p. 200.

2. John P. Kaminski and Gaspare J. Saladino, eds., *The Documentary History of the Ratification of the Constitution*, vol. 13, *Commentaries on the Constitution*, vol. 1 (Madison: State Historical Society of Wisconsin, 1981), p. 245.

3. "The Blessings of the New Government," *Philadelphia Independent Gazetteer*, October 6, 1787, in Kaminski and Saladino, *Documentary History*, pp. 345–46.

4. "Brutus V," December 13, 1787, Herbert J. Storing, ed., *The Complete Anti-Federalist*, vol. 2 (Chicago: University of Chicago Press, 1981), pp. 396–97.

5. "Essay by a Farmer and Planter," *Maryland Journal*, April 1, 1788, Storing, *Anti-Federalist*, vol. 5, p. 76.

6. Patrick Henry, "Speeches in the Virginia Ratifying Convention," June 1788, Storing, *Anti-Federalist*, vol. 5, pp. 222, 242; "Mr. Martin's Information to the General Assembly of the State of Maryland," Storing, *Anti-Federalist*, vol. 2, p. 55.

7. Thomas Jefferson to Edward Carrington, December 21, 1787, in *The Papers of Thomas Jefferson*, vol. 12, pp. 445–46.

8. "Letters of Cato," *New York Journal*, September 1787–January 1788, Storing, *Anti-Federalist*, vol. 2, p. 120.

9. Henry quotation and details from Massachusetts Convention from Wood, *Creation*, p. 526; George Mason, "Speech in the Virginia Ratifying Convention," June 4, 1788, Storing, vol 5, p. 255.

10. Cecelia Kenyon, "Men of Little Faith: The Anti-Federalists on the Nature of Representative Government," in Gordon S. Wood, ed., *The Confederation and the Constitution* (Washington, DC: University Press of America, 1979), p. 61.

11. "Essays of John DeWitt," *(Boston) American Herald*, October–November 1787, Storing, *Anti-Federalist*, vol. 4, p. 27.

12. Kenyon, "Men of Little Faith," p. 68.

13. "Brutus I," *New York Journal*, October 18, 1787, in Kaminski and Saladino, *Documentary History*, pp. 414–16.

14. "Centinel I," *The Philadelphia Independent Gazetteer*, October 5, 1787, in Kaminski and Saladino, *Documentary History*, pp. 332–34.

15. "Centinel II," *Philadelphia Freeman's Journal*, October 24, 1787, in Kaminski and Saladino, *Documentary History*, p. 465.

16. "Speech of George Mason, etc.," Storing, *Anti-Federalist*, vol. 5, p. 257; Letters of Centinel," Storing, *Anti-Federalist*, vol. 2, p. 162.

17. James Monroe, "Some Observations on the Constitution," 1788, Storing, *Anti-Federalist*, vol. 5, p. 306; William Symmes, "Speech in Massachusetts Convention," January 22, 1788, Storing, *Anti-Federalist*, vol. 4, pp. 64–65.

18. Jonathan Elliot, *The Debates of the Several State Conventions on the Adoption of the Federal Constitution*, vol. 2 (New York: Burt Franklin, reprint of 1888 edition), pp. 190–95.

19. Elliot, *Debates*, pp. 36, 482, 237.

20. *The Federalist Papers*, introduction by Clinton Rossiter (New York: Mentor Books, 1964), p. vii.

21. Hamilton, No. 7, *The Federalist Papers*, pp. 60–66.

22. Hamilton, No. 12, *The Federalist Papers*, p. 92.

23. Ibid., pp. 94–96.

24. Hamilton, No. 22, *The Federalist Papers*, pp. 141–43.

25. Hamilton, No. 17, *The Federalist Papers*, p. 119.

26. Hamilton, No. 30, *The Federalist Papers*, p. 188.

27. Ibid., pp. 189–92.

28. Hamilton, No. 35, *The Federalist Papers*, pp. 211–13.

29. Hamilton, No. 31, *The Federalist Papers*, pp. 195–97.

30. Hamilton, No. 32, *The Federalist Papers*, pp. 198–200.

31. Hamilton, No. 34, *The Federalist Papers*, pp. 208–11.

32. Hamilton, No. 36, *The Federalist Papers*, pp. 221–22.

33. Madison, No. 56, *The Federalist Papers*, pp. 346–50.

34. Hamilton, No. 35, *The Federalist Papers*, pp. 214–15.

35. Hamilton, no. 12, *The Federalist Papers*, p. 93.

36. Hamilton, No. 36, *The Federalist Papers*, p. 223.

37. Madison, No. 41, *The Federalist Papers*, p. 262.

38. General Defense of the Constitution at the Virginia Ratification Convention, June 6 and 11, 1788, *Madison Papers*, vol. 11, pp. 86–87, 107–9 and 117.

39. Elliot, *Debates*, p. 361.

40. Petaliah Webster, "Remarks on the Address of Sixteen Members of the Assembly of Pennsylvania, to Their Constituents" (October 12, 1787), in Webster, *Political Essays*, pp. 406–7.

41. Elliot, *Debates*, pp. 466 and 535.

42. Ibid., p. 486.

43. Edward Dumbauld, *The Bill of Rights and What It Means Today* (Norman: University of Oklahoma Press, 1957), pp. 32–33.

44. Joseph T. Keenan, *The Constitution of the United States*, 2d ed. (Pacific Grove, CA: Brooks/Cole, 1988), pp. 31–32.

45. Dumbauld, *The Bill of Rights*, p. 174.

46. Keenan, *The Constitution*, pp. 31–32.

47. Ibid., pp. 32–33.

48. Dumbauld, *The Bill of Rights*, p. 176.

49. Symmes, Speech, Storing, *Anti-Federalist*, vol. 4, p. 65.

50. Keenan, *The Constitution*, p. 33.

51. Dumbauld, *The Bill of Rights*, p. 179.

52. Keenan, *The Constitution*, p. 33.

53. Dumbauld, *The Bill of Rights*, p. 180.

54. Keenan, *The Constitution*, p. 34.

55. Dumbauld, *The Bill of Rights*, p. 181.

56. Keenan, *The Constitution*, pp. 34–35.

57. Dumbauld, *The Bill of Rights*, p. 186.

58. Keenan, *The Constitution*, p. 35.

59. Dumbauld, *The Bill of Rights*, pp. 193–96.

60. Elliot, *Debates*, p. 341.

61. "Letter of North Carolina Delegates to Governor Richard Caswell," September 18, 1787, in Kaminski and Saladino, *Documentary History*, pp. 216–17.

62. Keenan, *The Constitution*, p. 36.

63. Ibid., p. 36.

64. "Introduction" and "*Baltimore Maryland Gazette*, May 22, 1788," in Kaminski and Saladino, *Documentary History*, pp. 31, 112.

65. Henry, Speech, Storing, *Anti-Federalist*, vol. 5, p. 235.

66. Hamilton, No. 21, *The Federalist Papers*, p. 140.

67. Thomas Jefferson, "Autobiography, 1743–1790," January 6, 1821, in *Thomas Jefferson: Writings* (selected with notes by Merrill D. Peterson) (New York: Library of America, 1984), p. 75.

Chapter 5

A NATIONAL REVENUE

The Federalists had won a narrow victory in getting the Constitution ratified. Now they had to form a government and carry out new policies in a way that would win over the opposition. At the same time, as Washington put it in his first annual message to Congress, the country would have to learn "to distinguish between oppression and the necessary exercise of lawful authority."[1] The full expression of the rights of citizenship required an appreciation for the duties as well. In a freewheeling society such as existed in the United States at the time, a policy asking for loyalty to a far-off government would not be readily accepted.

A critical variable that would define the popularity of Federalist policies was how they would handle taxes. To be effective leaders, the Federalists had to find enough revenue to establish the new government and take care of the debt of the old one. They had to make the new government popular with a people still set against taxes. Taxes would be part of the "exercise of lawful authority." There would be no reliance on paper money and inflation as an easy way to finance government spending. Taxes would be collected and the people would have to accept them as part of responsible governance.

In collecting taxes, government officials also had to cope with a country that was still essentially rural. Only six cities had a population of more than 7,500 persons. The largest, New York, barely exceeded 30,000. The economy was dominated by agriculture, and most farms were self-sufficient. What little industry that existed was still in the handicraft stage. It was an economy that today would be categorized with the less developed countries. Getting taxes from it would not be easy.

TAXES: THE FIRST TARIFF

The starting point was a tariff, first proposed to the new Congress by Madison on April 9, 1789, even before Washington had been sworn in as president. Not surprisingly, the tariff proposed was very similar to the one submitted to the old Congress in 1783. In a speech proposing the tariff, Madison acknowledged this similarity along with getting in a parting shot at the old system:

I take the liberty, Mr. Chairman, at this early stage of the business, to introduce to the committee a subject, which appears to me to be of the greatest magnitude; a subject, sir, that requires our first attention. . . .

The union, by the establishment of a more effective government, having recovered from the state of imbecility that heretofore prevented a performance of its duty, ought, in its first act, to revive those principles of honor and honesty that have too long lain dormant.

The deficiency in our Treasury has been too notorious to make it necessary to animadvert upon that subject. Let us content ourselves with endeavoring to remedy the evil. To do this a national revenue must be obtained. . . . Happy it is for us that such a system is within our powers. . . .

The propositions made on this subject by Congress in 1783, having received, generally, the approbation of the several States of the Union, in some form or other, seem well calculated to become the basis of the temporary system, which I wish the committee to adopt.[2]

It was still agreed that a tariff was likely to be preferable to Americans than excises or direct taxes. Madison's proposal called for a 5% tariff on imports, with higher duties placed on a list of items.

As the Federalists appreciated, a tariff on imported items was a good way for a government to raise revenue. In addition to the virtues set forth by Adam Smith, it had other advantages. Smith alluded to its fairness, certainty, and convenience as useful traits. In a less developed country a tariff is especially convenient to collect. Most imported items come through a few ports and are handled by a few merchants. It would be relatively easy to collect a tax from them and let them pass it onto their customers as well as possible. Moreover, the actual amount of the tariff would be hidden from the final consumer, and the price paid would reflect other variables, including the several markups in price by middlemen. These advantages were well understood by members of the first Congress.

Madison took this attitude into account in proposing "such articles of requisition only as are likely to occasion the least difficulty." He had learned Smith's lesson about moderate taxes on luxury items and suggested duties on alcoholic beverages, molasses, tea, pepper, sugar, cocoa and coffee—a list Smith would have approved.

Madison's fellows in Congress, however, immediately began pushing for special consideration for a variety of cases of other items to include or exclude from the tariff list. Congressman Thomas Hartley (Federalist of Pennsylvania) stated the principle of protection as "both politic and just that the fostering hand of the General Government should extend to all those manufactures which will tend to national utility." Since 1783, there had been a growth in manufacturing in the country, so the rates and list of dutiable items from that date were outmoded.[3]

This attitude, however, opened a Pandora's box of sectional interest that the Constitution had intended to close. The North wanted a higher duty than proposed put on rum and a lower one on molasses; this would help the rum industry of New England. Pennsylvania wanted higher duties for steel. The South wanted no duties on manufactured goods or salt. The debate over using tariffs for a national revenue foundered over a desire to protect regional interests.

Madison countered that "however much we may be disposed to promote domestic manufactures, we ought to pay some regard to the present policy of obtaining revenues." He went on to say that although his "general principle" was that "commerce ought to be free," there were exceptions. If the United States opened its ports to ships of all nations, while other nations discriminated against its ships, it had the right to retaliate to protect its interests. In addition, manufacturing might develop on its own, but in a weakened state, and "ought not to be allowed to perish," as it was "not possible for the hand of man to shift from one employment to another," without being injured by the change. Finally, protection must be given to industries crucial to national defense.[4]

Although Hamilton gets credit for making the case for protectionism, Madison's espousal of exceptions to free trade proceeded on the same ground and preceded Hamilton's case by several years. As will be seen later, however, Hamilton, like Madison, believed that the need for revenue took precedence over protectionism.

The Tariff Act of 1789, passed on July 4, placed taxes on thirty items. Some products such as steel and dishware carried a percentage rate based on their value. Others carried a specific rate such as 2.5 cents per pound for coffee and 10 cents per gallon for Jamaica rum. Duties were placed on rope and hemp, salt, boots and shoes, candles, cheese, coal, soap, tobacco products, and playing cards. Luxuries were on the list, as Smith recommended, but necessities were, too.

The act was limited to seven years' duration, which was extended. Tariff rates from 1790 to 1801 averaged about 10%. While some protection was intended, it was probably kept to a minimum. Customs collections amounted to $4.4 million in 1791 and rose to $10 million by the end of the decade; they accounted for more than 80% of tax collections during the Federalist era.[5]

This part of the Federalists' tax program should have satisfied their opponents. Madison and Hamilton had promised a heavy reliance on tariffs in *The Federalist Papers*, and they had delivered. To be sure, special interest taxes were added to the program in the guise of mild protectionism. Already politicians had started down the path whereby the tax system was used to influence the economy and not just to raise revenue. Revenue was raised, however, indicating that Smith's stricture that tariffs be kept moderate was followed.

TAX LIMITATIONS

In terms of amendments to the Constitution limiting the taxing power of Congress, the Federalists stuck to their original position. At the Constitutional Convention they had opposed a bill of rights and only begrudgingly agreed to consider one to get the document approved. They wanted as few limits as possible, especially with respect to taxes. On May 4, 1789, Madison raised the issue of amendments, and on June 8 the House went into a committee of the whole to consider them.

Madison picked what he thought were the important issues raised at the ratifying conventions and combined them into nine amendments. None related to taxes. Undaunted, Thomas Tudor Tucker, representative of South Carolina, proposed an amendment stipulating that no direct taxes be used unless tariffs, excise taxes, and requisitions on the states failed to raise sufficient revenue—much as several state ratifying conventions had wanted. After lengthy debate, the House defeated his motion by 39 to 9.

The House sent a final package of seventeen amendments to the Senate for consideration. Efforts were made there to place a limit on direct taxes unless requisitions failed, but to no avail. A House-Senate conference produced twelve amendments to submit to the states, with the House approving on September 24, 1789, and the Senate the next day. Ten of these were eventually approved as the Bill of Rights.[6] No restrictions on taxes were part of them. A strong desire of eight of the ratifying states had been circumvented. Anti-Federalists would have to rely on the word of the Federalists or their own political skills if taxes were to be limited.

The Anti-Federalists probably felt they had suffered another setback when the Treasury Department was organized. First, the administration of the department was placed in the hands of a single person, instead of the committee management that marked most of the Articles of Confederation era. Second, the person placed in charge was Alexander Hamilton, appointed on September 11, 1789, and very likely to draw fire from the opposition camp. For his own part, Hamilton took the job at a great financial cost, saying "he thought it would be in his power, in the financial department, to do the country great good."[7]

HAMILTON AS SECRETARY OF TREASURY

We can probably never get to the bottom of Hamilton's character, and it is futile to try. Ben Franklin once said of John Adams, "He means well for his country, is always an honest man, often a wise one, but sometimes, and in some things, absolutely out of his senses."[8] This statement could have applied to many of Franklin's contemporaries. It fitted Hamilton.

Hamilton's loss of his senses often came through in his pursuit of glory, but he hoped to be honored for accomplishment. While there was a lot of strut to Hamilton, he backed it up with ability. His wisdom and honesty came through in his financial plans for the government. Perhaps his early life clerking in a store on a small island gave him a flair for handling money and accounts. It surely must have given him a commercial attitude toward dealing with financial issues; he understood the importance of retaining a reputation that instilled confidence among creditors. In any event, his talents were recognized. At a time when the Treasury Department was being formed, Madison wrote to Jefferson that both John Jay and Hamilton were front-runners for head of the new department. In Madison's opinion, of the two men, Hamilton was "perhaps best qualified for that species of business and on that account should be preferred by those who know him personally."[9]

Of all the Federalist leaders, Hamilton had the best-defined vision of the United States as a continental power. Perhaps that vision came from seeing things whole, an attribute derived from growing up in the confined geographical space of an island. More plausibly, Hamilton, having spent his youth outside the colonies, did not develop the attachment to his adopted state, New York, that other Founding Fathers had for their native states. Whatever the reason, Hamilton was an ardent nationalist. As he wrote to Washington in 1783, "There are dangerous prejudices in the particular states opposed to those measures which alone can give stability & prosperity to the Union."[10] His policies always kept his continental vision in mind.

For example, he was often a spokesman for the aristocracy of wealth, and his personal and family contacts were with its members. Yet it is too easy to call him an avid believer in the virtues of the wealthy. He was practical enough to recognize that their political and financial support was essential to the success of the new government and his vision of the nation. His guiding principle was that humans acted mainly in their self-interest, and appeals to that self-interest were the means to get them to "co-operate to public good."[11] In terms of public finance this meant he emphasized the importance of keeping public creditors happy, even if they happened to be his friends.

It also helped that as secretary of the treasury he faced no elections. Hamilton made many decisions with regard to taxes that entailed unknown consequences and political risk. He acted as Washington's first minister, usually with the president's approval. Although his reports and recommendations were done at the request of Congress, he usually exceeded those requests to get things done. Not all of his advice was followed, but enough of it was that he was chiefly responsible for overall public finance during the first Washington administration.

He was often charged with overstepping his bounds, by members of Congress and by public writers. As one critic told his readers,

You express surprise . . . to find that the Secretary of the Treasury has been constantly intrusted with originating revenue bills. You further observe, that when the constitution was the subject of investigation, some citizens expressed the apprehensions, that the time might come, when the President himself, or he, with a majority of the Senate combined, might influence the legislative measures; but that there never were any suggestions, that a Secretary could have so much influence as has been ascribed to Col. Hamilton, both by those who applaud, and those who blame him.[12]

Here was centralization of power greater than the Anti-Federalists feared, and it was in the hands of an appointed official, a situation difficult to square with the notion of taxation with representation.

But perhaps Hamilton's not having to run for reelection was an asset. Certainly, he set no easy task for the new government. Keep taxes low, take care of the public debt, and spend on national defense. Managing the public finances under these conditions required adroitness and savvy. Hamilton's savvy enabled him to appreciate that the debt did not have to be paid off in order to keep bondholders happy. They simply needed the confidence that it could be paid off. This was the gist of the commercial attitude toward the public debt.

The basis of the Hamilton program was presented in three great state papers, written in 1790-91. In those papers, Hamilton outlined how the government could manage its finances and help establish the country's economy. Although taxes were not at the center of any of those reports, they hovered in the background, never far from Hamilton's thoughts.

DEBT: HAMILTON'S FIRST REPORT

Fiscal management such as Hamilton envisioned aimed at restoration of public credit. The first step in attaining this public credit was to service the debt accrued during the war. On January 9, 1790, Hamilton presented his first plan to Congress as a "Report Relative to a Provision for the Support of Public Credit," calling for a policy under which the government would assume responsibility for the public debt. As he put it, "States, like individuals, who observe their engagements, are respected and trusted."[13]

Hamilton proposed that all of the national debt, both principal and interest, be paid in hard currency, although creditors could exercise an option to take payment in the form of western land. At the same time, however, Hamilton would lower the interest rate on the debt from 6% to 4% by exchanging it for a new issue of debt in various combinations with land and lower interest securities. His aim was to reduce the burden of the interest payments, because a full-scale assumption "would require an extension of taxation to a degree and to objects, which the true interest of public creditors forbids."[14] Hamilton wanted to manage the debt but keep taxes as low as possible. He also proposed that the debt payments be made to current holders of the bonds and that the national government assume the debts incurred by the separate states for fighting the war.[15]

At the Constitutional Convention, debates had taken place over paying the debt of the original versus current holders of debt securities. As a way of heading off the opponents of his plan for paying current holders, some of whom were speculators purchasing government bonds in anticipation of full payment, Hamilton maintained, with some dissembling, that it would not always be possible to determine the original holders of the debt; in many cases loan certificates had been issued by agents in each state in direct payment to soldiers and suppliers, and the original name on the treasury register might have belonged to the state agent. Determining the market price paid by the holders of the debt would be equally difficult. In many cases the loan certificates had changed hands several times. It would be impossible to determine how the gains or losses could be allocated among original and present holders of debt certificates. The simplest plan would be to pay full value to current holders.[16]

It was also an honorable plan. The old Congress had agreed in 1783, in a report written by Madison, to settle its debt by paying whoever held it.[17] Doing otherwise was an injustice, "a breach of contract; in violation of the rights of a fair purchase."[18] If the new Congress wanted to aid its original creditors, it should do so directly and not at the expense of a breach of faith with subsequent bond purchasers.

Hamilton also thought that fiscal responsibility on the part of the central government dictated that it pay all the debt incurred in fighting the Revolutionary War, including that of the separate states. Assumption of the state debt would have the additional effect of loosening the allegiance of creditors to those states and tying them to the national government.

Hamilton linked this need to retain investor confidence in government to taxes. Collection of taxes, he argued, was more efficient in the hands of the federal government. It alone had the right to levy tariffs, giving it access to a secure form of revenue. For this reason, holders of state debt would be put in an inferior position compared to creditors of the national government. His best guess was that payment of interest on the entire debt could "be obtained from the present duties on imports" along with a few additional tariffs that he proposed in the report.[19]

In justifying the imported items he wanted taxed, Hamilton again followed Smith by indicating, "They are all of them, in reality—luxuries—the greatest part of them foreign luxuries; some of them, in the excess in which they are used pernicious luxuries. . . . The consumption of ardent spirits particularly, no doubt very much on account of their cheapness, is carried to an extreme which is truly to be regretted, as well in regard to the health and morals, as to the economy of the community."[20] If the tariff decreased consumption of these luxuries, so much the better.

He was also aware of how the debt could influence economic development. As Hume had argued, Hamilton considered that debt certificates that traded at a stable value could serve as a source of liquid capital. They either could function as money themselves or could be readily converted into money. As long as their value fluctuated, however, capital in the hands of speculators would be tied up waiting to move on changes in the government bond market. This speculative demand for money would create a credit crunch elsewhere in the economy.[21]

In summing up his case for assumption of the debt, Hamilton made a statement that would chase him forever: "The proper funding of the present debt, will render it a national blessing." But the context of the statement was more detailed. Hamilton did not intend this as a "position inviting to prodigality, and liable to dangerous abuse." Rather, the debt would be a blessing only if borrowing was always "accompanied with the means of extinguishment." Hamilton regarded this principle "as the true secret for rendering public credit immortal."

The means for extinguishing the debt that Hamilton proposed was a sinking fund system. Revenues from post office operations, duties, and public land sales were to be vested in a group of commissioners, consisting of the president of the Senate, the Speaker of the House, the chief justice, the secretary of the treasury, and the attorney general. They would use these funds to pay off the debt.[22]

The idea behind the sinking fund, which was borrowed from England, was simple. Surplus government revenues would be placed in the fund, which could then be used to buy government bonds on the open market. As interest on these bonds accumulated, the fund would grow. If the public debt were kept constant, the sinking fund would grow to equal it through compound interest, and the debt could be paid off without high taxes. Those were Hamilton's hopes.

Hamilton's espousal of a sinking fund was one policy where he went against the advice of Adam Smith. Smith doubted the ability of any government to devote surplus revenue to a sinking fund, as any excess of tax collections above normal operating expenses would be needed to pay for interest on public debt. Only when interest rates declined, would there be an increase in the sinking fund and any reduction in debt.[23] Smith proved more correct than Hamilton on this issue.

Hamilton's first report caused fierce debate in Congress. There was no opposition to his plans for funding the foreign held-debt. The first challenge came against the idea of assumption of the domestic debt. Prior to passage of the Constitution, government securities sold in the market at about one-quarter of their face value. The government, had it purchased its securities on the open market, could have retired a substantial portion of the debt at less than par, saving the Treasury millions. By assuming the debt at its stated value, the government instead conferred that money on holders of the debt.

There was opposition to rewarding those debt holders. In the House of Representatives, Madison wanted payment to be made to the original holders of the debt, with current holders being granted the market price they had paid in order to prevent speculators from making improper gains. Madison argued, "This will not do perfect justice; but it will do more real justice, and perform more of the public faith, than any other expedient proposed."[24] Hamilton felt Madison's argument was a turnabout from his earlier position in the Continental Congress, but Madison sincerely felt that since then the problem had worsened, with more debt having been transferred from original holders to speculators.[25]

Here was a case of the conflict between agrarian and commercial values. To an agrarian like Madison, payment of a debt was a mark of honor that was owed to those who had helped you in your time of need. You did not abandon that honor lightly. For Hamilton, debt was merely a commercial contract, assignable as a creditor saw fit, and, once assigned, the right of a contract had to be upheld. Hamilton's view prevailed. Madison's motion in the House of Representatives to discriminate between original and current holders was defeated by a vote of 36 to 13.

Madison and his good friend Jefferson were uneasy with Hamilton's attitude that the debt need not be paid off as long as creditors had confidence in the government. Writing to Madison in September 1789, Jefferson argued against "the received opinion, that the public debts of one generation devolve on the next." Instead, Jefferson wanted to see a limit placed on government debt such that it would be paid off by each generation, as part of his philosophy that the earth belongs to the living. He wanted to avoid the oppressive debt and taxes that characterized Europe at the time and urged Madison to make this generational limit part of U. S. policy, stating, "It would furnish matter for a fine preamble to our first law for appropriating the public revenue." Madison disagreed. Some government spending, such as in fighting a war for freedom, was for the benefit of future generations, so there was nothing wrong with their helping to pay for it.[26] (The debt philosophies of Jefferson and Madison are considered in more detail in Chapters 8 and 9.)

In principle, Jefferson won. The United States now pays its debt off at least every thirty years, by borrowing more; treasury bonds do not exceed a life of thirty years, and technically their refunding represents paying them off and borrowing again, from a new generation perhaps. In practice, Hamilton's view has prevailed. Refunding of the public debt requires confidence that creditors can get their money when they want it.

The issue of assumption of state debts also found Hamilton and Madison on separate sides. Madison led an opposition that believed an assumption of state debts discriminated unfairly between states that had paid their wartime debts and those that had not.

Other congressional opponents of the assumption of state debt linked the debt to the greater powers sought by the central government, especially with taxes. James Jackson pointed out that his state, Georgia, had paid off part of its debt by levying a tax payable in its bonds—much as colonial governments had eliminated bills of credit—and expected to continue. Samuel Livermore of New Hampshire agreed with Jackson that it was best to leave responsibility for the debt with the states and give them the taxing power to pay their debts separately, rather than consolidate all debt and taxes with the federal government. Each state could tailor its own tax system to the needs of its citizens, much better than a central government could. Virginia and North Carolina had also used a tax payable in debt certificates to reduce their obligations.[27]

Here again Hamilton prevailed, but only after Madison and Jefferson switched sides and supported his proposal. In return, Hamilton helped the two Virginia leaders secure a commitment to locate the capital of the new government on the Potomac River.[28] Jefferson later claimed he had been taken in this deal, but Hamilton might have made the same charge.

The issue of assumption of the debt, both national and state, had been raised many times in Congress during the 1780s and was considered at the Constitutional Convention. Madison had never objected, so his opposition to Hamilton was a switch. Madison and Jefferson might have been playing local politics. After all, Virginia had not sent Madison to the Senate, and he barely won election to the House of Representatives. Both also knew that Virginia would derive economic benefit from having the national capital in its region and were happy with the political swap.

For his part, Hamilton sacrificed the interests of New York, where the capital was located, for his vision of the national interest.

Not everyone was happy, however. Congressman John Steele of North Carolina wrote to his constituents, "Thus you see my Friend, that assuming, funding and excising have taken root in America. How these foreign plants will flourish in free soils, time must determine."[29]

MONEY: HAMILTON'S SECOND REPORT

In "The Second Report on the Further Provision Necessary for Establishing Public Credit (Report on a National Bank)," given to Congress on December 13, 1790, Hamilton proposed formation of a federally chartered private bank to be owned, in part, by the government while also holding government deposits. The banking program of Robert Morris was to be repeated. It was expected that such a bank, by issuing its own notes, would be able to establish a national currency. It would also help handle the government's finance and was part of a plan to reduce the public debt and steady its market.

As Smith had described in *The Wealth of Nations*, banks play an important role in market economies by accumulating individual savings into a source of loans and by helping to create credit and, in Hamilton's day, to introduce paper money into the economy through the issue of banknotes backed by gold. In 1790 there were only three incorporated banks operating in the country,[30] and even though the number of banks would increase to eighteen by 1794,[31] the banking system was still inadequate to serve the government's needs for collecting and handling its funds.

Hamilton's experience as a founder of the Bank of New York contributed to his understanding of the role of banks. As an economic agent, the proposed national bank would help the economy secure the capital it needed and also serve as a source for government borrowing. The bank would further help the government by making tax collections easier. It could make loans to taxpayers for paying taxes. More important, the supply of banknotes issued by the bank would be useful for paying taxes. There would be no problem due to a shortage of specie.[32]

Hamilton wanted the best of both worlds with regard to paper money. Previously, the states and the national government had excessively issued paper money because "the stamping of paper is an operation so much easier than the laying of taxes." Since they could not control themselves, the states and the federal government had been thwarted from this action by the Constitution. Now Hamilton was proposing that the power to print money be given to the Bank of the United States. What would keep the bank from printing excessive money? After all, Hamilton intended it to be a tool in securing public credit. The bank could simply print money to purchase government securities, thereby providing the government with funds to spend. A private bank had limits on how much money it could print, however. Its continued operation would depend on its redeeming its paper emissions in gold on demand, so it would not print too much money. In this way paper money would be available for helping the economy and for paying taxes, but emissions would be limited by prudent banking practices,[33] much as Smith had argued.

The bill to charter the Bank of the United States was passed by the Senate on January 20, 1791, and the House on February 8, 1791, both by 2-to-1 margins. The chartering of the Bank of the United States sparked another debate. Madison led the initial attack on the bank by questioning its constitutionality. The Constitution had not given the government any power to establish a bank, and if it took that power, Madison believed, it would set a precedent that would enable it to establish any other business. Madison knew what the framers of the Constitution intended regarding federal charters for business. His proposal to have the Constitution give the government the power to incorporate businesses had been defeated.[34]

In terms of the Bank of the United States itself, Madison had reservations about the impact the bank would have on government finances. He especially worried that having been given the power to borrow under the Constitution, Congress was now creating an instrument to lend to it. If the process of borrowing by the government became as easy as calling on the Bank of the United States for loans, there might be no limit to how much public debt the government could incur.[35]

Jefferson, although he admitted that the Bank of the United States might be a help to the government in organizing its finances, did not care to see concentrations of large amounts of wealth in a few hands, which he feared the Bank of the United States would create. He also felt that it would become so powerful that it would eliminate any competition from state-chartered banks, thereby abridging the right of the separate states to charter their own banks.[36] Jefferson expressed his views in a brief to the president on the constitutionality of the Bank of the United States, and Attorney General Randolph seconded this disapproving opinion in his own report.

Given this negative legal advice in his own cabinet, especially from fellow Virginians, Washington had doubts about the constitutionality of the Bank of the United States and asked Hamilton for his opinion. Hamilton responded with the doctrine of "implied power." Since the Constitution gave Congress the power to coin money and regulate its value, he argued, this clause implied that Congress had the power to establish the means to accomplish these tasks. The Bank of the United States was such a means, he concluded, so its constitutionality was secure.

As for the intent of the framers in not placing a power of incorporation in the Constitution, Hamilton maintained that it was not clear why they had refrained. He continued, "Some again alledge, that it was disagreed to, because it was thought improper to vest in Congress a power of erecting corporations—others, because it was thought unnecessary to specify the power, and inexpedient to furnish an additional topic of objection to the constitution. In this state of the matter, no inference whatever can be drawn from it."[37] The original intent of the framers could not be counted on, according to Hamilton's view.

Hamilton also linked the legality of the bank to the taxing power. The Constitution gave Congress the right to raise taxes for the general welfare. Suppose an emergency arose wherein a large amount of revenue was needed more quickly than taxes could be collected. Loans could be used in their stead. Creation of the Bank of the United States would make those loans easier to secure, in essence substituting for the taxing power.[38] Washington agreed and signed the Bank Act on February 25, 1791.[39] Anti-Federalist fears that the Constitution gave unlimited power to the government through the necessary and proper clause found confirmation.

The issue of the Bank of the United States proved a final straw in a string of battles between Hamilton and Madison over the nature of the new government's finances. The debate in Congress over Hamilton's funding of state debts dragged on for six months, and Hamilton lost several votes on it. Even after the deal had been made on assumption of state debts, Madison arranged for other members of the Virginia delegation to switch their votes so he could keep his negative vote. Hamilton would characterize Madison's opposition as "a perfidious desertion of the principles which he was solemnly pledged to defend."[40]

At heart the two former collaborators disagreed over how powerful the national government would be. Hamilton wanted to push that power to the limit, and his financial plans pointed that way. Madison was trying to strike a balance between federal and state government, and his opposition to the Bank of the United States and the debt assumption plans indicated this effort. Hence they were drawn from common ground to battleground, and the unity of Washington's first years of office deteriorated into the rough-and-tumble of partisan party politics.

TAXES: HAMILTON'S THIRD REPORT

The third part of Hamilton's program is the most famous. Hamilton's reputation as a thinker in economic affairs rests on his "Report on Manufactures," submitted to Congress on December 5, 1791. In that document he used the ideas of the French Physiocrats (and maybe Jefferson) to bow toward the importance of agriculture. Then he took the ideas of Adam Smith to point out the advantages of manufacturing. Finally, he argued against Smith's precepts of free trade and made the appeal for protectionism based on the infant industry case. Analysis of protectionism is outside our direct interest in taxation, at this stage; it is considered in more detail in Chapter 10.

At this point, however, there remains the question about the conflict between tariffs for protection versus the need for revenue. How can Hamilton's presumed protectionism be squared with his obvious following of Smith in believing that tariffs had to be moderate to raise revenue? As noted earlier, a high tariff that succeeds in protection will not produce much revenue. Hamilton had three answers to this question.

First, he thought that direct payment of a bounty to subsidize fledgling businesses was "one of the most efficacious means of encouraging manufactures, and is in some views, the best." Bounties did not raise prices of products or cause shortages, as did protective tariffs. Even better, though, was to combine the two by using a modest tariff on imports that would raise revenue and taking a portion of the proceeds to provide bounties. Perhaps some would object to this application of public funds, but Hamilton felt that it would lead to "a new and useful branch of industry . . . [and] . . . a permanent addition to the general stock of productive labor."[41]

This growth in manufacturing led to Hamilton's second and most important point. Even if the system of tariffs and bounties cost revenue, he pointed out, "there is no truth, which may be more firmly relied upon, than that the interests of the revenue are promoted, by whatever promotes an increase of National industry and wealth." As domestic industry grew, the internal tax base would also expand. The extent of national wealth determined "the capacity of every country to contribute to the public Treasury."[42] Internal taxes would replace the revenue lost from trade. Hamilton's plans for the nurturing of manufacturing also served as a stalking-horse for internal taxes.

Third, a policy of encouragement of manufacturing through tariffs and bounties needed to be undertaken on a case-by-case basis. In industries where no domestic production was feasible immediately, tariffs for revenue purposes could be laid. In other industries, protection would take place at the sacrifice of revenue. Hamilton aspired to what we now call industrial policy, in trying to pick winning industries to encourage. At the same time, he would use imports with no domestic competition for taxing purposes. He even went down a list of products to discuss how he would tinker with the duties on them.[43]

To be sure, the tariff rates Hamilton proposed were not high enough to be overly protective, and even protective tariffs would bring in some revenue. For Hamilton, the appearance of a secure source of revenue was as important for maintaining public faith in the debt-paying powers of the government as the reality. He saw little conflict between the two, especially since his long-run vision of the United States was of a prosperous economy led by a strong manufacturing sector. Not everyone agreed, however, and the recommendations made in the "Report on Manufactures" were not enacted. Congress tabled the report, except for helping out manufacturing vital for national defense, and Hamilton made no objection.

PUBLIC OPPOSITION

Along with the infighting over Hamilton's program in Congress, private citizens, both well known and not, voiced disagreement with parts of Hamilton's plan. The former treasury assistant Gouverneur Morris wrote to Robert Morris, his former boss and collaborator in public finance, "To assume payment of what the States owe, merely because they owe it, seems to my capacity not more rational, than to assume the debts of corporations, or of individuals."[44] Others argued that assumption would lead to higher taxes.

In the press there appeared a variety of forms of opposition. The *Boston Columbian Centinel* of March 20, 1790, carried the comments of a "Real Soldier" concerning the discrimination plan: "Thank God there lives a Madison to propose justice" for the "poor emaciated soldier, hungry and naked, in many instances wandering from one extreme part of the country to another." Along with soldiers, their heirs were called into play. The *New Haven Connecticut Journal* (August 11,

1790), in reviewing the funding plan, said that the "WIDOW should be able to comprehend the value of her note, and not be exposed to the artful calculation of some harpy, who is aiming to take advantage of her ignorance." The soldier, widow and orphan appeal became quite common.[45]

Despite these appeals, the idea that the government would not honor its obligation with regard to negotiable securities seems so foreign to us now that it is worth spending some time looking at how opponents to Hamilton's plan argued their case. A cogent case for paying the original holders was provided by Petaliah Webster in his essay "A Plea for the Poor Soldiers." Webster countered Hamilton's legal argument by maintaining that the government itself had breached the contract earlier when it issued securities whose market value was never equal to their face value: "If the public promise or faith is supposed to be given in the certificate, it was broken in the instant it was made." Furthermore, any person who bought the security was entitled only to what was paid for the security, just as anyone who accepted depreciated continental dollars was able to lay claim only to what those dollars would purchase. The real debt was with the original holders of the security. If Hamilton was concerned with identifying those holders, Webster countered that it was up to them to prove the validity of their claim, either by recourse to the government's records or by other evidence in a legal proceeding.

Webster also added three economic arguments linked to taxes. First, he maintained that a policy of paying the original holders would make taxes more acceptable among the public as being a necessary government expenditure, whereas "any tax to pay the speculators will sit very uneasy on the most quiet and peaceable citizens." Second, the Hamilton plan, by rewarding speculation, "encourages and supports idle and hurtful contrivances to procure fortunes by dexterity and sleight of hand, rather than by the old, painful methods of industry, economy and care." Industry and economic growth could create a larger tax base. Third, payment to the multitude of original holders, rather than to a few speculators, would spread money throughout the economy, foster economic growth, and again make tax collection easier.

As indicated earlier, Webster was a strong advocate of taxes to pay government expenses and to eliminate the public debt. Along with many others, he followed Adam Smith in favoring taxes on luxuries and alcoholic beverages. Indeed, he set a standard for government debt as the point where "the annual demand for money does not exceed the product of an impost on imported luxuries." He then estimated the public debt at $109 million, with annual interest charges of $6.4 million; based on revenue estimates of $2.6 million, there would be a deficit of $4.3 million, given other expenses of $600,000. Webster did not think taxes could be raised sufficiently to pay this amount but also opposed Hamilton's plan of deferring a portion of the debt. It made little sense in these circumstances to reward speculators.[46]

Pennsylvania politician William Findlay also criticized the Hamilton plan. He argued that revenues from land sales and timely purchases of the public debt on the open market when bond prices were low could have eliminated much of the debt and obviated the need to assume such a burden. Nor was Hamilton's plan honestly achieved. It would not have passed except for the "venal bargaining about the seat of government."[47]

The Bank of the United States also came under attack in the press. Philip Freneau, a Jefferson partisan and receiver of patronage from the then secretary of state (he was on the payroll as a translator), wrote a poem to Washington in his own paper, the *Philadelphia National Gazette* (June 22, 1793). Its closing lines take Jefferson's side in the question of the constitutionality of the Bank of the United States:

> That thou has long and nobly served the state
> The nation owns, and freely gives thee thanks.
> But, sir, whatever speculators prate,
> She gave thee not the power to establish BANKS.[48]

Another, more detailed attack on the bank was leveled by John Taylor, who called it "the master key of that system, which governs the administration." His understanding of how banks operate was rather simplistic: "The business of banking, is simply a reiterated exchange of obligations for payment of money. A. gives his bond to B. and receives B.'s bond in exchange. But A. pays B. an interest, whereas B. pays A. none. A. is the community, B. is the bank. How must this traffic end?" In answer, he added, "The profits of the bank are obviously an indirect tax on the community."

In the past, states had emitted paper currency to pay their bills, and it had circulated as money. Now with the Bank of the United States as issuer of paper money, it took borrowing by the public to get paper money into circulation. The public had to pay interest on that money, which was why Taylor could charge that, "the profits of the bank are a tax upon the community." Why the profits of other businesses were not also a tax on the community, Taylor indicated by saying the use of money was not voluntary, whereas the purchase of other goods was. As a result, he concluded, Hamilton's policy was dishonest in that while it "exclaims 'A national debt is a national blessing,' it filches all it can get."[49] Taylor had left out that the emissions of paper money by the states had carried with it an inflation tax as real as the interest charged by the bank and often higher.

The gain made by speculators in government bonds under Hamilton's funding plans was a constant complaint in the press. It was also pointed out that letting the government establish its credit on solid ground had dangerous consequences. With a sound credit, officials would find it easy to borrow and soon would do so. They could, for example, go to war without raising taxes. As one writer warned, with a clairvoyance that deserves recognition through quoting him at length,

Public credit, which our politicians esteem of the greatest importance to government, should be regarded as the most unjust and ruinous invention of modern times. It is only useful and convenient to serve the ambitious projects of government. . . . The facility of acquiring credit precipitates nations into wars and other expences beyond the revenues of the state; funding systems are adopted, and peace itself does not relieve the people from oppressive taxes; but the misery of the present generation is unjustly transmitted to posterity.[50]

The linkage between the people and their representatives over government spending would be lost through the use of credit. The people would lose the ability to control the powers of the purse, and politicians would take advantage of that loss.

The press also grumbled about the high cost of government, particularly expressing concern over the pay of members of Congress ($6 a day) and the president (Washington earned $25,000 a year). There were objections to money's being used to establish the Library of Congress, which the *Boston Gazette* wryly pointed out was the result of members' having "no Matters of Importance to call to their attention, and being willing to do *something* for their Six Dollars a day, they propose to expend a few Thousand Dollars of the public Money in procuring a Library . . . to spend their time . . . in reading Magazines and other entertaining Publications." There was even concern that Congress would vote its members lifetime pensions.[51] Congressional pay increases, special restaurants, and munificent pensions, which all have been recent concerns, have a long history.

CONCLUSION

The first phase of the new federal government saw the resolution of issues left ambiguous by the Constitution. The framers had set forth a general collection of rules for governance, but rules must be interpreted and implemented to become workable. Regarding public finance, Hamilton's genius and forceful personality were the major influences on making the taxing power of the government function. Where others might have hesitated, in two major reports he devised a system of money, debt, and taxes consistent with the needs of a commercial economy. It in no way detracts from his accomplishment to consider that his reports were an eclectic gathering from Hume and Smith.

The tax and credit plan set forth by Hamilton was grandly conceived but very familiar, as it replicated many of the components of the Morris plan, which failed of acceptance under the Articles of Confederation. Then it had been opposed by advocates of a weaker national government. While they supported a stronger government, Madison and Jefferson thought that Hamilton had gone too far. Regardless of the complaints of these two Virginians, the Federalists had faced up to the challenge of showing the nation that a central government could be entrusted with broad powers, including the power of taxes. Whether or not they would remain popular was another matter.

NOTES

1. John C. Miller, *The Federalist Era* (New York: Harper and Row, 1960), p. 2.

2. Wednesday, April 8, 1789, *Debates and Proceedings of the Congress of the United States*, Joseph Gales, Sr., comp. (Washington, DC: Gales and Seaton, 1834), First Congress, First Session, pp. 106–8.

3. Ibid., p. 114.

4. April 9, 1789, *Debates of Congress*, First Congress, First Session, pp. 116–19.

5. Dewey, *Financial History*, pp. 80–84, 110.

6. Dumbauld, *The Bill of Rights*, pp. 33–49.

7. John C. Miller, *Alexander Hamilton: Portrait in Paradox* (New York: Harper and Row, 1959), p. 226.

8. Fleming, *The Man Who Dared Lightning*, p. 420.

9. James Madison to Thomas Jefferson, May 27, 1789, in *The Papers of Thomas Jefferson*, vol. 15, p. 153.

10. Jacob E. Cooke, ed., *The Reports of Alexander Hamilton* (New York: Harper and Row, 1964), p. viii.

11. John R. Nelson, Jr., *Liberty and Property* (Baltimore: Johns Hopkins University Press, 1987), p. 24.

12. William Findlay, *A Review of the Revenue System* (Philadelphia: Dobson, 1794), p. 44.

13. Report on Public Credit, Cooke, p. 3.

14. Ibid., p. 22.

15. Ferguson, *Power of the Purse*, pp. 293–95.

16. George R. Taylor, ed., *Hamilton and the National Debt* (Boston: D. C. Heath, 1950), pp. 1–3.

17. McDonald, *The Presidency of George Washington*, p. 70. See also Report on Public Credit, Cooke, p. 12. In 1790, Madison justified his view by writing to himself, "At that time the debts were due to the original holders." Adrienne Koch, *Jefferson and Madison: The Great Collaboration* (New York: Oxford University Press, 1964), p. 104.

18. Report on Public Credit, Cooke, p. 8.

19. Ibid., pp. 14, 34, 36–38.

20. Ibid., p. 34.

21. Nelson, *Liberty and Property*, pp. 33–35.

22. David F. Swanson, *The Origins of Hamilton's Fiscal Policies* (Gainesville: University of Florida Monographs), Winter 1963, pp. 50–51; Report on Public Credit, Cooke, pp. 40–41.

23. Smith, *Wealth*, vol. 2, pp. 444–57.

24. Taylor, *Hamilton and the National Debt*, p. 32.

25. Banning, *The Sacred Fire*, p. 294.

26. Koch, *Jefferson and Madison*, pp. 64–68, 71–74.

27. Ferguson, *Power of the Purse*, pp. 311–12.

28. Ibid., pp. 306–23.

29. Circular Letter dated January 27, 1791, in Noble E. Cunningham, Jr., ed., *Circular Letters of Congressmen to Their Constituents* (Chapel Hill: University of North Carolina Press, 1978), vol. 1, p. 4.

30. Lester V. Chandler, *The Economics of Money and Banking*, 4th ed. (New York: Harper and Row, 1964), p. 133.

31. Ibid., p. 6.

32. Hamilton, "Report on the Bank," in Cooke, *The Reports of Alexander Hamilton*, pp. 48–52.

33. Ibid., pp. 62–64.

34. Banning, *The Sacred Fire*, pp. 326–27.

35. Richard H. Timberlake, Jr., *The Origins of Central Banking in the United States* (Cambridge: Harvard University Press, 1976), p. 7.

36. Bray Hammond, *Banks and Politics in America* (Princeton, NJ: Princeton University Press, 1957), p. 120.

37. Report on the Bank, Cooke, pp. 83–94.

38. Ibid., pp. 102–5.

39. Hammond, *Banks and Politics*, pp. 209–10.

40. Miller, *Federalist*, p. 41.

41. Hamilton, Report on Manufactures, in Cooke, *The Reports of Alexander Hamilton,* pp. 167–71.

42. Ibid., pp. 202–3.

43. Ibid., pp. 181–201.

44. Joseph Charles, *The Origins of the American Party System* (New York: Harper and Brothers, 1961), p. 24.

45. Cited in Donald H. Stewart, *The Opposition Press of the Federalist Period* (Albany: State University of New York Press, 1969), pp. 33, 41, 42.

46. Petaliah Webster, "A Plea for the Poor Soldiers" (January 2, 1790) and "A Review of the Principles and Arguments of the Two Foregoing Essays" (December 20, 1790), in Webster, *Political Essays*, pp. 306–44, 346–75, respectively, quotations from pp. 351, 362, 363, 364.

47. Findlay, *A Review of the Revenue System*, pp. 4–12, quotation on p. 23.

48. Stewart, *The Opposition Press*, p. 53.

49. John Taylor, *An Enquiry into the Principles and Tendency of Certain Public Measures* (Philadelphia, Dobson, 1794), pp. 7, 11, 19, 21.

50. George Logan, *Letters Addressed to the Yeomanry* (Philadelphia, 1791), p. 36.

51. Stewart, *The Opposition Press*, pp. 71–75.

Chapter 6

SUBJECT TO ALL THE BURDENS

Although the general plan proposed by Hamilton was well conceived, like all economic plans it was only a projection of what would happen. Any effort to create a government budget of necessity involves what will take place in that unknowable place, the future. As Hamilton and the Federalists appreciated, the future can be a very different place from when it was forecast. Adjustments had to be made in Hamilton's program, as he probably had known from his experience in the army.

Compounding this predicament, there was a conflict between tariff collections and foreign affairs. In 1789, 1791, and 1794 Madison and Jefferson proposed tariff plans aimed at discriminating against England with higher tariffs both as a direct punishment for its trading policies and as a way of encouraging trade with France. Hamilton accepted the fact that the bulk of foreign trade, around 60% of imports, was with England. Reliance on tariff collections as a chief source of revenue meant that the government could ill-afford to do anything that would disrupt that trade. He chided Jefferson that since his tilting of tariff policy toward France would cost the government revenue, "it would be essential that the same act which should destroy this source of revenue should provide an equivalent. This I consider a rule that ought to be sacred."[1]

For this rule to be followed, the tax base had to be broadened. New taxes would be necessary, but these needs showed themselves only after the program had been implemented.

IMPLEMENTING THE PROGRAM: DEBT

The end result of the debate over the assumption of the public debt was the Funding Act of 1790, which called for the issuance of new federal bonds to cover all the old debt, with interest payments on two-thirds of the former debt to begin immediately and interest on the remaining third deferred for ten years.[2] By assuming the obligation to pay this debt, the government established its credit rating. By February 1792, for example, the 6% immediate interest-bearing bonds were selling in the market at $1.20 on the dollar.[3]

Assumption of the debt and the concomitant interest payments turned out to be a budget buster for the new government. Hamilton had estimated that the debt of the government was about $54 million. He reckoned that if his plan were followed, interest payments would total $2.2 million. Combined with $600,000 in other government expenses, about $3 million in taxes would have to be raised.[4]

Assumption of state debts produced an estimated public debt of $77,124,464 as of December 1789. Interest payments on the public debt were about $3 million per year during the 1790s and accounted for over half of total spending during the Federalist era. Hamilton recognized that tariff collections would not bring in enough revenue to meet the government's spending needs, after all. He put the revenue shortfall at $827,000.

IMPLEMENTING THE PROGRAM: TAXES

He soon recommended to Congress that tariffs on imported alcoholic beverages be raised and that an excise tax be placed on domestically produced whiskey. He anticipated that the new taxes would raise $877,500, including $270,000 from the internal excise on whiskey. The surplus of about $50,000 would go into the sinking fund. In proposing the taxes, he considered other options, most notably a land tax, but felt they should be employed for more pressing needs, such as war, rather than for interest on the debt, which appealed only to the interests of a small group of bondholders. He also thought the internal excise was important to diversify the government's sources of revenue.[5]

Congress accepted part of his plan in the Tax Act of 1791. The excise tax on whiskey would appear to be a voluntary consumption tax along lines Adam Smith suggested, but America was different from England. Although alcoholic beverages might have been a luxury in England, in the United States whiskey represented a way for rural farmers to store their surplus corn production to ship east. Their daily consumption of it made them feel it to be a necessity; in an area where coins were scarce, whiskey also served as a unit of money.

Within Congress the tax passed easily, and even Madison voted for it. President Washington judged that "there remains no doubt but [the whiskey tax] will be carried into effect not only without opposition, but with very general approbation. . . . It is possible, however, and perhaps not improbable that some Demagogue may start up, and produce and get signed some resolutions declatory of their disapprobation of the measure."[6] His fears proved correct. There was public opposition to the whiskey tax, and on Hamilton's recommendation Congress yielded to the pressure by reducing the tax rate. On country stills, which were the major issue of contention, the tax fell from about nine cents a gallon to seven cents. The farmers out on the frontier were not impressed.

The whiskey tax retained a feature that had been a part of the tax plans of the Continental Congress. Proceeds from it were earmarked strictly for payment of interest on the public debt. Any funds left over would then be used to pay off a portion of that debt by going into the sinking fund.[7] Samuel Livermore of New Hampshire thought this debt payment feature would be popularized "as drinking down the national debt."[8] Despite this novelty, there was much discontentment.

OPPOSITION TO TAXES: THE WHISKEY REBELLION

The tax incited the notorious Whiskey Rebellion of western Pennsylvania, the largest internal conflict in the United States between the Revolutionary War and the Civil War. A variety of forces pushed the men of the frontier toward defiance of the government. There were class distinctions between western farmers and eastern merchants, and the people of the frontier always had sought independence from a distant government. In fact, the resistance to the whiskey tax existed all along the frontier region of the country, from Pennsylvania south through Maryland, Virginia, the Carolinas, and Kentucky. In Georgia opponents to the excise felt burdened because the peach brandy they preferred was a "necessary of life . . . in this warm climate."[9] It was truly a regional insurrection.

The direct idea behind the resistance was older than the country: internal taxes should not be laid by a distant government. As one petition put it, "To be subject to all the burdens and enjoy none of the benefits arising from government is something we will not submit to."[10] Readers of the *Maryland Gazette* (August 27, 1790) were told that the Continental Congress had very early determined that excise taxes were "the HORROR of ALL FREE STATES."[11]

On the Federalist side the idea of respect for a proper authority of law was as important as the need for revenue, but the need for revenue mattered. Excluding payment of interest, more than 80% of government spending went to fight the Indian wars in the West during 1790-96. The army was protecting the westerners, and the westerners should pay their fair share of the cost. Getting Congress to agree was not easy. Hamilton had suggested several bills to put an excise on alcohol but had been defeated in 1790. Some critics thought he was reneging on his promises in *The Federalist Papers* to rely on tariffs. He saw the issue as "whether the government of the United States will ever raise any revenue by any internal tax."[12]

The crisis was a while in coming. Antitax agitators in Pennsylvania first attacked the federal tax collectors in September 1791. Assaults on tax collectors continued in Pennsylvania through 1794. Actual tax collections along the western frontier were very meager for the first three years of the tax, and in Kentucky the tax was not paid at all. Even respectable citizens, such as Albert Gallatin, a future member of Congress and secretary of the treasury, led meetings to protest against the tax and sent petitions seeking its repeal to Congress. Liberty poles appeared, bearing the message, "Liberty, plenty of Whiskey, and No Excise."[13] For the most part the opposition was law-abiding, but the few outbursts of violence, eventually resulting in several deaths, set the tone as far as the government officials were concerned.[14]

A defense of the opposition to the whiskey tax, offered in William Findlay's *A Review of the Revenue System*, had as its theme that as a result of the assumption of the entire public debt, "a necessity was created, for the obnoxious and impractical excise on the produce of agriculture." He asked, with convoluted rhetoric,

Is the discouraging [of] agriculture by levying a partial excise in the produce of soil, improved by domestic manufactures, a tax the most insulting on the prepossessions of the people, which bears hardest upon those whose situation is the most unsuitable to support it, which is levied to pay the interest of the assumed state debts, the discharge of which had been already completed or provided for, and putting the power and energy of the government so early to a severe trial in executing a law, against which the minds of the citizens revolt, and to the execution of which they will not administer support, which is a fruitful source of perjury and smuggling and has been hitherto impracticable, I ask is this a national blessing?

If it were, he continued, "I cannot conceive what we are to term national curses."

Findlay went on to describe how the "plan for perpetual excise on spirits manufactured by the farmer from his fruit or grain" resulted in "the necessity of intrusting the collection of the revenue, and the liberty and peace of the citizens, to the discretion of such persons as no man would intrust with his private affairs." A poor system of tax collection meant that the tax was "not completely executed any where. We find people near Philadelphia who tell us . . . they are not called upon to pay the money, nor can find any that will receive it." Out on the frontier, few were asked to pay, and the stories that tax collectors in western Pennsylvania had been mistreated were unfounded, as the people of Westmoreland County, where the attack allegedly took place, "agree in asserting that they never knew of an excise-man residing or keeping an office in that county since the law was enacted."

The opposition to the tax could be seen in the fact that not much was being collected from it, at least, Findlay asserted, according to Hamilton's reports on its effectiveness. As important as opposition, however, was the state of the whiskey market. "No manufacture can bear a tax," Findlay argued, "until it is brought to perfection and to be in general demand. That whiskey is not in that state is too evident to need proof." In affluent areas the price of whiskey could bear the tax, but on the frontier the low prices meant that the tax was nearly half the price. The problem was the one constantly raised by opponents of the central government: "Congress cannot apply taxation laws to the particular circumstances of the respective states."[15]

Not everyone agreed. One writer parodied the anti-tax sentiment as, "I would have a government, but it should not govern me; that is my first article. My second is, I would govern it. And thirdly, I and my government should govern everybody else according to my pleasure."[16] Another writer gave a more thoughtful analysis of the views of the tax rebels that the tax was unequal, immoral, dangerous to liberty, and oppressive. In terms of its inequality, he pointed out that the tax on domestic liquor was lower than on imported, so the inequality favored the home brew. As to the immorality, what could be more immoral than "engendering drunkenness as an epidemic." With regard to the danger to liberty, the tax rebels were "at variance with almost all the civilized world." The claim of oppressiveness was answered with the counterclaim, that if the tax on liquor "be on the same foot with taxes of every other denomination, then how can the western people be oppressed or injured by it?" Underlying the opposition to the tax, he concluded, was "a residue of anti-federalism," which led people "long accustomed to stand loose to everything but their wills . . . to oppose a new dispensation that should teach them the duties of citizens."[17]

In Virginia, Edward Carrington, the federal revenue agent for the state, expressed confidence that the whiskey tax would work. He wrote to Madison that the excise "daily becomes better understood and consequently better liked." He reported that he had visited two counties under his jurisdiction "on account of the uneasiness which prevailed there, attended, in the former with a riot against the Collector." "Indeed," he went on, "the rioters were not numerous and are discountenanced by the body of the County."[18] Madison was not so optimistic. He later reported to Jefferson from Virginia, "The unpopularity of the excise has evidently increased in this quarter."[19]

The first tax revolt did keep alive the Anti-Federalist attitude that oppressive taxes would be the result of Federalist government. If the sides of this argument appear to be reminiscent of the controversy recently settled with England, that was how the westerners viewed it. As Thomas Slaughter writes in reference to the opponents of the whiskey tax, "To these men, the issues raised by the excise seemed precisely analogous to those of the Stamp Act."[20]

Although he really wanted to crack down on the tax rebels, Hamilton tried various ways to make the tax more acceptable. For example, the tax was collected directly from producers, based on assessed value, even before they sold the whiskey. He eased up on this feature. He also permitted some payment of taxes in whiskey itself and used these payments to supply the army. To the cry that the tax was ruining business, he replied that taxes might hurt an industry in its infancy, but a mature industry such as distilling would not be endangered. Nevertheless, he responded to complaints about the excise's being too high by asking Congress to lower it.

Hamilton also pointed out to the distillers that they would be able to pass the tax onto consumers easily. He contended that with relatively small changes in price, the demand for alcohol would not decline.

He then had Washington issue a proclamation decrying noncompliance with the law, especially in light of Hamilton's efforts to mitigate its harmful effects. Jefferson gave a terse account of the events in a report from Philadelphia to Madison:

The people in the Western parts of this state have been to the excise officer & threatened to burn his house &c. They were blacked & otherwise disguised so as to be unknown. He has resigned & H. says there is no possibility of getting the law executed there, & that probably the evil will spread. A proclamation is to be issued, and another instance of my being forced to appear to approve what I have condemned uniformly from it's first conception.[21]

Jefferson would later be very effective in using this antitax sentiment to his advantage.

As part of a lawful exercise of authority, the Federalists would counter that the Constitution said that taxes had to be uniform throughout the nation, and on this issue Hamilton was a strict constructionist; no farmers on the frontier would be allowed to be tax cheats.[22] At this point Washington was against using the army to quell the resisters, noting that it would permit Anti-Federalists to say with truth, "The cat is out; we now see for what purpose an army was raised."[23]

Washington was overly hopeful. His opponents were called to the Armageddon: "The fate of the excise law will determine whether the powers of the government of the United States are held by an aristocratic junto or by the people." Hamilton disagreed. He could find no difference, in terms of liberty, between a tariff and an excise.[24] His frustration on this issue was similar to that experienced by the English. Ultimately, Hamilton saw the problem being the legality of indirect excise taxes in general: "If precautions of this nature are inconsistent with liberty, and immoral, as there are very few indirect taxes, which can be collected without them, the consequences must be, that the entire weight of the public burthens must, in the first instance, fall upon fixed and visible property, houses and land."[25]

The English helped bring the issue to a close in 1794 by restricting trade with the United States, thereby cutting off tariff revenues at a time when this action brought about a need for more money for defense spending. A committee of the House of Representatives looked into the need for revenue that the government would have. It found that Hamilton's earlier estimate had projected a small deficit of $400,000. New spending of $650,000 "for the addition to the military establishment" and a loss of $1.3 million in tariff revenues, however, had led to a $2.4 million deficit. A loan of $1 million still meant that about $1.4 million in taxes had to be raised. Following Hamilton's advice, new taxes were proposed on carriages, stamps, snuff, sugar, and land.[26]

Action also stepped up in the collection of the whiskey tax. In May 1794, a federal district judge served processes on seventy-five distillers who were not in compliance with the tax, ordering them to appear in federal court in Philadelphia. More violence took place.

Finally, in autumn 1794, Washington called out the militia of several states to form an army of 12,950 soldiers (as large as the Continental Army he had commanded) to restore the peace in Pennsylvania and collect the tax. The ease with which this army was raised indicates that the unpopularity of the whiskey tax was not widespread. An article in the *Gazette of the United States*, admittedly a pro-administration paper, remarked, "The spirit of true patriotism appears to electrify every class of citizen—the number of volunteers that flock to the standard of the constitution and the laws, exceeds the most sanguine expectations of the warmest friends to the unity, indivisibility and honor of the American Republic."[27]

The *Gazette of the United States* repeated this point in a series of stories reporting on the mustering of the militia throughout the mid-Atlantic region. It also reported comments of Governor Thomas Mifflin to the Pennsylvania legislature that despite the "defects in the militia system," he was happy to recount, "I have found our fellow citizens, in the counties of Chester and Delaware, eager to support the honor of our government, and the authority of the laws against the violence of the present lawless combination."[28] The *Gazette of the United States* repeated this charge of lawlessness, headlining the rebels as anarchists and calling them worse: "The views of the Pennsylvania Western Insurgents, so plainly appears to be the views of the Anti-federalists, (consequently destructive to the government of the United States) that no man of common sense, or common honesty, can possibly mistake them." When ignorant men take up arms against the law, they must be stopped, was the gist of the article.[29]

For his part, Hamilton, who rode with the army, wanted to ensure that the government's tax-collecting powers were respected. The charges made by Anti-Federalists that the army would be used to collect taxes proved true—the cat was out of the bag after all. Nevertheless, the march brought in few rebels, and the leaders escaped. Henry Lee, governor of Virginia and commander of the militia, offered rewards for the capture of some of the leaders,[30] but no one collected them. The *Gazette of the United States* reported on Governor Mifflin's speech describing the success of the operation and recounted several occasions where the members of the militia were "received by their fellow citizens with the most cordial and respectful attention" and joined them "to celebrate the happy issue of the late expedition against the western insurgents."[31]

Despite the praise and celebration, only two rebels were convicted of anything, and Washington pardoned them. Still, the point that taxes would be collected uniformly throughout the nation had been made. In fact, the whiskey tax had been collected elsewhere with little fanfare and brought in $422,000 in 1793 and $347,000 in 1794, although $60,000–70,000 of that went for collection costs in each year.[32] This collection of the tax exceeded Hamilton's estimate. As David Whitten has shown, distillers were able to shift the tax onto consumers.[33]

It is often forgotten that the whiskey tax was imposed nationwide, and most regions paid it without complaint. Washington believed that "this insurrection is viewed with universal indignation and abhorrence."[34] Although there were no polling data to support this belief, the stories in the *Gazette of the United States* and the overwhelming success of the expedition lend credence to it.

Since the *Gazette of the United States* was a Federalist paper, however, it is only fair to let Jefferson's version of the rebellion stand as the opposition view. On December 28, 1794, he wrote Madison from Monticello:

The excise-law is an infernal one. The first error was to admit it by the constitution. The 2d. to act on that admission. The 3d. and last will be to make it the instrument of dismembering the Union, & setting us all afloat to chuse which part of it we will adhere to. The information of our militia returned from the Westward is uniform, that tho the people there let them pass quietly, they were objects of their laughter, not of their fear . . . that their detestation of the excise law is universal, and has now associated to it a detestation of the government, & that separation which perhaps was a very distant & problematical event, is now near & certain & determined in the mind of every man.[35]

Jefferson exaggerated the threat of disunion, but he did recognize a seat of disgruntlement he would later endeavor to appease.

Jefferson was right about the Federalists' paying a high price for their action on the whiskey tax. The expedition to Pennsylvania alone cost about $800,000[36] and resulted in a further breakup of the coalition that had created the Constitution. Disgruntled western farmers would form a key part in the Republican Party that Jefferson was building. Meanwhile, Hamilton and the Federalists continued to expand the tax base.

EXPANSION OF THE TAX BASE

In 1794 Congress passed taxes on carriages, snuff, and refined sugar. It also considered taxes on the transfer of certificates of the public debt and stock in the Bank of the United States. In the debate over the tobacco tax, members of the House of Representatives argued that since snuff was a luxury, the tax would fall on the wealthy. Others asked whether direct taxes would not be more appropriate. Congressman George Smilie (Republican of Pennsylvania) believed that "taxes ought to be raised in such a way, that the public might not only pay them, but at the same time, *feel* them. This would teach them to think a little better in what way their money goes." An awareness of the tax burden would make citizens more careful of how the government spent their money.

Members of the House of Representatives also worried over how the tax would affect the industry being taxed. Representative Samuel Smith (Republican of Maryland) thought it "a very odd scheme to crush American manufactures in the bud. Men of capital and enterprise advanced large sums of money in erecting snuff mills. After long exertion, they began to reap the reward of their expense and their labor. At that critical moment, the Government souses down upon them with an excise, which ends not in revenue but in extirpation." The tax would double the price of raw tobacco, making the business very unprofitable.

Smith also worried that the snuff dealer and tobacco processor would be required to keep records for the tax collector. This would be another hardship on them, requiring them to hire another clerk to keep the records, and in his district, where "tobacco spinners are poor ignorant creatures" who could not read, might lead to unwitting perjury.[37]

The tax on tobacco products, especially snuff, led to protests in Philadelphia. Manufacturers of these products felt that the tariff program gave them insufficient protection, while the excise raised their costs unfairly. On July 4, 1794, they toasted the anniversary of the country with: "EXCISE, may this baneful exotic wither in the soil of freedom." The protests were never violent enough to warrant physical suppression, but opponents did get the tax on tobacco suspended several times before its final repeal in 1800.[38] Hamilton might wonder, indeed, if an internal tax would ever be collected or even be constitutional. Such was the case with the carriage tax.

The carriage tax was an annual fee that ranged from one dollar to ten dollars on carriages used in transporting persons, with an exemption for wagons used in farming or transporting merchandise. The debate over the tax in Congress raised the first constitutional issue over taxes and over a law of Congress.

The Constitution had said that a direct tax had to be imposed in proportion to the population of the states, but it had not made a clear distinction between direct taxes and indirect taxes. Indeed, the latter term was never mentioned. At the time, there was agreement on certain items that fell into each category, but not on any general principle of how the distinction was made. Economic thinkers gave little help. The Physiocrats thought all taxes eventually fell to land, so argued that it be taxed directly; from Adam Smith it could be inferred that excises and tariffs were indirect. What was a carriage tax?

To Madison, it was obviously a direct tax, and as such he opposed "this tax on carriages as an unconstitutional tax." The case for construing the tax as direct was whether or not it could be shifted to consumers. An excise on snuff, for example, could be added to the price and at least partially imposed on consumers. A tax on the personal use of a carriage could not be shifted, making it a direct tax.

An alternative view, presented by Theodore Sedgwick (Federalist of Massachusetts), was that if Congress "be authorized to impose a tax on every subject of revenue (and surely pleasure carriages, as objects of luxury, and in general, owned by those whose contribution would not be inconvenient, were fair and proper objects of taxation) and a tax on them could not be apportioned by the Constitutional ratio, it would follow irresistibly that such a tax, in the sense of the Constitution, is not 'direct.' " If a tax could not be made to fit the proportionality rule, the rule could not apply. Furthermore, "it would astonish the people of America to be informed that they had made a Constitution by which pleasure carriages and other objects of luxury were excepted from" taxation.

The varied use of carriages in the separate states was also an issue. One representative pointed out that in some states such as Vermont and Kentucky there were no carriages, so these states were voting to tax other states. Fisher Ames (Federalist of Massachusetts) believed that in the South "a carriage was not always a mark of wealth, but that it was a necessary article." William Murray (Federalist of Maryland) pointed out that if the tax were direct and apportioned by population, Connecticut would have to pay as much in taxes as Maryland. Since only two coaches existed in Connecticut, "the owner or owners of those two coaches would pay as large a sum as all the owners of coaches in Maryland." This would be unjust, and "of course the Constitution could not be constructed to carry such a meaning."[39]

The constitutionality of the carriage tax would eventually be decided by the Supreme Court, as is described in Chapter 7, but that case would be argued after Hamilton left office. While he remained in office, however, Hamilton encountered continual opposition to his program.

Madison, for example, attacked the tobacco excise as an unequal burden that "fell upon the poor, upon sailors, upon day-labourers, and other people of these classes, while the rich will often escape it." Although the case had been made in favor of the tobacco tariff as a luxury tax, Madison felt tobacco was a simple pleasure of life. Instead of excises, he favored the use of direct taxes, such as on land, which he felt would be much cheaper to collect than indirect taxes like the excise.[40]

One anonymous critic of the tax system also expressed dismay that the Hamilton plan had not taxed the wealth of the rich, instead using taxes that hit the laboring classes especially hard. It was argued, he wrote, that "it is often very difficult to ascertain the real wealth of an individual." In his view the existing system carried "as much difficulty as would attend a universal examination of property." He went on, citing a respected authority, to give the real reason he thought that taxes were not collected in proportion to wealth: "Government is usually in the hands of the rich, and, as Dr. Smith says, All for ourselves, and nothing for other people, has, in all ages, been the maxim of the masters of mankind." Taxes should be levied in proportion to wealth. This was only fair, since wealth was "the great cause of expence to government for its protection."

Instead, the government relied on the excise, with poor results: "That on distilled liquors has produced a rebellion, suppressed at an expence of two million dollars. An Act past [*sic*] in the session of Congress before the last one, for imposing an excise upon the manufacture of refined sugar and snuff. With regard to the latter of these two, the gentlemen who were foremost in promoting the excise, have since acknowledged, in the last session of Congress, that their own act was absurd and impractical." If the government intended to rely on excise taxes, he asked, why not extend it to cover "superfine flour, potash, cyder, paper, malt, beer, leather, or even the light of Heaven itself, than which we know no greater luxury?" Instead of these, this writer wanted resort to a tax on land.[41]

Several writers argued against the use of excise taxes and suggested a tax on land be used in its place or at least to supplement it.[42] One writer found a regional bias in the use of excise taxes: "It is in those states which are most concerned in commerce and manufactures, that excises will always most abound. The states north of the Patowmac, I conceive to be such, and that they would pay three-fourths of an excise laid on distilled spirits, strong beers, snuff and other proper subjects of excise." To even out the tax burden regionally, a land tax was needed.[43] This perspective overlooked that a tariff hit the southern states more heavily than the North, at least so its residents believed.

This effort to use land as a basis for taxation also derived from an unequal burden on the wealthy as opposed to the rest of society. Another writer, George Logan, in 1791 wrote, "The legislators of a free people, influenced by the just principles of political economy, will look only to the land for a source of revenue." Logan was an apparent follower of the French economic school of the Physiocrats, for like them, he believed that "the cultivation of the earth is the only productive employment." As a result, every tax ultimately fell on agriculture; merchants and manufacturers simply passed taxes on them onto farmers. It would be simpler and more efficient, to levy all taxes directly on farmers. As he told farmers, "[I]f you refuse to pay to government a just proportion of the net produce of your farms, by a direct tax, and you will submit to be deceived and ruined by the arts and projects of crafty financiers, you must expect that, by circuitous impositions, the free state of your produce will be circumscribed." In addition, "an indirect tax, upon articles of consumption, requires a great expence to support a host of revenue officers."[44] Despite these arguments, it would not be until the Adams administration that a land tax was tried.

The problem with a land tax was that under the Constitution, it very likely had to be levied as a direct tax in proportion to population. This provision could be construed as establishing that the wealthy did use the government to protect their wealth. In his classic book *An Economic Interpretation of the Constitution of the United States* (1913), Charles Beard used bondholdings of the framers to allege that a conspiracy of wealth formulated the Constitution.[45] Perhaps he should have based his case on their attitude toward taxes. "Soak the rich" has often been a battle cry in tax debates. But with respect to a land tax, it did not carry the day at this point.

TAX ADMINISTRATION

In setting up the Treasury Department, Congress had placed it in an unusual situation. Even though it was part of the executive branch, the secretary of the treasury was also responsible to Congress and reported straight to it. This Hamilton did, perhaps to an extreme. All of his reports were addressed to Congress, and many of his recommendations were nearly directives for Congress to act. The power to raise revenue bills seemed to reside in Hamilton as much as in the House of Representatives. There was continual conflict between Hamilton and members of the House of Representatives on this issue.[46]

Hamilton held the upper hand in those conflicts, due to his control over the flow of information and his unrivaled knowledge of public finance. His opponents in Congress would try to trap him with requests for information about the state of the government's finances, and he would respond in short order with one of his massive reports. His expertise was very difficult to challenge.

The operation of the actual collection of taxes was also of concern to Hamilton. His Report on Public Credit had stated, "The Secretary, in the plan submitted, has taken scrupulous care, that those citizens upon whom it is immediately to operate, be secured from every species of injury by the misconduct on the officers to be employed." Protection in terms of punishment for abusive tax collectors was promised along with compensation for wrongful seizures.

In addition to these safeguards, the focus of the tax plan would be to secure the public credit. Taxpayers, "drawn from an enlightened class of citizens, zealously devoted to good government," would cooperate by making their proper contributions. As a result, Hamilton had concluded, his plan would "experience the chearful and prompt acquiescence of the community."[47]

In his later plan for new taxes in December 1790, Hamilton further expounded on his philosophy of tax collecting. There were two ways to collect taxes effectively: rely "on the vigilance of the public officers" or "on the integrity of the individuals, interested to avoid the payment of it." Self-interest was a paramount human trait to Hamilton, and his statement certainly loaded the decks against individual integrity. Not surprisingly, he concluded that "taxes or duties, relying on [integrity], wholly, or almost wholly, are uniformly unproductive." The net result was that "the most conscientious will pay the most." The sacredness of oaths was also undermined.

Thus, it was necessary to rely on tax collectors. To protect the public, tax collectors would not have any "summary jurisdiction" that precluded the right to a trial by a jury. In addition, while tax collectors would have a right to inspect the premises of taxpayers in a probe for taxable items, in this case alcoholic drink, that search would be limited to places specified by the sellers.[48] Tax collectors were given detailed instruction as to the rules they would follow with the whiskey tax, and Hamilton told collectors to go easy on distillers who misunderstood the law.[49]

To collect the internal taxes, Hamilton divided the country into fourteen districts, which were further subdivided; each unit was placed in the hands of appropriate supervisors, who were given the authority to enforce the tax laws with the assured backing of the federal government. As a result, Hamilton reported, "The revenues of the government were perhaps never collected under a more simple organization, or through a smaller number of channels."[50]

If people thought this meant Hamilton would go easy on wealthy taxpayers, he proved them wrong. On taking office, he gave no extra time to importers who failed to post their bonds, filing suit the moment they were past due. Weekly reports were required of tax collectors, and those who did not do a good job were fired. He put as much energy into tax collecting as he did in all his endeavors.[51]

He did not make the mistake, however, of assuming that tax collectors were as dedicated as he was. He worried that the low pay given to them would not attract persons of character and trust. Hamilton pushed for higher pay for them and wanted to have customs collectors given rank in the navy.[52] In return, he pushed customs collectors to work hard. One later reported, "The incessant application I was obliged to pay to the duties of my office for the past 2 ½ years, has injured me more, than all the fatigue . . . which I experienced thro' the late war."[53]

Given the responsibility for collecting taxes, both internal and external, the Treasury was the largest department in the government, with more than a thousand employees during Hamilton's regime. By 1801 the department had 78 officials in the capital and more than 1,600 in the field.[54] Hamilton proved a very able administrator.

Despite this ability, Hamilton was able to make little progress in debt reduction. His foes criticized him for this failing, and that criticism may have been part of his decision to give up his post, effective January 31, 1795. Before he quit, however, he offered a plan for eliminating the public debt.

HAMILTON'S FINAL REPORT

Just as he left office, Hamilton issued a final report on the state of the finances. The "Report on a Plan for the Further Support of Public Credit" (January 16, 1795) contained a lengthy review of Hamilton's entire fiscal plan. It also contained a tally of the debt at that time of $76,096,468.67, indicating that about $1 million in debt reduction had taken place. He expressed concern that deferred interest of about $1.2 million a year on part of the debt would be coming due starting in 1800 and urged that additional plans be made to prepare for the extra burden.

He presented the outlines of such a plan and characterized opponents of it as "declaiming against a Public Debt, and for the reduction of it as an abstract thesis; yet vehement against every plan of taxation which is proposed to discharge old debts, or to avoid new." He maintained that if his plan were followed, the debt "would be extinguished in 30 Years."

The gist of Hamilton's plan was the sinking fund. The sinking fund policy was passed by Congress on May 8, 1792. Hamilton's concrete proposal for the sinking fund was that money from land sales, the post office, and unspent taxes be put into a fund, as described earlier. As an example of how a sinking fund would work, he calculated that annual payment of $7 would take care of the interest and eliminate the principal of a $100 debt carrying 6% interest in about 33 years.[55] Under this type of payment plan, $5 million a year would pay the interest on the $70 million debt and eliminate it in about the same time. Since interest payments of about $4 million a year were already being made, this meant that about $1 million per year was needed for the sinking fund.

The key was putting that amount into the sinking fund. Hamilton believed part would be raised from land sales. The rest could be gained by having all the internal taxes in effect at that time extended until the debt was paid off. At this time, Congress always put an expiration date on taxes. If taxes were assured, each year the sinking fund commissioners would purchase a portion of the government debt. In future years, interest payments on debt held by the sinking fund would continue to be paid into the fund and used to purchase additional debt. In this way, taxes dedicated to paying interest on the debt would be used to retire additional debt.[56]

A sinking fund can work only if the government has a budget surplus, but there were budget deficits in three of Hamilton's years in office (1792, 1794, and 1795) of from $1 million to $2 million, about 30% of the annual budgets. These deficits took place even though the economy enjoyed prosperity throughout this time. The surplus years did not fully compensate for the deficits. Military expenses associated with fighting Indians and external conflicts with France, Spain, and Algiers contributed to the deficit. As Adam Smith had argued, payments into the sinking fund held a low priority.

The sinking fund was little used in actual practice. Hamilton was shrewd enough to foresee this possibility. He pointed out "that a simple appropriation of an adequate sinking fund is not a complete barrier against its being diverted when immediate exigencies press." In those cases, government officials would be tempted "to lay hold of this resource, rather than resort to new taxes." He felt that additional legal conditions had to be added to the sinking fund's provisions. He wanted the fund to be a part of the contract made with public creditors by detailing how they would be repaid.[57]

Hamilton's last funding plan was very much debated in Congress. Much of the debate centered on what to tax rather than on whether or not to extend the expiration date of the taxes. On February 15, 1795, Madison wrote Jefferson about the plan for the reduction of the debt and its extension of taxes, maintaining that the plan would not work without new taxes. He wrote, "Hamilton has in an arrogant valedictory Report presented a plan for the purpose. It will require about 30 years of uninterrupted operation. . . . You will judge of our ever being out of debt, if no other means are to be use(d). It is to be lamented that the public are not yet better reconciled to direct taxes, which alone can work down the debt faster than new emergencies will probably add to it."[58] Jefferson and Madison would get their chance to deal with the problem during their own terms as president.

Critics of the Hamilton system readily found faults with the sinking fund. William Findlay alleged that of the $3.4 million designated for the fund, only $675,000 had been used to purchase bonds. He was bothered because the price of bonds was rising and the sinking fund was not purchasing them as cheaply as possible. As the force behind the fund, Hamilton should be charged with a "misapplication of the funds."[59]

John Taylor pointed out that less than $1 million was in the fund in 1793 and that even as money went into the fund, the government was borrowing larger sums overseas. He asked, "How was the debt sunk, by the erection of a fund, producing the necessity of incurring a new debt, to a greater amount than the fund itself?" A good question for which Taylor provided an answer: "If keeping up, or raising the price of certificates be considered as the primary object, all these difficulties are solved."[60] The sinking fund itself was the explanation for rising bond prices.

Here was further evidence of Hamilton's alleged abuse of power concealing his futuristic policies. In its early years the sinking fund probably helped to stabilize bond prices and interest rates through its open market purchases. Today, the Federal Reserve Bank performs a similar function with government securities. Hamilton was capable of elaborating such a policy and seeing the usefulness of it. That he controlled the sinking fund commissioners, who after all included John Adams and John Jay, was doubtful. He could have done so only if they were so busy with their other duties that they did not give a priority to the sinking fund.

Besides, the sinking fund was doing a little better than Findlay and Taylor claimed. In December 1796, Adams reported that the fund held $2,307,641.71 in bonds, which had been purchased for $1,618,936.04, including $544,066.54 purchased in the previous year (Hamilton's last year in office).[61] The fund was purchasing bonds, even after Hamilton left the government, and the total saving had been respectable—about a 30% discount. Not an outstanding record, but not a bad one given the state of the fledgling government's finances.

CONCLUSION

Overall, the Hamilton plan placed the government's finances on a sound basis. Interest on the debt was paid, and the investing public seemed satisfied to hold on to its securities. The banking plan also worked out well for the government. The Bank of the United States was set up to have a total capital of $10 million. Subscriptions were begun on July 4, 1791, and the entire $8 million in stock available to the public was taken. The remaining $2 million was bought by the federal government in a complicated arrangement concocted by Hamilton.[62] The Bank of the United States soon did its part in taking care of the government's tax collections and in creating a steady supply of banknotes. The government made money on its investment in the Bank of the United States when it sold its shares. As a result of the Hamilton plan, President Washington reported, "Our public credit stands on ground which three years ago it would have been considered a species of madness to have foretold."[63]

Hamilton's financial plan aimed at pulling the nation, especially its wealthy members, together in support of the new government. Included in that plan was an avoidance of an inflation tax that hit the wealthy most heavily. This part of his program apparently worked; at least the bond market signaled its approval. The taxes necessary to pay for it, however, were higher than he expected. The process of raising them caused problems that pulled apart the coalition that had supported the Constitution and unified the first years of the Washington administration.

In the short run, when it mattered, Hamilton had sustained Washington's policy of creating confidence in the new government. His special role in securing public credit was vital. Given the antipathy to taxes that pervaded American life, the government would resort to borrowing many times in the future. The intent of Hamilton's plan to establish firmly the public credit worked. But that was as far as it went. Hamilton had won the first round in the fight over the nature of the United States government. It would be a long time before anyone with his philosophy would win another one as completely.

NOTES

1. Cited in Nelson, *Liberty and Property*, p. 52.

2. G. R. Taylor, *Hamilton and the National Debt*, pp. 3–4.

3. Ferguson, *Power of the Purse*, p. 330.

4. Report on Public Credit, Cooke, *The Reports of Alexander Hamilton*, pp. 32–33.

5. "First Report on the Further Provision Necessary for Establishing Public Credit," December 13, 1790, PAH, vol. 7, pp. 225–35.

6. George Washington to David Humphreys, July 20, 1791, in Fitzpatrick, *The Writings of George Washington*, vol. 31, p. 319.

7. Dewey, *Financial History*, pp. 105–6.

8. Broadus Mitchell, *Alexander Hamilton: The National Adventure, 1788–1804* (New York: Macmillan, 1962), p. 116.

9. Stewart, *Opposition Press*, p. 83.

10. Thomas P. Slaughter, *The Whiskey Rebellion* (New York: Oxford University Press, 1986), p. 164.

11. Stewart, *Opposition Press*, p. 83.

12. Slaughter, *The Whiskey Rebellion*, pp. 94–99, 193.

13. Stewart, *Opposition Press*, p. 87.

14. Slaughter, *The Whiskey Rebellion*, pp. 113–21.

15. Findlay, *A Review of the Revenue System*, pp. 41–42, 59–61, 120.

16. "Whiskey versus Government," *The American Museum, or, Universal Magazine*, Philadelphia, April 1791, p. 171.

17. "Remarks on the Resolves of the Inhabitants of the Western Country of Pennsylvania against the Excise Laws" (signed "A"), *The American Museum, or, Universal Magazine*, Philadelphia, September 1791, pp. 149–50.

18. Letter from Edward Carrington, September 21, 1791, *Madison Papers*, vol. 14, pp. 76–77.

19. Letter to Thomas Jefferson, June 12, 1792, *Madison Papers*, vol. 14, p. 317.

20. Slaughter, *The Whiskey Rebellion*, p. 111.

21. Letter from Thomas Jefferson, May 19, 1973, *Madison Papers*, vol. 15, p. 19.

22. Alexander Hamilton, "Report on the Difficulties in the Execution of the Act Laying Duties on Distilled Spirits," March 6, 1792, PAH, vol. 11, pp. 77–106.

23. Slaughter, *The Whiskey Rebellion*, p. 122.

24. Ibid., pp. 130–40.

25. "Report of the Secretary of the Treasury, on the Act for Laying Duties on Spirits & C.," read in the House on March 6, 1792, copy in collection of American Antiquarian Society, p. 5.

26. "Report of the House Committee Appointed to Enquire Whether Any, or What Further Revenues Are Necessary for the Support of Public Credit; and If Any Further Revenues Are Necessary, to Report the Ways and Means," 1794, copy in collection of American Antiquarian Society, no page number.

27. "Philadelphia," *Gazette of the United States*, September 18, 1794, no page numbers.

28. "United States—Easton, September 6 and Cambridge, September 11," September 25, 1794; "Alexandria, September 27," and "Baltimore, October 2," October 6, 1794; "Philadelphia, September 18," September 18, 1794, all in *Gazette of the United States*.

29. "From the Rights of Men to the Enemies of Anarchy," *Gazette of the United States*, September 15, 1794.

30. "Philadelphia, December 11," *Gazette of the United States*, December 12, 1794.

31. "Address," December 12, 1794; "Philadelphia, December 11," December 12, 1794; "Lancaster, February 9," February 18, 1795, all in *Gazette of the United States*.

32. Dewey, *Financial History*, pp. 105–6.

33. David O. Whitten, "An Inquiry into the Whiskey Rebellion of 1794," *Agricultural History* 49 (July 1975): pp. 491–504.

34. George Washington to Governor Henry Lee, August 26, 1794, in Fitzpatrick, *The Writing of George Washington*, vol. 33, p. 475.

35. Letter from Thomas Jefferson, December 28, 1794, *Madison Papers*, vol.15, pp. 427–28.

36. Mitchell, *Alexander Hamilton*, p. 312.

37. *Debates of Congress*, Third Congress, First Session, May 1794, pp. 617–24.

38. Roland M. Baumann, "Philadelphia's Manufacturers and the Excise Tax of 1794: The Forging of the Jeffersonian Coalition," in Steven R. Boyd, ed., *The Whiskey Rebellion: Past and Present Perspectives* (Westport, CT: Greenwood Press, 1985), pp. 135–64.

39. *Debates of Congress*, Third Congress, First Session, May 1794, pp. 644–46, 648, 652–53, 730.

40. Madison's Remarks on Excises, Committee of the Whole House, May 2, 1794, *Madison Papers*, vol.15, p. 321.

41. James Callender, *A Short History of the Nature and Consequences of Excise Laws* (Philadelphia, no publisher, 1795), pp. 6–7, 92–93.

42. See "To the American Farmers and Planters," *The American Museum, or, Universal Magazine*, Philadelphia, February 1790, pp. 12–15.

43. "Hints Respecting an American Excise," *The American Museum, or, Universal Magazine*, Philadelphia, September 1790, pp. 136–40.

44. George Logan, *Letters, Addressed to the Yeomanry* (Philadelphia, no publisher), pp. 15, 18, 25–26.

45. Charles A. Beard, *An Economic Interpretation of the Constitution of the United States* (New York: Macmillan, 1960).

46. Leonard D. White, *The Federalists: A Study in Administrative History, 1789–1801* (New York: The Free Press, 1948), pp. 68–76.

47. "Report on Public Credit," Cooke, *The Reports of Alexander Hamilton*, pp. 39–40.

48. "Report on a Plan for the Further Support of Public Credit," pp. 229–31.

49. Slaughter, *The Whiskey Rebellion*, pp. 144–45.

50. Cited in Miller, *Alexander Hamilton*, pp. 398–99.

51. Ibid., pp. 322–23.

52. "Report on the Improvement and Better Management of the Revenue of the United States" (January 31, 1795), PAH, vol. 18, pp. 218–19.

53. Cited in Mitchell, *Alexander Hamilton*, p. 31.

54. White, *The Federalists*, p. 123.

55. "Report on a Plan for the Further Support of Public Credit," pp. 84–106.

56. Ibid., pp. 82–102.

57. Ibid., pp. 105–9.

58. Letter to Thomas Jefferson, February 15, 1795, *Madison Papers*, vol.15, p. 474.

59. Findlay, *A Review of the Revenue System*, pp. 96–97.

60. John Taylor, *An Enquiry*, p. 45.

61. "Report of the Commissioners of the Sinking Fund," December 16, 1796, copy in collection of American Antiquarian Society, p. 1.

62. Hammond, *Banks and Politics*, pp. 123–24.

63. George Washington to David Humphreys, July 20, 1791, in Fitzpatrick, *The Writing of George Washington*, vol. 31, p. 319.

Chapter 7

A Choice of Evils

Hamilton's departure from office might be thought to have reduced the controversy surrounding his plans for public finance. After all, Hamilton had a personal style that lent itself to confrontation. The controversy, it soon became clear, was as much about the plans as about Hamilton. To be sure, the plans for public finance set forth after Hamilton resigned still bore his stamp. By maintaining close personal ties with his successor and protégé, Oliver Wolcott, Hamilton remained influential in the government's policymaking, and his political opponents regarded Wolcott as Hamilton's tool.[1] The opposition was not yet able to match Hamilton's expertise in public finance.

With the election of Albert Gallatin to the House of Representatives in 1795, however, the Jeffersonians finally had someone with financial expertise to match Hamilton's. Gallatin did his own study of the government's books and concluded that the government's debt was rising, not declining as Hamilton had hinted. In fact, Gallatin alleged, it was $5 million more than it had been in 1789. Gallatin went further and suggested that direct taxes on houses and land be levied and that military spending be cut to reduce the debt. Hamilton provided Federalists with figures to challenge Gallatin's estimate. Madison, however, was pleased with Gallatin's performance, while Jefferson wrote in response that he, too, had always felt "that our public debt was increasing by about a million dollars a year."[2]

For the remainder of Washington's term of office and for all of John Adams' years as president, the wrangling over public finance would continue. The sides were clearly drawn in the case of the constitutionality of the carriage tax.

THE CONSTITUTION AND THE CARRIAGE TAX

While these debates over Hamilton's system continued, the carriage tax was winding its way through the courts. When Congress first passed the tax in 1794, Washington had asked the Supreme Court for advice on whether or not it was a direct tax under the Constitution. The Court answered that it would not give an opinion unless there was a case before it. To produce that case, Daniel Hylton of Virginia refused to pay the tax on his chariot. The amount involved was only $16, an $8 tax and an $8 penalty, while the requirement to get the case before the district court was a sum of above $2,000. As a result, the government charged Hylton with delinquency on 125 carriages, agreed to settle any judgment against him for the $16 he really owed, and paid all his legal fees.

When the case first went to the circuit court in Virginia, the government deemed the issue so important that it tried to retain John Marshall, then practicing law in Richmond, to assist the attorney general.[3] But Marshall was too busy with another case, which eventually went to the Supreme Court. The Hylton case was heard in circuit court, with the outcome handed down on June 2, 1795; the judges were split, which meant a decision against Hylton.

The advocates on both sides of the issue tried to define direct taxes in ways that supported their cause. It will be recalled that the Constitution prohibited direct taxes except in proportion to population in each state but never distinguished between direct and indirect taxes. Now two top legal minds went to work on the problem, making their case in separate pamphlets.

In support of the opposition to the law, John Taylor, who had argued the case for Hylton in circuit court, started with the premise that taxation had to be based on representation. Efforts to construe the carriage tax as an indirect tax created a contradiction in the Constitution: "If this carriage tax, and the excise, so far as it taxes stills and liquors, kept and made simply and extensively for a man's own use, are to stand as expositions of the Constitution, the fundamental principle is gone for ever."

That lofty ground covered, Taylor then defined both forms of taxes: "An indirect, is a circulating, a direct a local tax. The first being annexed to article of traffic, is itinerant, can travel from state to state in search of the actual payer, and eludes human fore sight so far, as to preserve to each state a chance for justice. . . . An indirect tax applies to the actual payer in the soothing voice of solicitation—'will you buy sir, and contribute to the revenue.' A direct tax extorts by the rough mandate of authority, enforced by pains and penalties." In short, an indirect tax was placed on items of consumption, luxury, and so on, that could be avoided, while a tax on carriages already purchased could not be avoided. Thus, "the voluntary quality of an indirect tax constitutes the striking difference."

In addition, a key point was whether or not a tax could be apportioned as the Constitution prescribed. Excise taxes on commodities could not be apportioned to the states because the commodities flowed about in the course of trade. In contrast, "all taxes possessing locality and capable of apportionment, were by that instrument considered as direct." Since "an apportionment of a tax laid upon a number of carriages, is as possible as one laid on a number of men; and a capitation, is the example stated, of a direct tax," it followed that the carriage tax was a direct tax.

To be sure, carriages were also itinerant, and their population could be readily altered, so Taylor's arguments seem weak. We must remember that new legal ground was being entered. We must also keep in mind that the issue was not carriages but direct taxes and how they would be levied, as the debates in the Constitution indicated, on slaves. Taylor observed, "Unhappily for the southern states, they possess a species of property which is peculiarly exposed, and upon which, if this law stands, the whole burden of government may be exclusively laid." Would they have agreed to an indirect tax on things like carriages, knowing it could be extended to slaves? The intent of the framers on the Constitution was to limit the direct tax as completely as possible.[4] The issue of taxing slaves lurked beneath the surface of the fight over the carriage tax.

An argument in favor of construing the carriage tax as an indirect tax, presented by John Wickham, a prominent Richmond lawyer who had assisted the government in the case, rested on a different definition of the terms. Wickham maintained that the antitax argument contained a contradiction. In addition to requiring direct taxes in proportion to population, the Constitution required indirect taxes to be uniform among the states. Acceptance of defense counsel's definition, which Wickham characterized as whether or not the tax was paid directly, as when a person paid an excise for liquor personally consumed by its producer, meant that taxes such as the carriage tax would have to be both proportional and uniform.

Then Wickham gave his own distinction, based on "approved writers on the subject of taxation," especially Adam Smith, on whose writings Wickham based most of his argument. He said, "I shall contend that, long before the Constitution of the United States was framed, a tax upon the revenue or income of individuals was considered and well understood to be a direct tax. A tax upon their expenses, or consumption an indirect tax." Because it was difficult to determine a person's income, resort was made to the indirect taxing of expenditures—as in the carriage tax. Since those with higher incomes spent more, they paid a proportionally higher tax.

The fact that the wealthy paid a higher tax did, indeed, violate the idea that taxation should be in proportion to representation. If that principle were applied to all taxes, the collection of tariffs and excises could also be challenged. Had the framers wanted taxation in proportion to representation, they would not have stipulated that indirect taxes be uniform among the states. If Congress pushed indirect taxes to the point where they were unequal among the states, it was up to the electorate, not the courts, to remedy the defect. Finally, he pointed out, if a carriage tax were levied in proportion to population, it would be unjustly unequal: "The numerous and opulent citizens who indulge in this luxury would be paying farthings, while the inhabitant of Connecticut, Vermont, or Kentucky, who can afford the expence of a carriage, must submit to a prohibition or sacrifice perhaps his income."[5]

Wickham got to the crux of the direct tax issue and why the southerners liked it. Perhaps a numerical example will help. Suppose a direct tax on carriages was intended to raise $1 million. If Virginia had 20% of the population, carriage owners in that state must pay a total tax of $200,000, while in, say Delaware, with 5% of the population, the tax would be $50,000. If affluent Virginia had 100,000 wealthy carriage owners, each would pay a $2 tax. Supposing Delaware to have only a thousand carriages, each owner would pay $50. Apply the same argument to other property, including slaves, and Massachusetts would have to pay in total nearly as much as Virginia, both having nearly equal populations, but the property owners in Massachusetts would find the tax prohibitive. No wonder the southern states wanted to keep the direct tax prohibition sacrosanct.

As the case awaited its turn at the Supreme Court, Attorney General William Bradford wrote to Hamilton describing how the case was going. He told the former secretary of the treasury, "I consider the question as the greatest one that ever came before the Court, & it is of . . . importance not only that the act should be supported, but supported by the unanimous opinion of the Judges and on grounds that will bear the public inspection. This is more necessary because J. Taylor who argued the cause below intends to publish the speech he delivered on the occasion & which I am told is calculated to mischief." Bradford then mentioned that Washington had given him permission to hire Hamilton as "auxiliary counsel." Not only was Hamilton's expertise on taxes needed to present the case, it was also "necessary to expel the poison of Taylor's publication."[6]

In addition to the previously mentioned unusual features of the case, when it reached the Supreme Court, there was another bizarre twist. On Taylor's advice, Hylton declined to present a defense before the high Court. As a result, the government hired two well-known lawyers, Jared Ingersoll, attorney general of Pennsylvania, and Alexander Campbell, U.S. attorney for Virginia, to argue on Hylton's behalf. These two were paid $233 each, while Hamilton earned $500.[7]

The case went to the Supreme Court in 1796 as *Hylton v. United States*. The case for the defense did little more than repeat Taylor's arguments at the circuit court and was not recorded.

In presenting the case for the government, Hamilton relied on Smith's view that a tax on luxuries was an excise, not a direct tax, and a carriage was certainly a luxury. His notes exhibit a heavy reliance on Smith's *The Wealth of Nations* and assert that usage of direct tax was "probably contemplated in his sense by [the] Convention— Smith Oracle."[8] As he put it, mocking Taylor's argument that the carriage tax was involuntary, "It so happens, that I once had a carriage myself, and found it convenient to dispense with it. But my happiness is not in the least diminished!"[9] He also thought it a "matter of regret that terms so . . . vague in so important a point are to be found in the Constitution."[10] Hamilton then followed the arguments that had been made in Congress and by Wickham that to call the carriage tax a direct tax would create ambiguity in the taxing system in general.

The Court sided with the government in the case, with three justices writing separate opinions. All admitted that the term "direct tax" was vague. Justice Samuel

Chase, for example, believed that "some taxes may be both direct and indirect at the same time." He then made a distinction between the two types: "The constitution evidently contemplated no taxes as direct taxes, but only such as Congress could lay in proportion to the census. The rule of apportionment is only to be adopted in such cases where it can reasonably apply." The rule of reason as to when the direct tax clause applied was if it created "great inequality and injustice." The carriage tax was clearly an indirect tax under this rule. The only direct taxes, in Chase's opinion, were capitation or poll taxes and a tax on land.[11]

Justice William Paterson considered the carriage tax in the context of the language of the Constitution. The counsel for Hylton had argued that since "a tax on carriages does not come within the description of a duty, impost or excise . . . [it is] . . . therefore a direct tax." The other side argued the reverse. To resolve the circularity of this argument, he asserted, "The constitution declares that a capitation tax is a direct tax; and, both in theory and in practice, a tax on land is deemed to be a direct tax. In this way, the terms direct taxes, and capitation and other direct taxes are satisfied." In support of this assertion, he added, "I never entertained a doubt, that the principal, I will not say, the only, objects that the framers of the constitution contemplated as falling within the rule of apportionment, were a capitation tax and a tax on land." Since he was one of the framers, he could speak with some authority. The basis for this rule, he went on, was to protect the South from having its concentration of slaves and vast acreage subjected to high taxes.

As to the plaintiff's argument that the direct tax clause took precedence over the uniformity clause, Paterson responded, "The constitution has been considered as an accommodating system; it was the effect of mutual sacrifices and concessions; it was the work of compromise. The rule of apportionment is of this nature. . . . The rule, therefore, ought not to be extended by construction." Efforts to extend it would come close to restoring the system of requisition, and that had failed. Finally, Paterson agreed with Hamilton that the carriage tax was a tax on expense and cited two passages from Smith's *The Wealth of Nations* in support of this opinion.[12]

Justice James Iredell agreed with his brethren and stated a clear principle: "As all direct taxes must be apportioned, it is evident that the constitution contemplated none as direct but such as could be apportioned." He then provided numerical examples to show how unevenly the tax would fall if apportionment were carried out, holding that, in an extreme case, "[i]f any state had no carriages, there could be no apportionment at all." This result would be too absurd to be thinkable.[13]

This was the first case ever of Supreme Court review of the constitutionality of an act of Congress. The affirmative votes of Chase, Paterson, and Iredell decided the issue for the government. Justice James Wilson declined to vote because he had previously given a favorable opinion in the circuit court but indicated he would have voted had the other three not formed a favorable majority. Justice William Cushing missed the argument due to illness so did not vote, while the new chief justice, Oliver Ellsworth, had just taken his seat and had not heard the case.[14] The upshot of the decision was to limit direct taxes to head or poll taxes or a tax on land. This limitation would be observed very shortly in the tax plans of the administration of John Adams.

THE ADAMS ADMINISTRATION AND NEW TAXES

As president, John Adams continued many of the policies of the Washington administration as well as the service of its cabinet members. The opposition party of Jefferson had barely lost out in the election, however, and continued to criticize the fiscal policies of the government. The hallmark of the Adams administration was foreign policy and the impetus this gave to military spending.

Diplomatic difficulties with France led to large increases in military spending in 1798-99, and the government's budget went from $6 million in 1797 to nearly $11 million in 1800. In 1789, the total operating expenses of the government were $900,000; by 1800 Adams was earmarking $6 million just for the military. The battle cry of the day became "millions for defense, but not one cent for tribute."[15] At the outset of this expansion, in 1797, Adams told Congress, "The national defence must be provided for, as well as the support of government; but both should be provided for, as much as possible by immediate taxes, and as little as possible by loans."[16]

The first tax to pay for this increase in spending was put in place by a Stamp Act in 1797, which made legal transactions include a stamp on them.[17] This tax, too, proved unpopular. As one newspaper warned, "LOOK OUT! This day the Stamp Act begins its career—God only knows where it will end."[18] Congressman Robert Goodloe Harper (Federalist) of South Carolina thought that opposition to the Stamp Act was related to the name itself. Habit opposed stamp acts in general, but this one had been passed by elected representatives, while the one that sparked the Revolutionary War had not. To him, the tax was "one of the best, most equal, and least inconvenient modes of raising money. It executes itself, requires few officers, very little expence, and few or no prosecutions."[19]

Despite these advantages of excise taxes, public opposition to them began growing. One broadside issued in Philadelphia in 1797 maintained that indirect taxes operated "as to have destroyed even the appearance of liberty." It went on: "We should be guilty of a folly equal to the madness of those against whom we complain should we at this critical moment silently submit to the introduction of similar measures, with an expectation that they would not be followed by similar effects, and that the procuring of revenue by the insidious and filching means of excise, stamps, and other indirect taxes, will not terminate in the destruction of the rights and liberties of the people." The problem with these taxes was that they were hidden, with no one knowing for sure how much was paid in from each source. This concealment was by design: "To keep the People ignorant of these things is the great secret of the modern science of finance." The entire method of indirect taxes was wrong because it was based "on the great antisocial principle that men must be governed by fraud." Instead, taxes should be based on a system where "the revenue is confined to an equal direct tax on property."[20]

The Weekly Museum of Baltimore reprinted an article on indirect taxes, introducing it with the statement, "The subject of direct and indirect Taxation has . . . been the subject of conversation among our citizens." The article itself pointed out that indirect taxes, being taxes on consumption, "had no fixed limit," with the consequence that no "calculation can ascertain it with precision." If people consume many goods, tax collections go up, but if consumption declines, so do government revenues. Hence, management of government budgeting became difficult. A direct tax on the value of property would be more certain. In addition, the voluntary feature of the excise made it very unequal: "As the dispositions of mankind vary, so does the operation of the law:—one man may purchase as much as another who is ten times as rich, and thus pay ten times more than he ought to pay; or both may purchase ten times less than they ought to purchase, and thus deprive the government of its revenue . . . and bring ruin and poverty on the whole family of politics."[21] Here again the proper solution was a resort to direct taxes.

DIRECT TAXES

While it is not clear how widespread these sentiments were, Congress eventually resorted to direct taxes. The efficacy of direct taxes had been debated in Congress for several years. In 1796, for example, Representative Jeremiah Smith (Federalist of New Hampshire) indicated that "he did not like direct taxation; he thought it could only be justified by necessity." Others, however, recognized that indirect taxation meant that "almost the whole of the present revenue depends upon commerce—on a commerce liable to be deranged by wars in Europe." To protect against a revenue shortfall if European wars reduced imports and thereby tax receipts, direct taxes should be enacted on a trial basis. Albert Gallatin went further by advocating a tax on land and houses, since they were "the chief property in this country."[22]

The outcome of the debate was a resolution that asked Secretary of the Treasury Oliver Wolcott for a report on the feasibility of a direct tax. He responded in a way that would have made Hamilton proud. First, he compared the government's revenues with its expected spending, especially on debt service, and found that since "it ought to be a fixed principle to establish a permanent revenue, adequate to every permanent expence," new taxes were needed. He then gave a lengthy account of how the individual states raised their own taxes. The purpose of the account was to examine three alternatives for raising the direct tax: (1) a requisition on the states, (2) a tax in each state that was added onto the state's own tax, or (3) a uniform federal tax.

The first alternative Wolcott rejected out of hand, because it "utterly failed under the late confederation." The second alternative had the merit of letting taxes rest on local circumstances, with the federal tax being put on items that each state had found best, but Wolcott's survey of state taxing systems found a great deal of disparity in types, from head taxes to land taxes. This violated the spirit of uniformity and the principle that a fair tax should "protect every taxed article by a proportional tax upon its competitor." Separate states might give economic advantages to their citizens in how they taxed them, but the federal government had to maintain fair competition among the citizens of all states. Wolcott's analysis included the use of the difference between value (labor cost) and price (market-based), a consideration of how well different taxes could be passed on to consumers, and concern about the trade-off between certainty and fairness; his economic thinking was advanced for the day and in line with what Adam Smith had taught.

In terms of specific taxes, Wolcott rejected a tax on farmers' equipment as too difficult to assess and did not ruminate over taxes on professional incomes and business profits because "taxes of this nature cannot be considered as of that description which the Constitution requires to be apportioned among the states." This left taxes on land, houses, and slaves.

Since a tax on land had been approved by the Supreme Court as a direct tax, it had to be included. The problem was how to devise a system of taxing and assessment that made a land tax as uniform as possible in terms of both quality and quantity. The best way was to base the tax on the value of the land; in a growing country like the United States, however, value had to be revised, and assessments would be needed not as often as every year, but every ten to fifteen years.

A tax on houses Wolcott considered a tax on expense and questioned whether or not it was proper to levy a direct tax on them. The key was the extent to which the expense was necessary, and Wolcott recommended an exemption on houses below the value of "the average of those occupied by farmers and laborers." This feature, however, would also require much work in assessing the value of houses.

With respect to slaves, Wolcott did not see how they could be left out, as they enhanced "the quotas of several of the states," and it was unfair "to exempt a species of property which enhances the proportions of certain states, and thus to relieve one class of landed proprietors at the immediate expence of another." Slaves were as much a part of the landowner's property as the land itself, was the point Wolcott wanted to make.[23]

Wolcott's report set off another debate on the feasibility of direct taxes. Gallatin got in the first blow by arguing for their cheapness in collection. He maintained that the excise on alcohol cost about 33% of revenue to collect. Surely a direct tax on land would cost less. Others pointed out that a direct tax would be easy to increase, just by raising the percentage charged. It also would ensure "that every man of property should pay his equal proportion" of taxes.

In opposition, it was argued that the tax would weigh heavily on the frontier, where individuals did not have enough cash to pay an involuntary tax. Opponents also thought that assessing property as to its value would be very costly. Indirect taxes were easy to collect, as the purchase of taxed items held to the principle that "money should be looked for where it is, and not where it is not." Ownership of property did not mean that a person had money to pay taxes. History recorded many examples of nations that had been ruined by direct taxes.

Then representative William Craik (Federalist of Maryland) got to the heart of the matter. The issue was whether or not everyone would be required to pay a fair share of taxes. He continued, "Gentlemen ought not to expect anything like perfection in any scheme of taxation. Taxes were only a choice of evils; they were unpleasant, but they were necessary." There was no way to make them acceptable. For example, a tax on hearths and windows, which had been suggested as an alternative to a land tax, was merely another house tax and would prove unpopular. Nevertheless, direct taxes needed to be considered as one option. It was also charged as "not a little surprising . . . to see the members of that House, whose estates were mostly on land, so desirous of avoiding a land tax."[24]

This argument could not be made against the owners of slaves, and for good reason. They wanted the tax levied on both land and slaves, to spread it out over both forms of property dominant in their state. Gallatin described the situation, "A land tax, unaccompanied with a tax on slaves, would be very unpopular in those States, as it would throw too great a burden upon farmers who did not hold slaves, and fall too lightly upon those whose property chiefly consisted of slaves." In addition, as one southerner pointed out, since slaves counted as three-fifths in the census under which the tax would be apportioned, they should also be counted in the tax.

Jeremiah Smith felt that the counting of slaves would contribute toward inequality. Landowners in his state would pay a higher land tax than would landowners in the South. He was reminded, however, that the tax was in proportion to population and not to land value. Indeed, that was the whole point of the direct tax clause. Representative John Page (Republican of Virginia) placed a moral value on the issue, noting that a person living in a state without slaves might pay a higher land tax, but the extra amount "was certainly not equal to the satisfaction he must enjoy in reflecting that his State is free from this evil." Representative Richard Brent (of Virginia with no party affiliation) pointed out that "it was a very extraordinary thing that gentlemen who represented States where there were no slaves, should oppose a tax on that species of property, and that the Southern States where slavery existed, should be advocating that tax."[25] The direct tax clause did, indeed, work mischief that the framers never intended.

After the debates, Congress determined that $2 million in direct taxes on houses, land, and slaves would be apportioned among the states. In the event that the total tax raised in a state exceeded that state's quota, the individual tax rate would be reduced accordingly.

A fifty-cent tax was placed on slaves. States without slaves would have to pay a higher part of their portion of the tax in house and land taxes, with the result that the northern states had a higher tax on these items than did the southern states.[26]

The tax on houses was progressive, 0.2% on homes worth between $100 and $500 and rising in increments to 1% on those valued at more than $30,000. Congressman Goodloe reported this progressivity to his constituents, explaining "that a man who lives in a house worth 30,000 dollars must have an income that will enable him to pay 300 dollars, as easily as one inhabiting a house worth only 100 dollars can pay 20 cents. Thus the burden is made to fall on those who are able to bear it, and on every one in proportion to his ability."[27] A progressive tax policy was to be followed, in line with what Smith suggested.

Assessing commissions were appointed in each state to place a value and tax rate on land and houses. The house tax was called the "window tax," but this was a misnomer. The law called for individuals to measure their windows as part of the assessment of their homes, not for a tax on windows. The House Ways and Means Committee investigated this issue and reported, "Discontentment has proceeded in part, from the trouble people find in measuring their windows, and in a much greater degree, from an apprehension, among the country people, that this return of windows was intended as the ground work of a window-tax. Wholly unfounded as this apprehension is, it has produced already embarrassing effects." Since the idea underlying the requirement—"that the number and dimensions of the windows in a dwelling house, would, in general, afford a pretty just criterion of its value"—had proved less applicable that had been thought, the committee recommended that the requirement be dropped.[28]

TAXES: ANOTHER REBELLION

The house tax set off another rebellion in Pennsylvania, this time in the east. Officials making the rounds to assess the value of homes, in part by counting and measuring the windows, were mistreated, in some cases by having hot water poured on them. When these perpetrators of harassment were arrested, an armed group of 150 men led by John Fries went to Bethlehem and broke them out of jail.

The federal marshal for the Pennsylvania district, William Nichols, was sent out to issue warrants on these perpetrators and subpoenas for witnesses. He reported that in one attempt to serve a subpoena on a witness, "His wife came to the door; on being asked for her husband she abused me and the gentlemen with me. He came to the door with a club of green oak which seemed to have been procured for the occasion and called us every abusive name the German language can afford, refusing at the same time the subpena." During an attempt to arrest one man, the marshal was met by "upwards of fifty men (chiefly armed with clubs) prepared to prevent the execution of the law." The man "refused to submit to the arrest; the mob swore that before he should be taken, they would *to a man* fight till they died." Then a melee broke out involving the marshal and his two companions. Members of the crowd "tore the cockade from Colonel Balliot's hat, and many others . . . rushed on in the most violent torrent of abuse . . . calling to each other strike! strike!" Physical blows were avoided when Nichols "showed some little resolution which seemed to strike terror into them." That was fortunate, for in his opinion, "If one single blow had been struck, the whole of the radicals would have fallen on us and we three should have been killed."[29]

President Adams issued a proclamation ordering the insurgents "to disperse and retire peaceably to their respective abodes." He also proclaimed that the "combinations to defeat the execution of the laws for the valuation of lands and dwelling places" along with other activities amounted, he was advised, "to treason, being overt acts of levying war against the United States."[30] Adams directed troops to be made ready, and about 500 soldiers were sent in to restore order.

As calm was being restored, Fries was arrested and charged with treason, apparently, from the presiding judges' comments to the grand jury and the jury, under the Sedition Act.[31] At the trial Fries was depicted by the prosecution as having "threatened to shoot one of the assessors, Mr. Foulke, through the legs, if he did proceed to assess the houses." In an even more colorful description, the prosecution also said, "John Fries was armed with a sword, and had a feather in his hat."[32]

Counsel for the defense argued that Fries "thought that the acts for the assessment and collection of a direct tax did not impose the quota upon the citizens equally, and therefore was wrong." Judge Ireton, presiding over the case, told the jury, "During the western insurrection the excise was unpopular; in this case it is the house tax act, and if this is permitted, it will be impossible to know where we can rest secure nor how soon the government itself will fall prey." The issues at the trial were discussed, he also said, "[d]uring the trials of the persons concerned in the western insurrection," and the jury had decided in favor of the prosecution. The Fries Rebellion was suppressed as readily as had the Whiskey Rebellion, and with similar results for the defendant. The jury convicted Fries of treason and sentenced him to death, but Adams pardoned him.[33]

Nevertheless, those taxes were not successful initially. Collections were slow and never filled the $2 million expected.[34] Wolcott reported that in the first year direct taxes raised about $1.2 million at a collection cost of $360,000.[35] In 1800 he estimated that tariff duties would bring in the bulk, $7 million, of the government's revenues, with various excises contributing $800,000 and the direct tax adding $1.2 million (not deducting $215,000 in expenses for "valuation of land and houses").[36] It was not a very efficient tax, and not a popular one either.

Its collection expense of 20% to 30% was even worse than that for the excise taxes. In 1798 Wolcott estimated that it cost $141,000 to collect $800,000 in excises, a 17% rate. Over half the collection expense was for commissions paid "to supervisors at 1 ½ per cent, to inspectors at 1 ½ per cent, to collectors on 600,000 dollars at 7 percent and on 200,000 dollars at 4 per cent." The same estimate reported an average collection expense of 14% to 16% on tariffs.[37]

INDIRECT TAXES

Even at the time direct taxes were being approved, members of the House of Representatives were considering additional indirect taxes. An increase in the tax on sugar was suggested, leading Representative John Swanwick (Republican of Pennsylvania) to wonder if "this increase of duty would produce an increase of revenue." Just because a tax raised a certain amount of money did not mean that a 50% increase in the tax would bring in 50% more in tax receipts, "for, as Dean Swift had justly said, two and two does not always make four in custom-house collection. If it were so, nothing would be more easy than for a financier to calculate the certainty of revenue."[38] Smith's quote certainly made the rounds.

Representative Swanwick understood that the ability to raise a revenue from a tax depended on the availability of substitute items. Hence, he proposed a higher duty on molasses to correlate with the increased tariff on sugar. Along with this taxing package, Representative Harper wanted the tariff on salt raised by five cents a bushel. Everyone bought salt, there were no substitutes, the bulk made smuggling difficult, and the smallness of the increase would all make this a good revenue raiser. Representative Robert Rutherford (Republican of Virginia) objected: "A tax on salt was almost like taxing the common air." An increased tariff on cotton goods was also proposed as "one of the cases in which two plus two would make four."[39] Tariffs were raised throughout the 1790s, but the exceptions were always adjusted.

In addition to raising tariffs, the House of Representatives considered modifications in other taxes. Proposals for extending the Stamp Act to banknotes and debentures were considered. The most controversial addition was to require a stamp on naturalization papers. The debates show little concern with the idea of charging a fee for citizenship but centered on the amount—with proposals ranging from four dollars to as high as twenty dollars, a substantial sum in those days. Gallatin, an immigrant himself, pointed out "the hardship under which a tax of twenty dollars would lay the poor man" and pushed for a lower rate.[40]

Despite the efforts of Congress, tax collections lagged, and with spending on the military rising, the government had to borrow $5 million in 1798, paying the very high rate of 8% interest. This new debt issue more than offset the $2.3 million that had been purchased by the sinking fund up to December 1798; instead, the commissioners reported that no purchases of the debt for the sinking fund had taken place in 1797–98.[41] Gallatin summed up the situation as a choice "between loans and taxation" and admitted he "should certainly resort to taxes rather than loans."[42]

In 1799, however, large numbers of individuals signed petitions seeking the elimination of the army and a reduction in taxes.[43] One petition from York County, Pennsylvania, stated, "We cannot but express our concern at several acts passed in the two last Sessions of Congress: the law for erecting a standing army, the Sedition and Alien Laws, the Stamp Act, the Direct tax on land, and the great increase in Revenue officers."[44] Despite this surge of discontentment, in 1800 Adams reported to Congress, "I observe with satisfaction, that the product of the revenue, during the present year, had been more considerable than during any former equal period. This result affords evidence . . . of the wisdom and efficiency of the measures which have been adopted by Congress for the . . . protection of public credit."[45] Adams' political opponents did not see it that way.

OPPOSITION TO FEDERALIST TAXES

In addressing Adams' plan of public finance, for example, Congressman Samuel J. Cabell (Republican of Virginia) told his voters that he opposed the use of loans "from my hatred to the creation of a public debt." He preferred "direct taxation [as] by far the most eligible mode for raising money" on the ground that it would "rouse the attention of the people to the outgoing of their money." Thomas T. Davis,

Republican representative from Kentucky, agreed, saying he opposed loans to "support the army" on the principle that "I have a great aversion to the increase of the public debt," and it was better "to resort to new taxes, when public exigency require additional expenditure."[46]

Attacks like these helped bring down the Adams' presidency. To be sure, the struggles against France and the Alien and Sedition Acts did not help the president's case with the people. Nevertheless, all of the tax difficulties over the Adams years as well as the increased spending took their toll. The opposition party of Jefferson attacked the fiscal system of the Federalists often.

For example, Gallatin updated his 1796 estimates of the public debt in a full report published in 1800. Part of the discrepancy in how much the debt had grown was in Hamilton's original estimate; Gallatin recalculated it at a lower figure of $72 million—meaning an increase of $7 million over the decade. Gallatin also differed with the Federalists over what other items should be included in defining the debt. He challenged Wolcott's estimates of collection expenses, coming up with an average figure of 6% for tariff collections over the decade and 24% for all internal taxes.[47] Gallatin's analysis anticipated his own program as secretary of the treasury and played upon the hostility toward the internal taxes.

The Jefferson opposition often cited the fiscal policies of the Federalists in its attacks, although the target was more often Hamilton than Adams. *The National Magazine* of Richmond led up to the campaign with a series of articles, "History of the National Debt," which went over the debt assumption plan in great detail, by reprinting John Taylor's "Review of the Revenue System." Following these it gave a small piece, "What Are the Objects of the Hamiltonian Federalists?" The piece reviewed the revenue and debt history of England, from Elizabeth to George III, to show how rising debt and taxes went hand in hand with despotism. It concluded, "Such is the example held out to us by *Hamiltonian federalists*—and the progress we have made is easily compared with that of Britain."[48]

The election campaign of 1800 was especially acrimonious and filled with double-dealing. Hamilton led a covert "dump Adams" campaign and, when that failed, expressed favor for his old enemy Jefferson. Adams lost decisively, and the opposition to his tax and spend program for national defense played a key part in that loss.[49]

The Federalist Congress stuck to its guns, however. In late 1800 the House Committee on Ways and Means reported on whether or not to repeal the direct tax. Since the tax was intended to give a source of revenue for Congress to use in emergencies, "to relinquish this object, after the expence of accomplishing it has been incurred, might be a proof of instability, but not of wisdom."[50] The need for taxes was apparent to them. Under their administration, however, even with unpopular taxes, the public debt grew by about $7 million, to a total of $83 million by 1801. The Federalists never held power again.

CONCLUSION

In 1790, early in his administration, Washington wrote to a friend, "That the government, though not absolutely perfect, is one of the best in the world, I have little doubt."[51] He understood that the success of the new government required confidence in it, and this he and his fellow Federalists in the government had achieved. More important, in terms of public administration, they had created the future, and it worked.

No part of that future was more important than how to handle the new government's finances. Throughout the period, from the Revolution to the Federalist administration, taxes had been discussed in a variety of terms. External taxes might be acceptable, but internal ones were not; the Constitution approved of indirect taxes, but direct taxes had limits. No one was ever sure what these terms meant, but they were sure that they did not like taxes at all.

This dislike held, even though taxes were low. Congressman Harper pointed out that if the $10 million in taxes raised in 1798 were divided among the population, the result would be about $1.33 per person, representing from one to three days' labor depending on the part of the country. Since not everyone worked enough to pay taxes, he assumed that only one-quarter did, but still found that "the whole of our contributions to the government, as now increased, amount to about ten days labour in the year, for each person capable of labour." Looking at other countries, he concluded that "we pay nothing in comparison with them."[52] But that was not the comparison that mattered. The Federalists had not gotten to the depths of tax antipathy, so their virtue in terms of sound finance ultimately became a defect with respect to their electoral prospects.

NOTES

1. Dewey, *Financial History*, p. 117.

2. Raymond Walters, Jr., *Albert Gallatin: Jeffersonian Financier and Diplomat* (New York: Macmillan, 1957), p. 92.

3. Letter from Tench Coxe, commissioner of the revenue, to Hamilton, January 14, 1795, PAH, pp. 40–41.

4. John Taylor, *An Argument Respecting the Constitutionality of the Carriage Tax* (Richmond: Davis, 1795), pp. 5–6, 10–12, 20.

5. John Wickham, *The Substance of an Argument . . . in . . . The United States vs. Hylton* (Richmond: Davis, 1795), pp. 5–6, 11–12, 15.

6. Bradford to Hamilton, July 2, 1795, PAH, vol. 18, p. 396. Bradford continued to worry about Taylor's influence. See his letter to Hamilton, August 4, 1795, PAH, vol. 19, pp. 86–87.

7. Julius Goebel, Jr., and Joseph H. Smith, *The Law Practice of Alexander Hamilton*, vol. 4 (New York: Columbia University Press, 1980), p. 330.

8. Ibid., pp. 334, 344–45.

9. Dewey, *Financial History*, pp. 106–9; Miller, *Alexander Hamilton*, p. 402.

10. Cited in Mitchell, *Alexander Hamilton*, p. 381.

11. A. J. Dallas, *Cases Argued and Decided in the Supreme Court of the United States*, vol. 3 (Rochester, NY: Lawyers Co-operative, 1926), pp. 174–75.

12. Ibid., pp. 177–81.

13. Ibid., pp. 181–82.

14. Ibid., pp.184; Goebel and Smith, *Law Practice*, p. 335.

15. Ralph Adams Brown, *The Presidency of John Adams* (Lawrence: University Press of Kansas, 1975), p. 53.

16. Cited in John Wood, *The Suppressed History of the Administration of John Adams (From 1797 to 1801), As Printed and Suppressed in 1802* (Philadelphia: Printed for the Editor, 1845), pp. 102–3.

17. Sidney Ratner, *Taxation and Democracy in America* (New York: John Wiley and Sons, 1967), p. 29.

18. Stewart, *Opposition Press*, p. 90.

19. Circular Letters dated July 14, 1797, and March 9, 1798, in Cunningham, *Circular Letters*, pp. 106, 109.

20. "Excise," a broadside addressed "To the Citizens of the United States," presumed published in Philadelphia in 1797, copy in collection of American Antiquarian Society.

21. "Of Indirect Taxes," *The Weekly Museum*, Baltimore, February 5, 1797, p. 33.

22. *Debates of Congress*, Fourth Congress, First Session, April 1796, pp. 841–49.

23. "Letter from the Secretary of the Treasury Accompanying a Plan for Laying and Collecting Direct Taxes," December 14, 1796, pp. 5–12, 57–67. Scholars interested in the taxing systems of the separate states should consult pp. 12–46.

24. *Debates of Congress*, Fourth Congress, Second session, January, 1791, pp. 1827, 1862, 1866, 1879, 1888, 1902, 1906, 1908.

25. Ibid., pp. 1932–34, 1935–36, 1939.

26. As explained by Robert Goodloe Harper, Circular Letter dated March 13, 1797, Cunningham, *Circular Letters*, pp. 83–84.

27. Circular Letter dated July 23, 1798, Cunningham, *Circular Letters*, p. 137.

28. "Report of the Committee of Ways and Means," January 21, 1799, pp. 4–5.

29. "Report of the Marshal of the District of Pennsylvania," March 11, 1799, included in *Message from the President of the United States*, December 5, 1799, published by order of the House of Representatives, pp. 6–8.

30. "By the President of the United States of America, a Proclamation," March 12, 1799, included in *Message from the President of the United States*, December 5, 1799, published by order of the House of Representatives, pp. 15–16.

31. *The Two Trials of John Fries*, taken in shorthand by Thomas Carpenter (Philadelphia: William Woodward, 1800), pp. 2–8, 165.

32. Cited in Wood, *Suppressed History*, pp. 205, 207.

33. Stewart, *Opposition Press*, p. 92; White, *The Federalists*, pp. 422–23.

34. Dewey, *Financial History*, pp. 106–10.

35. Stewart, *Opposition Press*, p. 79.

36. Table included in "National Debt, from the Appendix of Mr. Abraham Bishop's celebrated Oration on Political Delusion," *The Political Magazine and Miscellaneous Repository* (Ballston, NY) vol. 1, number 1 (November 1820), pp. 75–76.

37. Statement dated May 17, 1798, copy in collection of American Antiquarian Society.

38. *Debates of Congress*, Fourth Congress, First session, February, 1797, p. 2171.

39. Ibid., pp. 2187, 2189, 2196–97, 2267.

40. *Debates of Congress*, Fifth Congress, June 1797, pp. 394–96, 400, 424–28.

41. *Reports of the Commissioners of the Sinking Fund*, December 9, 1797, and December 17, 1798, p. 1 in both cases.

42. *Debates of Congress*, Fifth Congress, Third session, June, 1798 p. 1919.

43. Brown, *Presidency*, p. 133.

44. Cited in Stephen G. Kurtz, *The Presidency of John Adams* (Philadelphia: University of Pennsylvania Press, 1957), p. 336.

45. Wood, *Suppressed History*, p. 314.

46. Circular letters dated March 28 and 29, 1800, Cunningham, *Circular Letters*, pp. 179, 186.

47. Albert Gallatin, *Views of the Public Debt, Receipts and Expenditures of the United States* (New York: M. L. and W. A. Davis, 1800), pp. 8, 15, 40–41.

48. "History of the National Debt" and "Review of the Revenue System," *The National Magazine*, vol. 2, Richmond, 1799, various pages; "Miscellaneous," pp. 302–3.

49. Kurtz, *Presidency*, pp. 359–64; Brown, *Presidency*, p. 190.

50. Report of the Committee of Ways and Means, December 30, 1800.

51. White, *The Federalists*, p. 4.

52. Circular Letter dated July 23, 1798, in Cunningham, *Circular Letters*, p. 135.

Chapter 8

A Wise and Frugal Government

The arrival of Jeffersonian democracy ushered in a new period of government in the United States, but the shift can easily be overrated. The Anti-Federalists had not taken power in a counterattack on the centralizing powers of the Constitution. While the national government would be influenced by proponents of agrarian democracy, they had no thought of a return to the loose governance of the Articles of Confederation. That debate was over and won. The crowning achievement of the Federalists was to prove that a national government could be made to work.

The change of administration in 1801 brought about a shift in political philosophy and tax policy. In the main, tariffs would become the sole form of federal taxation. This reliance on tariffs ended debate over the constitutionality of direct versus indirect taxes for nearly a century, although a few constitutional issues would arise relating to federal finance. Remarkable at the time, it was a peaceful transformation, despite rough beginnings. The tie vote in the electoral college between Thomas Jefferson and Aaron Burr necessitated a long series of inconclusive votes in the House of Representatives before Federalists finally acquiesced, not by voting for Jefferson but by abstaining. From this difficult beginning, however, a significant tax and spending program emerged that would overthrow many of the centralizing trends of the Federalists.

JEFFERSONIAN PHILOSOPHY

Jefferson often referred to his policies as revolutionary, but he meant a return to the democratic principles of 1776, not a complete upheaval in the course of government. The new administration had as its aim the repair of what its leaders saw as mismanagement and abuses of power by their predecessors.

Those shortcomings had taken three broad forms. First, the government had grown large and central in its power over the people. Second, that power had been concentrated largely in the executive branch as opposed to the Congress. Third, the government was too expensive to operate, which required the levy of unpopular taxes. In its place, Jefferson proposed "a wise and frugal government, which shall restrain men from injuring one another, shall leave them otherwise free to regulate their own pursuits of industry and improvement, and shall not take from the mouth of labor the bread that it has earned. This is the sum of good government."[1] This laissez-faire policy was not aimed only at economic activities. Jefferson believed more than the Federalists that the will of the people mattered on public policy issues. He also appreciated that bowing to it was a way to attain electoral popularity.

In essence, Jefferson set forth a vision of the night watchman state. The federal government was to protect liberty, property, and the rights of the people and then let them alone as much as possible. Government intervention had to have the invitation of the people in its ideal form, but short of that ideal, popular support for any policy was absolutely essential. As Lynton K. Caldwell described the differing philosophies, "For Jefferson . . . government by the people was the governing principle of politics; for Hamilton, government for the people was the driving principle of policy."[2]

To attain a government by the people, the people had to be capable of making wise decisions about policies. Hamilton did not think the masses had this wisdom, which was why he favored an enlightened government to rule for the people and to use its power to push the people to the correct action. Jefferson agreed that the citizens of the United States were ill equipped for government but believed that they could attain a capacity for self rule. As he put it, "[S]ome preparation seems necessary to qualify the body of a nation for self government."[3] An enlightened elite could educate and lead them to that capacity but could not go beyond what popular feeling assented to.

With respect to the executive powers of the president, Jefferson had been a member of the executive branch and respected what it could do. He appreciated that Congress was often disorganized and divided. Executive initiative was still needed to get things done. In his relations with Congress, Jefferson had a position new to the United States; he was president of the country and the leader of his party. Party leadership made it easier for him to get things done in Congress by indirect means. His directives were made more subtly than Washington's and Adams', but they were heeded by Congress nonetheless. Indeed, Hamilton's perception of Jefferson's attitude, based on their common experiences in the Washington administration, was near the mark: "It is a fact which I have frequently mentioned, that while we were in the administration together, he was generally for a large construction of executive authority and not backward to act upon it in cases which coincided with his views."[4] The real difference was that Jefferson had fewer items on his agenda than did Hamilton.

Equally important, however, Jefferson viewed government by the people with a limited executive as an ideal. His own actions as chief executive of the nation often had to set aside that ideal under the press of events. He understood the need to attain harmony within the government and with the people and often compromised his ideals in the name of consensus.

This spirit of consensus also required an accord with prior policies. The Jeffersonians recognized limits on what they could accomplish. There was, after all, a government in place, with laws, procedures, and a Constitution to direct the affairs of state. Jefferson's inaugural address made conciliatory references to "the successful experiment" in government and set forth the notion that "we are all republicans: we are all federalists." To Hamilton these statements meant that Jefferson would "not lend himself to dangerous innovation, but in essential points will tread in the steps of his predecessors."[5] In some respects he had to. As Jefferson begrudgingly admitted with regard to Hamilton's fiscal policies, "We can pay off his debts in 15 years: but we can never get rid of his financial system."[6]

The key to that financial system was the public debt, which Jefferson deemed a corrupting influence on government and society. As Merrill Peterson has described this outlook, "In the Jeffersonian scripture, debt and taxes were public evils of the first magnitude. They drained capital from the mass of citizens, diverted it from production, and supported a system of coercion, corruption and privilege that was the bane of every government and necessarily fatal to a free one."[7] So strongly was he opposed to a funded debt by the government that in 1798 Jefferson had written to his old friend, John Taylor, "I wish it were possible to obtain a single amendment to our constitution. . . . I mean an additional article, taking from the federal government the power of borrowing."[8] That amendment would have restricted the Federalists from adding to the debt.

As noted earlier, the philosophy underlying Jefferson's repugnance for public debt can be found in his conviction that "the earth belongs to the living." Jefferson developed this conviction after a meeting with a poor woman in France. He pondered over the state of the poor and saw it caused by the unequal distribution of wealth. In particular, much of the land of France was concentrated in a few hands and often withheld from production at the whim of the wealthy, who had no need of income from it.[9]

The unequal distribution of wealth was related to public debt in two subtle ways. First, in aristocratic France, the royalty could exist in splendor by borrowing instead of using its landholdings productively. Take one of Jefferson's examples of a bad public debt: "Suppose Louis XV & his contemporary generation had said to the money-lenders of Genoa, give us money that we may eat, drink & be merry in our day; and on condition you will demand no interest til the end of 19 years you shall then for ever after receive an annual interest of 12 5/8 percent."[10] Although Jefferson wanted to make the point that such a debt should not encumber a future generation, his example also indicates his distaste for a system of finance that permitted luxury and idleness.

Second and more important, Jefferson realized that such a financial system could lead to a further concentration of wealth. Jefferson's admiration for the small farmer as the backbone of society was based on a Lockean principle that no person should accumulate more land than can be used without spoilage of its produce. Locke had pointed out, however, that financial wealth could be accumulated in large amounts without any spoilage. A large public debt could be concentrated in a few hands, and paying it off could hurt the middling classes: "If we run into such debts as that we must be taxed in our meat and in our drink, in our necessaries and our comforts, in our labors and our amusements, for our callings and our creeds, as the people of England are, our people, like them, must come to labor sixteen hours in the twenty-four, give the earning of fifteen of these to the government for their debts and daily expenses." To pay such high taxes, taxpayers would be forced to labor for anyone who would hire them at any wage, just to get a subsistence. Jefferson painted a picture of ruinous debt equal to that of Hume and agreed with him that public debt brought taxation "and in its train wretchedness and oppression."[11]

High public debt thus resulted in high taxes, which, in turn, forced taxpayers to work extra to pay them. This low-wage workforce could foster manufacturing and diminish the ranks of the small land owners and create further concentrations of wealth. To avoid a high public debt, Jefferson insisted that each generation pay off its debt: "Then I say, the earth belongs to each of these generations, during it's course, fully, in their own right. The 2d. generation receives it clear of the debts & incumberances of the first . . . , & so on." This way the generational cycle Hume had despaired of could be broken. In theory Jefferson argued based on a generation's being born at the same time, dying at the same time, and living the same life. In application he used actuarial tables to derive nineteen years as the time within which a majority of any generation above age twenty-one would have died, turning that generation into a minority of its time.[12]

Underlying Jefferson's mistrust of debt was an agrarian attitude drawn from his personal experiences. As Herbert E. Sloan has pointed out, in 1774 Jefferson became saddled with debts from his wife's father's estate and spent the rest of his life in debt. The legal wrangles and refinance schemes associated with this debt occupied a great deal of his time and energy and tied up the land his wife had inherited.[13] He felt this long-term debt as an unproductive burden and could never see a commercial perspective of a long-term debt as a way of using debt productively. He was not in favor of chartered corporations, as they were another way a past generation legislated for the future ones.

In his writings from France, Jefferson was justifying the manner in which the present generation of the French Revolution was loosening itself from the dead hand of the past, including the repudiation of the debt incurred by the crown, but he never wanted the debt of the United States disavowed. Rather, it should be paid. Once free of debt, a nation should adopt a plan whereby the legislature "can validly contract no more debt than they may pay within their own age."[14] In operational terms, Jefferson translated this plan into a policy: "Never borrow a dollar without laying a tax in the same instant for paying the interest annually, and the principal within in a given term."[15]

As president, Jefferson could adopt his financial views by his own actions. With the right policies, he could keep the government's budget in a surplus and pay off the debt in a generation.

TAX REFORM

To do so while keeping taxes low, however, was another trick to be pulled off. Jefferson's answer for the unpopularity of taxes was to promise to keep them low and live up to that promise. He had run on a platform of eliminating the internal taxes and had to deliver. He did. In his first annual message to Congress, Jefferson stated that "there is a reasonable ground of confidence that we may now safely dispense with all internal taxes, comprehending excises, stamps, auctions, licenses, carriages and refined sugars . . . and that the remaining sources of revenue will be sufficient to provide for the support of government to pay interest on the public debt, and to discharge the principals in shorter periods than the laws or the general expectations had contemplated."[16]

If those taxes were essential for paying off the debt, as Hamilton had insisted in proposing them, how would Jefferson handle the government's finances? His answer was to cut back on government spending. Economy in government would enable him to reduce taxes and pay off the debt. As he continued in his first annual message, "War, indeed, and untoward events, may change this prospect of things, and call for expenses which the imposts could not meet: but sound principles will not justify our taxing the industry of our fellow citizens to accumulate treasure for wars to happen we know not when."[17] It was an ambitious plan that could leave the country in peril if a war did come. The stakes were high, but Jefferson held that tax relief for the common person was a priority over national defense.

Jefferson's interest in taxing the common person as lightly as possible reflected his appreciation that what taxes were levied could be used to favor the poor against the rich. Too great an inequality of wealth might bring about the leveling spirit that had set the French Revolution on its course of cruelty. As a result he was willing to make limited use of the tax system to bring about some measure of equality by exempting "all from taxation below a certain point, and to tax the higher portions of property in geometrical progression as they rise."[18] The wealthy should pay a larger portion of their income in taxes than did the poor.

In the early days of the government, Jefferson had formulated his own plans for funding the debt, and at the time of the formation of the new federal government Hamilton had written to a friend that Jefferson had "marked out for himself the department of the finances."[19] Despite this background, Jefferson well knew of his limited interest in the details of public finance. To help formulate and manage his debt and tax program, Jefferson chose Albert Gallatin as his secretary of the treasury. Gallatin served in that post for more than twelve years.

As a member of the House of Representatives from Pennsylvania, Gallatin had been a gadfly of Federalist finance. He had challenged both the numbers and the policy backing them and qualified himself as an expert on government fiscal policy.

Jefferson was reported as referring to Gallatin as "the only man in the United States who understands, through all the laberinths that Hamilton involv'd it, the precise state of the Treasury."[20] His views on taxes and debt reduction corresponded to Jefferson's. His unpopularity with the Federalists was so strong that Jefferson did not nominate him to the post until after the lame-duck Federalist Congress adjourned.

Gallatin had in common with Hamilton a foreign birth. He had migrated from Geneva and settled on the frontier. He had also dabbled in local politics, serving in the Pennsylvania legislature. Although he considered his tepid backing of the Whiskey Rebellion to have been his chief political mistake, Gallatin overcame this setback and established a solid reputation as a leader. He was committed to the Jefferson tax and debt reduction programs, along with whatever reforms of Hamilton's system were possible. The need to streamline government operations he took for granted. Above all, however, he was a practical person who used reasoned choice as well as political ideology in the policies he recommended. He was an equal to Hamilton on the details of public finance but had only a smattering of Hamilton's grand national vision.

To give an example of the difference between them, one of Gallatin's first acts as secretary of the treasury was to initiate, at the request of the Congress he and Jefferson led, an annual report on the government's finances, a series that continued until the 1980s. Instead of the unique, magisterial reports that Hamilton had handed down, Gallatin set forth a methodical series of accounts backed by a wealth of data. Treasury records were put on a routine basis.

In the first of those reports, Gallatin outlined the new fiscal policy. Using data for the previous decade on population growth and imports, he estimated that the government could count on $9.5 million annually in customs receipts at a collection cost of 4%. Internal revenue would produce about $650,000 annually, with collection expenses running at 20%. The sale of public land and postage stamps added another $450,000, for a total estimated annual revenue of $10.6 million. With the ordinary expenses of the government estimated at $3.5 million, this left $7.1 million per year for payment of interest and principal of the debt. Since government expenditures had been budgeted at the high prices existing due to war in Europe, an additional $200,000 could be saved, leaving $7.3 million a year available for the debt reduction program.

As will be seen, Gallatin's estimates were conservative and cautious, which made for a very solid plan. If followed, the result of the plan would be that "[t]he public debt would, therefore, on the 1st January, 1810, be reduced to $45,592,739 and 59 cents." If the plan were continued, it would "discharge the whole of the public debt in seven years and a half, after 1809, or within the year 1817."[21] The Jeffersonian ideal of paying off the public debt within a generation was realizable.

In terms of meeting the goals set by Jefferson and his party, the record was even better. Through a reduction in the size of the army and the termination of the building of several navy ships, the government's operating budget, exclusive of interest payments and debt reduction, fell from $3.5 million in 1801 to $2.7 million in 1802, while customs receipts increased to more than $12 million. Gallatin sensibly, in light of the disruptive possibility of war, estimated that $10 million a year in revenue could be counted on, so the $7.3 million debt package was still feasible.[22]

The feasibility of the plan was not hindered by a tax cut during the year. On December 8, 1801, Jefferson presented his first annual message to Congress, indicating "that we may now safely dispense with all the internal taxes, comprehending excises, stamps, auctions, licenses, carriages, and refined sugars."[23] Congress got the message, and in March 1802 the House Ways and Means Committee, under the chairmanship of John Randolph, moved to repeal all internal excise taxes, especially the whiskey tax, which were bringing in about $600,000 a year. In opposition, the Federalists pushed for a reduction of tariffs on necessities such as coffee, tea, and salt.[24] They also wanted the internal excises retained.

Jefferson expressed his support for tariffs as the linchpin of his agrarian democracy:

We are all the more reconciled to a tax on importations, because it falls exclusively on the rich, and . . . constitutes the best agrarian law. In fact, the poor man in this country who uses nothing but what is made in his farm or family, or within the U.S., pays not a farthing of tax to the general government, but on his salt. . . . Our revenues once liberated by the discharge of the public debt . . . , and the farmer will see his government supported, his children educated, and the face of his country made a paradise by the contribution of the rich alone, without his being called on to spare a cent from his earnings. The path we are now pursuing leads directly to this end.[25]

Jefferson predicted that development of a domestic salt industry would free the poor of the salt tax.

The Federalists could give only a weak response. Hamilton reminded that the internal taxes had been pledged to make payments of interest and principal on the public debt, and eliminating them would undermine the confidence of investors. In the Senate, Gouveneur Morris argued that higher tariffs would increase smuggling and draw specie from the western frontier to the seaports. He followed Hamilton's manner by asking, "Do you suppose your creditors will be the dupes of this new-fangled logic?"[26] The Federalists also warned that tariffs were an unsteady source of revenue that could dry up in a war.

From Hamilton's perspective, Jefferson was sacrificing the needs of investors for the prominence of ending unpopular taxes—demagoguery in Hamilton's book. The people needed to be made to pay taxes. Jefferson's conviction that the people needed to learn good government meant that they had to be educated to the need for internal taxes, perhaps in an emergency. Meanwhile, the will of the people had to be followed in tax policy. Moreover, his debt reduction plan would do a better job of paying the debt and securing public credit than had Hamilton's.

Although outnumbered decisively in the House of Representatives, the Federalists engaged their opponents in a quarrelsome set of hearings on the tax bill. They particularly asked how Jefferson's plan could be soaking the rich when it continued the tariff on such necessities as coffee, tea, sugar, and, salt while it ended the tax on the luxury of carriages. After all, tea and sugar carried tariffs of 50%, and coffee 40%. They also warned that high tariffs encouraged smuggling, leading to the principle "that revenue is diminished when taxes are carried too far." The speaker of this principle, Roger Griswold (Federalist of Connecticut), also worried about the fairness of a plan that taxed salt and tea, as "these articles are of prime necessity, and used principally by the poor, and it is determined that the rich shall not pay for their carriages." Representative James Bayard (Federalist of Delaware) specifically resolved "to have the salt tax compared with the tax on carriages, and thus determine which would be the most beneficial to the country to be reduced or abolished."[27]

The debate over repeal of the internal taxes versus tariff increases was heated. Thomas Morris (Federalist of New York) wondered why the repeal of all internal taxes was necessary. The Republicans claimed that the end of the internal taxes would eliminate the patronage posts of tax collectors. John Randolph (of Virginia, no party affiliation) indicated that "his object in repealing the excise was as much to get clear of this host of officers as to be relieved from the taxes." Morris believed that elimination of the whiskey tax—a tax on the poor—would serve that purpose but felt that it did not follow that "other taxes, such as the taxes on carriages, on refined sugar, &c., which fall on the rich, and which are not expensive in the collection" ought to be repealed.[28]

The Republicans countered by claiming that the carriage tax was levied unfairly among the states and hurt the poor. Henry Southard (Republican of New Jersey) claimed that his state paid $5,252 compared to $7,325 for Pennsylvania and $7,807 for New York—both of which were substantially larger. Joseph Varnum (Republican of Massachusetts) said that in his state chaises and other two-wheeled carriages paid $12,000 of the total tax of $14,096, and those vehicles were "by no means owned exclusively by the opulent." Moreover, if the carriage tax had been levied as a direct tax in proportion to population, Massachusetts' share of the total tax of $77,871 would have been $10,284. Its citizens were paying more than their share compared to Connecticut and South Carolina. Samuel Smith continued this disposition, arguing that in his Baltimore district two-thirds of the carriage tax was paid by relatively poor owners of carriages for hire. The tax on carriages was a tax on small business. Moreover, Maryland contributed more in the carriage tax than several smaller states combined. A tax that fell that unequally should be repealed.[29]

The Federalists countered that all of the taxes fell unequally, so having a diverse system balanced things out. Benjamin Huger (Federalist of South Carolina) pointed out that Virginia paid $800,000 in tariffs, while the much smaller South Carolina paid $804,000; Virginians paid $134,000 in internal taxes, compared to $23,000 collected in South Carolina. Repeal of the internal taxes created greater inequality. Samuel Dana (Federalist of Connecticut) went further in this fairness criterion to remind the House of the tax and slave compromise of the Constitutional Convention. The Constitution had provided for representation and direct taxes to be levied on the three-fifths rule "on the principle of making representation conformable to internal taxation." If all internal taxes were repealed, the slave states would have representation in greater proportion than they paid in taxes.[30]

As to the Republican view that "by taking off the internal duties, you abolish a host of offices" and save on the collection costs, the Federalists had a ready reply. The internal taxes were too low. The tariff brought in a high amount of taxes per collector because the tax was high, as much as 50% on some items. If the carriage or whiskey tax had been that high, this efficiency rating would have been higher for internal taxes, too. Besides, the carriage and stamp taxes had not been expensive to collect. Retention and an increase in selected internal taxes would reduce their collection costs.[31]

Even if these selected internal taxes were increased, it is doubtful that they could have been raised sufficiently to counter another Republican objection. The Federalists had argued that the tariff would prove very unreliable during a war. In response, the Republicans pointed out that the potential loss of customs receipts in a war would be in the millions of dollars, whereas the internal taxes were bringing in only $650,000. How could internal taxes ever make up that difference?[32]

Whatever the merits of each side of the debate, Jefferson's plan passed. A resolution to have the Ways and Means Committee consider a drop in the salt tax "passed in the negative," to use the charming phrase of the day, by 32 yeas to 57 nays on January 25. The bill to repeal the internal taxes passed the House of Representatives by a 61 to 24 vote,[33] and the internal taxes were repealed on April 2, 1802. Certainly, the move was popular, as the internal taxes had led to the outbursts of the Whiskey Rebellion and the Fries Rebellion, as Jefferson well knew.

The Federalists were also wary of Jefferson's ability to cut the costs of government. This wariness extended to their disapproval of the intention to appropriate $7.3 annually to reduce the public debt until the debt was extinguished. They contended that this permanent appropriation would tie the hands of future Congresses, especially if the cost-cutting program did not pan out.

Randolph responded with his usual acerbity, in a sentiment that echoed Hume's words about paying the public debt, "The gentleman says, and I agree with him in the opinion, that future Congresses will be as wise as we are, and equally competent to provide for the discharge of the public debt. Those Legislatures may say the same thing of their successors, and in this way provision will never be made." The purpose of the annual appropriation was to have a consistent debt payment strategy, rather than the haphazard scheme of using any surplus funds that might appear at year's end. The bill passed on April 15, 1802, by a 55 to 19 vote.[34]

The Jeffersonians had won a complete victory for their plan, albeit on party lines. Taxes were reduced on the premise that government spending could be cut by more, enabling the debt payment plan to operate.

The end of the internal taxes eliminated the jobs of 500 tax collectors. Gathering the internal taxes had required a lot of manpower. In the case of the whiskey tax, there were 22,000 stills strewn throughout the country to be assessed. In comparison, the tariff was collected in a few major ports. For 1801 to 1804, for example, the ports of New York, Philadelphia, Boston, and Baltimore accounted for 68% of total customs receipts. Tariffs averaged about 15% of total imports during the Jefferson years, much more than the 10% average of the Federalist era.

In other cost-cutting measures, the army saw eighty-seven officers discharged, and its duties reduced to manning a few forts on the frontier. The navy was reduced to a total of 195 men, and most ships were placed in dry dock. The reduction of the bureaucracy in Washington was slight. The total of 127 government employees in the capital (73 in the Treasury Department) in 1801 was reduced to 123 (67) by the end of Jefferson's second term. Embassies were closed to reduce the diplomatic corps.[35]

With the reduction in tax collectors, the military personnel, Jefferson heralded the accomplishments of the Congress:

They have reduced the army and navy to what is barely necessary. They are disarming executive preponderance, by putting down one-half the offices of the United States, which are no longer necessary. These economies have enabled them to suppress all the internal taxes, and still to make provision for the payment of the public debt as to discharge that in eighteen years.[36]

If these efforts stayed the course, a fiscal revolution was indeed afoot. Before that revolution could be completed, the Jefferson fiscal program would be strained by several outside events.

THE LOUISIANA PURCHASE

The first test was a great opportunity. Jefferson, along with nearly everyone else, recognized the importance of the Mississippi River to the economic development of what was then the West, and especially the ability of westerners to trade freely in New Orleans. The winds of European war threatened the fragile system, especially after Spain agreed to transfer its North American holdings to France. The U.S. response was an offer to purchase the Floridas, which also included New Orleans. This purchase would consolidate the borders of the United States from the Atlantic to the Mississippi and from Canada to the Gulf of Mexico.

The offer to purchase this territory was consistent with Jefferson's political beliefs. It represented an acquisition of territory by peaceful means, even if the cuts in military spending made that option a short-term necessity. Jefferson and Gallatin based their fiscal plans on a perpetuation of peace. In the long run, it was possible to rearm, although that might have been a more expensive option. As Hamilton described the alternatives facing the United States with respect to acquiring the desired territory, "First, to negotiate, and endeavor to purchase; and if this fails, to go to war. Secondly, to seize at once on the Floridas and New Orleans, and then to negotiate." Hamilton favored the second choice.[37]

Jefferson favored the first, and not because he was a pacifist. His efforts in the Revolutionary War showed his willingness to engage in warfare, even if not directly in combat as had Hamilton. A war would upset his fiscal policy, especially since the expense of war was uncontrollable and led inexorably to higher taxes and greater debt. It was better to negotiate a purchase and go to war only as a last resort.

In 1802 Napoleon made a counteroffer to sell the United States not the Floridas but New Orleans and France's claims to territory in Louisiana for $15 million. A deal was negotiated by James Monroe, and word of it reached Jefferson on July 3, 1803. He fretted about the constitutionality of the purchase. The Constitution said nothing about the power of the government to acquire land, and there were no constitutional procedures for administering the new territories. Of special legal concern, the treaty called for accepting the population of Louisiana as United States citizens.

Jefferson raised these issues with his confidants. He also drafted an amendment to the Constitution to cover the legalities of the purchase. Gallatin gave three concise answers to the legal issues. First, the country had "an inherent right to acquire territory." Second, the approval of the purchase treaty by the Senate would cover the constitutional question. Third, Congress had the authority to set procedures for governing and disposing of the new lands.[38] Hamilton would have been proud of this use of implied powers. Indeed, they were more than implied, for what was the constitutional end for which the purchase of Louisiana was the means?

Under the press of a time limitation set by Napoleon for concluding the deal, Jefferson agreed to press forward. He also feared that there would be opposition to the purchase, and the fight for an amendment would be a delaying tactic. Nevertheless, after the deal had been completed, he admitted, "The Executive have done an act beyond the Constitution."[39] Later he would justify breaches of the Constitution with the tenet that while "a strict observance of the written laws is doubtless one of the high duties of a good citizen," there were higher ones.[40] In the case of the Louisiana Purchase, Congress wholeheartedly agreed, for in a special session during October 1803 the Senate approved the purchase treaty by 24 to 7, and both Houses passed the enabling legislation by wide margins. The purchase received widespread public favor, which also eased Jefferson's mind.

To settle the deal, Gallatin used $2 million of surplus funds in the treasury, the result of very high tariff collections in 1802, the issuance to France of $11,250,000 in new 6% bonds, payable in four installments starting in fifteen years, and a short-term loan for the remaining amount. The total debt, which had been reduced from $83 million in 1801 to $77 million in 1803, jumped up to $86.4 million in 1804.[41] As Jefferson observed in his third annual message, "Should the acquisition of Louisiana be constitutionally confirmed and carried into effect, a sum of nearly thirteen millions of dollars will be added to our public debt, most of which is payable after fifteen years; before which term the present existing debts will all be discharged by the established operation of the sinking fund." Given the increase in tariff duties added by the new territory and additional economies in government, he added, the interest on the new debt should be paid "without recurring to new taxes."[42]

Although this purchase by debt seemed to go against the Jeffersonian debt philosophy, it was a good investment. Hamilton had argued that the public debt would serve as a fund of capital. Gallatin disagreed, maintaining that "a public debt does not increase the existing amount of cultivated lands, of houses, of consumable commodities; it makes not the slightest addition either to the wealth or the annual labor of the nation."[43] The Louisiana Purchase, however, was an addition to the public debt that did add wealth to the nation. Not only did the geographic area of the United States greatly expand with new land for the spread of agriculture, but the developed parts of the acquisition had a thriving economy. The customs receipts of $200,000 a year that Gallatin estimated would come in from New Orleans helped pay for the interest charges on the new debt. To allow for the larger debt to be paid, he got Congress to increase the annual debt reduction appropriation to $8 million. The purchase was a good deal for the country.

PEACE AND PROSPERITY

The second trial of Jeffersonian finance came with a small war with the Barbary pirates of Tripoli in 1804. To pay for beefing up the navy, Congress in March 1804 increased tariffs slightly by placing a 2.5% surtax on each item, which raised the average from 13.5% to 16%, and increased the duties on goods carried by foreign ships by 10%. In an administrative innovation, the funds from this tax increase went into a restricted "Mediterranean fund." In this way the spending on the war would be highlighted and not hidden in the overall budget.[44] The fund was to expire three months after peace was negotiated, but Congress kept renewing it until 1812.[45]

Due to the increased tariff rates and general economic prosperity, customs collections rose form $10.5 million in 1803 to $16.4 million in 1808. Direct taxes, still on the books, amounted to less than $50,000 per year in this period, with land sales adding less than $1 million annually to the government's coffers. The tariff was effectively the only source of revenue for the government, and Jefferson had delivered on his campaign promise.

He had done so well that the election of 1804 seemed a formality. A mere comparison of the record between Jefferson and Adams was campaign enough. As Peterson has described it, "New taxes—no taxes; profusion—economy; mounting public debt—rapid extinguishment of the debt."[46] The new term of office promised more of the same.

The second Jefferson administration started favorably, and the tax and debt reduction trend continued. In his annual report for 1806, Gallatin indicated that the public debt had been reduced by $24.7 million, and the treasury faced a problem in that only a small amount of the debt was due in the next few years. Purchases by the treasury of bonds in the open market might bid up their price above par, which was higher than Congress allowed. He suggested that Congress authorize new issues of redeemable bonds with features attractive enough to induce investors to swap them for the older issues. Otherwise, there would be a surplus of $5.5 million a year in the debt appropriation. Such a swap would permit payment by 1815 of all the debt except for the Louisiana bonds owed to France. Payment of the fourth installment to France in 1821 would eliminate the entire debt.[47] Even with the purchase of Louisiana, Jefferson's goal of eliminating the public debt was on track.

Although Congress ultimately approved of Gallatin's debt swap plan, in March 1807 it responded to his good financial news by repealing the salt tax, the one tariff that hit the nonrich very hard. This was a significant cut, as salt was in common use, and the tariff on it alone contributed about 5% of the government's revenue.

The debate in the House of Representatives over the salt tariff raised the issue of protection. Josiah Quincy (Federalist of Massachusetts) asked that the tax be reduced but not eliminated. As a result of the salt tariff, in just a few years a flourishing salt industry had arisen on Cape Cod. With a few more years of protection, which a reduced tariff would continue, the industry would grow enough to make the country self-sufficient. As to the tax's hitting the poor, Quincy estimated that a poor person paid about forty-two cents a year in salt taxes, compared to $10.50 for a wealthy farmer or plantation owner. The wealthy benefited from the tax cut. George W. Campbell (Republican of Tennessee) chimed in that his constituents produced a surplus of salt and had no interest in eliminating the tariff. Protection of manufacturing was not a part of Jefferson's agenda, however, and the elimination of the salt tax passed by a vote of 122 to 5.[48]

GALLATIN AS SECRETARY OF TREASURY

This cut in taxes came at a time when international affairs were again turning hostile, so Gallatin felt obligated to establish a wartime fiscal policy. He did well, for his policy endured for 175 years. The design of the policy called for the government to raise enough revenue during the war to pay for its normal operations, interest on existing debt, and interest on new debt; this latter amount was essential, for Gallatin believed that the war should be paid for by borrowing. This plan would require new taxes to pay the anticipated interest from the new debt, but "the losses and privations caused by war should not be aggravated by taxes beyond what is strictly necessary." After the war, there would be "ample resources for reimbursing whatever may have been borrowed during the war."

In assessing the relative merits of taxing versus borrowing during a war, Gallatin pointed out that while taxes were paid by everyone, only a few individuals lent money to the government. Fairness would indicate that taxes be used to spread the burden of the war to all. A war at sea would reduce the exports of Americans, however, and "the reduced price of the principal articles exported from the United States and will operate more heavily than any contemplated tax." The best that could be hoped for in the way of war taxes was a continuation of the Mediterranean fund and a doubling of tariffs. Indirect internal taxes might work as a war tax and but not a direct tax. Loans would be needed.[49]

Gallatin's program was impressive for its reach. At the time it was written, the need for borrowing was not obvious. The treasury was filled with surplus funds. His recognition that war would tax farmers with lower prices proved prophetic. In 1809, during that substitute for war, the embargo, the price of corn fell to seventy-one cents a bushel from its 1804 high of ninety-four cents, and wheat prices went from $1.56 to $1.10 a bushel in the same period.[50] That problem lay in the uncharted future.

In the present, 1807, with an excess of money in hand, Jefferson began looking for constructive ways to spend it. In his second inaugural address, Jefferson had indicated the possibility of using excess funds for "rivers, canals, roads, arts, manufactures, education and other great objects within each state."[51] Here, too, Jefferson worried about the constitutionality of using tax money for projects of internal improvement and requested an amendment to the Constitution to give the federal government clear authority. In the meantime, he preferred to return the money directly to the states, to use as they thought best.

As a citizen of the frontier, Gallatin was more concerned with building roads than in preserving constitutional technicalities. He had told the president that in some cases "an improvement is as useful or more useful to an adjacent State than to that through which it passes."[52] There was a national interest in improving transportation, which made that a concern of the federal government.

In 1808 Gallatin prepared his well-known "Report on Roads and Canals." In it he narrated the advantages of a national transportation system, including coastal canals, canals linking the coast to the interior, canals that connected interior rivers, and roads that crossed the mountain ranges where canals were not feasible. He described efforts undertaken up to that time, by state governments and private companies, in starting various components of the system he proposed. These individual efforts, he argued, had proved inadequate due to the time it would take for profits to pay off investors. The projects were too big and risky for private finance to undertake. He wrote, "Some works already executed are unprofitable and many more remain unattempted, because their ultimate productiveness depends on other improvements, too extensive or too distant to be embraced by the same individuals. The general government alone can remove these obstacles."[53]

Gallatin proposed that the government fund a turnpike and canal system parallel to the coast ($7.8 million); roads, canals and river improvements on east-to-west routes ($4.8 million); navigational improvements in the Great Lakes region ($4 million); and a fund to support local projects ($3.4 million)—for a $20 million total. The projects would be completed over a period of ten years, with annual appropriations of $2 million. This annual appropriation was well within the means of the government. He reiterated that unless his debt swap was adopted, the government would have an extra $3.4 million, "applicable to any other object." Even if the debt swap plan were adopted, estimated revenues for the future still showed a surplus.

To be sure, Gallatin qualified his argument by twice remarking that the plan would apply "in times of peace" only. He explained, however, "that the facility of communication, constitutes, particularly in the United States, an important branch of national defence." Even this justification, however, did not mitigate the constitutional difficulties of the plan, and Gallatin asked Congress to submit an amendment to the Constitution to the states to permit internal improvements.[54]

Of Gallatin's two great plans, for wartime finance and for internal improvements, the former was most useful right away. The affairs of life and government are not always capable of human control. The Jeffersonians soon were beset by external forces that undermined their well-laid plans.

THE EMBARGO

War had been raging in Europe for over a decade, as Napoleon set on his course of empire, and the British and their allies fought him. The Federalists had pushed for increased military spending to keep the United States prepared in case the war touched here. Jefferson had canceled that preparedness campaign. He hoped that neutrality and a wide ocean would keep the country protected. Events began to prove otherwise, as British impressment of sailors and seizure of commercial shipping began to take their toll. The final straw was the firing on the U. S. Navy frigate *Chesapeake* by a British man-of-war in July 1807.

Congress first passed an anti-importation act aimed solely at England. Before it went into effect, however, in December 1807, Jefferson proposed and Congress enacted a full-scale embargo on commerce, which kept American ships from sailing overseas and stopped foreign ships from picking up shipments in United States ports.[55]

The embargo started out successfully, although several additional laws were needed to close loopholes and step up enforcement. In the beginning, enforcement was the responsibility of the customs service, as the agency with intimate knowledge of foreign trade and the facilities for monitoring it. As time went on, violations spiraled, and smuggling took place. The navy began taking part in enforcement, penalties were increased, and land routes from Canada were closed. This last policy earned the enmity of those same backwoodsmen who rebelled over the whiskey tax, and proved equally unenforceable. Along the New England seacoast, the idling of many sailors also proved unpopular.

Despite these fulminations against the power of the government and the prospect that they might become as unpopular as their predecessors, Jefferson and his party in Congress held firm for a time. In fact, in 1808 customs officials were empowered to seize a ship merely on the suspicion that it was in violation of the embargo, pending a decision by the president. This certainly was a broad exercise of executive power. Had Hamilton still been alive, he might well have been shocked.

Even Gallatin pointed out to the president that, under the embargo, "not a single vessel shall be permitted to move without the special permission of the Executive ... the collectors [shall] be invested with a general power of seizing property anywhere," adding that these "arbitrary powers" were "dangerous and odious."[56] Seemingly unperturbed, Jefferson went to extreme measures of telling customs officials to assume every shipment was suspicious, and when they lacked the manpower for such draconian enforcement, he began beefing up the navy. These measures eventually proved counterproductive, and opposition grew. In 1808 a special session of Congress ordered a repeal of the embargo effective March 4, 1809—the date Jefferson left office.[57]

The embargo placed Jefferson's fiscal policy under quite a strain. Customs receipts fell from $16.4 million in 1808 to $7.3 in 1809. With this drastic decline in its main source of revenue, the government experienced a shift in its budget from a $7 million surplus to a $2.5 million deficit (about 25% of the $10.3 million in total spending), the only one of the Jefferson administration. Tariff collections rose slightly to $8.6 million in the following year, and only draconian cuts in military spending of more than 30%, from $5.7 million in 1809 to $4 million in 1810, brought the budget a surplus of $1.2 million above total spending of $8.2 million.[58]

Gallatin had responded to the decline of revenue in his annual report for 1808. He gave several scenarios, ranging from ending the embargo to all-out war. His judgment was, "If the embargo, the suspension of commerce shall be continued, the revenue arising from commerce, will, in a short time, entirely disappear." The government had enough reserves to survive for two years, but after that, loans would be needed. Given that creditors recognized the ability of the United States to survive a war intact, and then be able to amass custom receipts when peace resumed, there would be no difficulty in securing loans. "No internal taxes, either direct or indirect, are therefore contemplated," Gallatin assured Congress.[59]

Tariffs were another matter, and Gallatin recommended that they be doubled. His war-time financial plan was to be put in initial operation. Congress disagreed with him and kept to a pledge of no new taxes. The small deficit of 1809 was the outcome. Gallatin repeated his request for tariff increases in his 1809 report,[60] with the same negative outcome.

As a result, Jefferson left office with his program in disarray. He had reduced taxes and the debt. To maintain a balanced budget, spending on the military was cut at a time when the world was growing increasingly hostile. Despite setbacks, at the end of his second term Jefferson's fiscal program had worked well. Taxes, especially on the poor and middle class, had been cut, and the public debt had been reduced to $57 million. Had the Louisiana Purchase not been made, Gallatin's initial forecast of a $45 million debt level by this time would have been accurate. The public debt was being diminished at a rate that made Jefferson's claim of being able to pay it off in fifteen to nineteen years more realistic than Hamilton's thirty year plan. Jefferson could claim to have made headway in reforming Hamilton's system of finance.

CONCLUSION

The Jeffersonian tax plan proved very effective in times of peace. Taxes were cut, and the public debt was reduced. As a bonus, an important feature of Hamilton's plan, internal taxes, was eliminated. It all worked well, and the country was happy. The Hamiltonian system was dismantled as much as possible, and the government was kept small. The Jeffersonians saw little need for wasteful military spending as long as negotiations could hold off a war. They placed a priority in tax cuts and debt reduction.

The Jeffersonian plan reflected an agrarian policy of small government, little debt, and low taxes. The public finance triad of money, debt, and taxes was limited to taxes, as few as possible. Whether this system could survive the crisis of war was another matter.

NOTES

1. Cited in Dumas Malone, *Jefferson the President: The First Term, 1801–1805* (Boston: Little, Brown, 1970,) p. 22.

2. Lynton K. Caldwell, *The Administrative Theories of Hamilton and Jefferson*, 2d ed. (New York: Holmes and Meier, 1988), p. xiii.

3. Cited in Ibid., p. 122.

4. Cited in Robert M. Johnstone, Jr., *Jefferson and the Presidency* (Ithaca, NY: Cornell University Press, 1978), p. 53.

5. Cited in Malone, *Jefferson the President*, pp. 20–21.

6. Cited in Ratner, *Taxation and Democracy*, p. 32.

7. Merrill D. Peterson, *Thomas Jefferson and the New Nation* (New York: Oxford University Press, 1979), p. 687.

8. Cited in James D. Savage, *Balanced Budgets and American Politics* (Ithaca, NY: Cornell University Press, 1988), p. 106.

9. Thomas Jefferson to James Madison, Fountainbleau, October 28, 1785, in Lance Banning, *Jefferson and Madison: Three Conversations from the Founding* (Madison, WI: Madison House, 1995), pp. 162–63.

10. Jefferson to James Madison, Paris, September 6, 1789, in Banning, *Jefferson and Madison*, p. 166.

11. Jefferson to Samuel Kercheval, July 12, 1816, in Banning, *Jefferson and Madison*, p. 45.

12. Jefferson to Madison, September 6, 1789, in Banning, *Jefferson and Madison*, p. 167.

13. Sloan, *Principle and Interest*, p. 3.

14. Jefferson to Madison, September 6, 1789, in Banning, *Jefferson and Madison*, p. 169.

15. Thomas Jefferson to John Wayles Eppes, Monticello, June 24, 1813, in Banning, *Jefferson and Madison*, p. 176.

16. Thomas Jefferson, *Public and Private Papers* (New York: Vintage Books, 1990), p. 177.

17. Ibid.

18. Cited in Caldwell, *The Administrative Theories*, p. 169.

19. Hamilton to Edward Carrington, May 26, 1792, as cited in Donald F. Swanson, "Thomas Jefferson on Establishing Public Credit: The Debt Plans of a Would-be Secretary of the Treasury?" *Presidential Studies Quarterly* 23 (Summer 1993): p. 499.

20. Cited in Walters, *Albert Gallatin*, p. 141.

21. "Report on the Finances, for 1801," in *Reports of the Secretary of the Treasury of the United States*, vol. 1 (Washington, DC: Duff Green, 1828), pp. 217, 219, 226.

22. "Report on the Finances, for 1802," in *Reports of the Secretary of the Treasury*, pp. 252–53.

23. Cited in Noble E. Cunningham, Jr., *The Process of Government under Jefferson* (Princeton, NJ: Princeton University Press, 1978), p. 74.

24. Dewey, *Financial History*, pp. 119–20.

25. Cited in Ratner, *Taxation and Democracy*, pp. 32–33.

26. Both cited in Claude G. Bowers, *Jefferson in Power* (Boston: Houghton Mifflin, 1936), pp. 91–92, 136–37.

27. *History of Congress*, 6th Congress, 2d Session, 1802, pp. 434–37.

28. Ibid., pp. 440, 449.

29. Ibid., pp. 1027–31, 1061–62.

30. Ibid., pp. 1028, 1073.

31. Ibid., pp. 1033, 1041.

32. Ibid., p. 1036.

33. Ibid., pp. 461, 1073.

34. Ibid., pp. 1164–65, 1192.

35. Cunningham, *The Process of Government*, pp. 90, 127–28.

36. Cited in Peterson, *Thomas Jefferson*, p. 702.

37. Cited in Malone, *Jefferson the President*, p. 277.

38. Ibid., p. 312.

39. Cited in Caldwell, *The Administrative Theories*, p. 128.

40. Cited in Malone, *Jefferson the President*, p. 320.

41. Dewey, *Financial History*, pp. 121, 124.

42. Jefferson, *Public, Private Papers*, p. 188.

43. Cited in Studenski and Kroos, *Financial History*, p. 69.

44. Dewey, *Financial History*, pp. 121–22.

45. Cited in Studenski and Kroos, *Financial History*, p. 68.

46. Peterson, *Thomas Jefferson*, p. 799.

47. "Report on the Finances, for 1806," in *Reports of the Secretary of the Treasury*, pp. 333, 335, 336.

48. *History of Congress*, 9th Congress, 2d. Session, 1807, pp. 301–20.

49. "Report on the Finances, for 1807," in *Reports of the Secretary of the Treasury*, pp. 360–61.

50. Robert Allen Rutland, *The Presidency of James Madison* (Lawrence: University Press of Kansas, 1990), p. 23.

51. Cited in Caldwell, *The Administrative Theories*, p. 165.

52. Cited in Walters, *Albert Gallatin*, p. 183.

53. Albert Gallatin, *Report of the Secretary of the Treasury on the Subject of Public Roads and Canals* (1808) (New York: Augustus Kelley, 1968), pp. 6–7.

54. Ibid., pp. 69–73.

55. Peterson, *Thomas Jefferson*, pp. 882–83.

56. Walters, *Albert Gallatin*, p. 202.

57. Johnstone, *Jefferson, the Presidency*, pp. 254–93.

58. Studenski and Kroos, *Financial History*, pp. 68–70.

59. "Report on the Finances, for 1808," in *Reports of the Secretary of the Treasury*, pp. 376–77.

60. "Report on the Finances, for 1809," in *Reports of the Secretary of the Treasury*, p. 401.

Chapter 9

A PROPER SELECTION OF MODERATE INTERNAL TAXES

Although Jefferson had decried his inability to rid the nation of Hamilton's system, he had done a fairly good job. Tax reduction and the elimination of internal taxes had minimized the unpopularity of taxation that had marked the later years of Federalist governance. Tariffs constituted the government's revenue needs, which were modest, and there was no talk of protecting manufactures. With reductions in government spending, the federal budget surpluses had been consistently large enough to make a real dent in the public debt, even after the purchase of Louisiana.

Having passed from the scene, Hamilton could make no comment on this state of affairs. Yet, his shade surely would have wondered how long it could last. Europe was ablaze with war, as Napoleon endeavored to impose a new world order. Sooner or later the United States would be dragged in. What would happen to Jefferson's fiscal plans then? Fortunately for him, Jefferson never had to answer that question. Instead, his friend and confederate, James Madison, would be forced to relearn the message Hamilton had preached.

MADISON TAKES OVER

Although Jefferson and Madison maintained a relationship of undisturbed cordiality for fifty years, their views on debt and taxes were not identical. To be sure, Madison agreed with Jefferson on the detrimental effects on democracy of an unequal distribution of wealth and how debt and taxes could contribute to that inequality; he also worried that a commercial order was dangerous for society.[1] Regarding Jefferson's generational limit on debt and taxes, while Madison thought the idea "a great one" in principle, he worried over its practical value.

Perhaps because he had not been as burdened by debt as Jefferson, Madison could see some merit in Hamilton's views on the usefulness of debt, and he noted that "the improvements made by the dead form a charge against the living." With regard to that note, he replied to his friend,

Debts may be incurred for purposes which interest the unborn, as well as the living: such are debts for repelling a conquest, the evils of which descend through many generations. Debts may even be incurred principally for the benefit of posterity: such perhaps is the present debt of the U. States, which far exceeds any burdens which the present generation could well apprehend for itself. The term of 19 years might not be sufficient for discharging the debts in either of these cases.[2]

Madison had the better of the argument here. In time of war, legislatures could plan neither how much to borrow nor how much to tax. Efforts to fight a war could exceed the ability of any single generation to pay the costs associated with those efforts. Madison's words, written in 1790, proved very true in his own administration.

Despite his recognition that wars made debt and taxes necessary, Madison did not favor war as a policy except as a last resort—that was what separated him from Hamilton. As he put it in 1795, when the Federalists were building up the military, "War is the parent of armies; from these proceed debts and taxes; and armies, debts, and taxes are the known instruments for bringing the many under the dominance of the few."[3]

To no one's surprise, the Madison administration continued the policies of Jefferson, and the new president's inaugural address repeated the dictum of low taxes and debt reduction. Madison, however, did not have Jefferson's stature, physically or politically. Hence his following of the philosophy that Congress should lead on policy became more of a practice. Key members of the Jeffersonian party also challenged Madison's leadership, forcing him to abandon his desire to name Gallatin secretary of state. This challenge was especially unseemly, given that Gallatin had overseen the dismantling of Hamilton's system, albeit with some reluctance.

THE OVERTURN OF HAMILTON'S SYSTEM

When he first became secretary of the treasury, Gallatin surely took it for granted that he had been selected to modify the Hamiltonian system. That was the aim of the debt and tax reduction programs, but he also sought to modify two other features of the Federalist finance, the Bank of the United States and the sinking fund.

The Bank of the United States had operated much as Hamilton had anticipated in his proposal. It had been a source of loans for the government, although the debt reduction plan had reduced its holdings of government securities from $6.2 million to $2.2 million—certainly not the forceful amount that Jefferson and Madison had feared. It had acted reasonably and responsibly in issuing its notes and in supervising the amount of notes issued by state banks. It also performed well as the government's fiscal agent, earning Gallatin's praise. He admitted to being helped by having a safe depository for government funds and a means for shifting those funds to different regions of the country. The management by the Bank of the United States of the nation's money supply along with its own issuance of banknotes made the collection of taxes much easier.[4]

When the charter of the Bank of the United States came up for renewal in 1809, Gallatin supported it, but with modification. To offset its central control, he wanted the bank's capital increased from $10 million to $30 million, with the states purchasing $15 million of the increase. This change would permit the states to elect directors to the bank and let them exercise some control over its branches in their jurisdiction. The House of Representatives approved of a new charter on this basis in 1810, by a 75 to 35 vote. A decision in the Senate, however, was adverse, when vice president George Clinton broke a 17 to 17 tie by voting against renewal.[5] As is often the case in politics, the argument centered on the supposed antidemocratic tendencies of the bank, rather than on its economic functions.

Gallatin was more successful in modifying the sinking fund. As Hamilton had proposed it, the fund would use surplus funds to purchase government bonds and hold them, using interest payments into the fund to buy additional bonds. Gallatin pointed out the flaw in this plan: "If you spend more than you receive, you may have recourse to sinking funds, you may modify them as you please, you may give a scientific appearance to additions and subtractions; you must still necessarily increase your debts."[6] He felt that the diversion of money into a sinking fund was an unnecessary complication of the government's accounts and that the payment of interest into the fund merely a subterfuge.

To put the fund on a sounder basis, in 1802 he recommended and Congress concurred that a set amount be budgeted for payment into the sinking fund before other appropriations were made. The appropriation would cover the payment of principal and interest. For the next decade, Congress appropriated annual amounts of $7.3 million to be put in the fund, with the amount raised to $8 million after the addition of debt for purchase of Louisiana.[7] Giving the sinking fund commissioners responsibility for payment of interest on the debt produced the curious result that they paid interest to the fund itself, on bonds it held. This odd policy was not eliminated for another fifteen years.

Gallatin's two great reports on war finance and internal improvements have overshadowed his own "Report on Manufactures," in which he countered the need for Hamiltonian policies for economic development. The report listed all the industries whose production was adequate for domestic consumption needs, which Gallatin defined as domestic production being greater than imports, and followed with a description of each industry. Manufactures had done well, thanks to the Jeffersonian system under which tariffs had "operated as a premium in favor of American manufactures," and "the frugality of the government" had made "unnecessary any oppressive taxes."[8]

Jefferson's tax policy was aiding economic development, was Gallatin's conclusion, but it was possible more could be done. He rejected Hamilton's idea that manufacturing could be encouraged by protective tariffs and bounties. These incentives would pull resources into areas the government dictated and not necessarily where they would be most productive for the economy. The real problem, according to Gallatin, was "the comparative want of capital" in the United States in contrast to England. Gallatin then proposed that the federal government could lend low-interest circulating bonds to businesses as a way to increase capital in the country. He wrote, "A plan might be devised by which five millions of dollars a year, but not exceeding in the whole twenty millions, might thus be lent, without any material risk of ultimate loss, and without taxing or injuring any other part of the community."[9] With such a generalized loan program, the government could avoid the problem of favoring some industries that bedeviled protectionism. To be sure, this type of loan program was not compatible with agrarian distaste for debt, but Gallatin had more background and experience with commercial matters than most Jeffersonians. Nevertheless, the report went nowhere, and it is not included among Gallatin's great plans.

These changes in the Hamiltonian system left the country both better and worse off. Debt reduction had a positive value that the changes in the sinking fund did not modify. The shift to a strict reliance on tariffs for revenue had lightened the tax burden of the agrarian community but left the nation exposed to danger in time of war, when there would be a need for greater spending just as tax collections were falling. The termination of the charter of the Bank of the United States eliminated a secure source of credit for the government that would be sorely missed.

The timing of the elimination of the Bank of the United States could not have been worse. War was looming on the horizon, and with it would come the need for credit to finance an expansion of the military, or else there must be new taxes. With respect to taxes, however, even in the face of the obvious need to plan for war, Congress was as intense in opposition to new taxes as Jefferson had been. Everyone remained as optimistic as the sage of Monticello, who in 1811 still believed "that, if war be avoided, Mr. Madison will be able to complete the payment of the national debt, within his term."[10]

GALLATIN PLANS FOR WAR

Gallatin was smart enough to anticipate that war must come and kept pushing Congress for a plan. From his earlier reports, he clearly had a program to meet the financial demands of war. By 1811, however, Congress' failure to recharter the Bank of the United States had eliminated it as a ready source of credit for the government. Gallatin estimated that the normal operations of government would continue to cost about $7 million, but if the war reduced tariff collections as much as the embargo had, tax collections would barely cover them, and a deficit of $2.6 million would exist. There would be no surplus funds to pay the interest on new loans. Given these projections, Gallatin proposed continued extension of the Mediterranean fund and a doubling of tariffs. If these proved insufficient, the salt tax could be restored, and "a proper selection of moderate internal taxes" could be enacted.[11] This return to Hamilton's scheme of internal taxes did not fare well, and although Gallatin's proposal passed in the House of Representatives, it failed in the Senate.

Thus rebuked, Gallatin offered his resignation, but President Madison refused the offer. Nevertheless, in 1812, with war declared, Gallatin's annual report contained no suggestions for new war taxes. Apparently discouraged, in 1813 he took a diplomatic mission as part of a committee sent to Europe in hopes of negotiating peace with England. In 1814, in return for Congressional approval of his participation on that mission, he officially resigned as secretary of the treasury.[12] As had Hamilton, Gallatin eventually left office as the victim of tax politics, but his overall record was very good. Jefferson's fiscal policies had continued under President Madison, so that by 1812, the public debt had been reduced to $45 million—a decline of almost half in less than a decade. As a result, interest payments on the public debt went from $4.4 million in 1801 to $2.5 million in 1812.[13]

THE WAR OF 1812

The War of 1812 has often been accorded the ignominy as a low point of U.S. military and political history, and for good reason. The campaign was filled with embarrassing military defeats, including the burning of the capital, and the one great victory at New Orleans was unnecessary. There was dissent about the war in Congress and in the northeast states, where governors held it unconstitutional to send their militia into Canada. War hawks dreamed of annexing Canada as part of the U.S. empire, but no one wanted to pay for the men and arms it would take. As would happen often in the United States, advocates of the war greatly underestimated how long the war would last and how much it would cost.

John C. Calhoun, then a representative from South Carolina, exemplified this optimism when he said, "I believe that in four weeks from the time a declaration of war is heard on our frontier, the whole of upper Canada and a part of Lower Canada will be in our power." This view became common in Washington, despite the fact that the U.S. military establishment, weakened by a decade of budget cuts, was outnumbered by British forces in Canada. The superiority of the British navy over that of the United States was overwhelming.[14]

In Congress, when Madison sent it his war message, his arch enemy John Randolph ridiculed it fiercely, "Go to war without money, without men, without a navy! Go to war when we have not the courage, while your lips utter war, to lay war taxes!"[15] Randolph was in a minority. Still, it was a consequential minority. The war declaration passed the Senate by 20 to 13 and the House of Representatives by 79 to 49, and war was effectively declared on June 18, 1812.

As war became more than a potential, Congress began authorizing loans, with the first, a 6% issue of $11 million in bonds being made in March 1812, three months before the war started. Additional loans were authorized throughout the war. Antiwar sentiment deplored this predicament. The electors of Worcester, Massachusetts, were warned that if the United States went to war with England, "We must resort to large and repeated loans, or burden the farming interests of the country with Direct Taxes." The law authorizing the $11 million loan would require higher taxes just to pay the interest.[16]

In addition to the new loans, the government also began issuing treasury notes to be retired in one year and to be used in payment of taxes. These were reminiscent of the continental dollars, except that they carried interest at 5.4%, were issued in large denominations, and were actually repaid. The treasury issued $36.7 million in these notes during the war. The largest amount of notes outstanding at any time was $17 million on January 1, 1816. As the war went on, the minimum denomination of the notes fell from $100 to $20 to $3 in the last issue. The notes were never declared legal tender, but the smaller-denomination ones did circulate as money. There was some inflation as a result, but it was kept reasonable.[17]

The tax collections during the War of 1812, although sufficient for the government's needs, showed the obstacles inherent to planning a budget during trying times. On July 1, 1812, Congress responded to the war's financial needs by doubling all tariffs. It ignored Gallatin's recommendation for internal taxes and a direct tax.

A substitute plan of permitting trade with England to enhance tariff revenue was considered, and members of the House of Representatives asked Gallatin for an opinion on the plan. Without endorsing the plan, Gallatin advised that goods imported from England had contributed one-half of total customs receipts before trade was disrupted, and reopening of that trade might add the same percentage to tariff collections.[18] The measure was barely defeated. With higher tariffs, customs collections rose from $8.9 million in 1812 to $13.2 million in 1813 but fell to $6 million in 1814. As tariff revenues began falling, financial stress deepened.

In June 1813, secretary of the Navy William Jones, serving as acting secretary of the treasury in Gallatin's absence, reported on the need for new internal taxes to make it easier to negotiate loans, telling Congress that "the terms of the loan, for the present year, would have been more favorable, if the taxes had been previously laid."[19] The warnings of the Federalists that tariffs were unstable and a poor support for public credit were coming to pass. Congress began looking at other taxes in the summer of 1813, including internal excise taxes and a direct tax.

The delay in imposing these taxes was caused by extensive debate over them. In fact, Congress dawdled over the issue for several sessions until Madison called a special session in the Summer of 1814. Finally, a direct tax on land, houses, and slaves of $3 million for 1814 was passed, to be levied in proportion among the states based on the 1810 census. Internal taxes were placed on carriages, refined sugar, liquor distillers, stamps, auctions, liquor retailers. Another special session in September 1814 made the direct tax $6 million annually, raised the internal taxes and added new ones on distilled spirits, and placed a property tax on personal items such as household furniture and watches.[20]

These direct taxes were apportioned to the states based on population, as had been done in the past. Each state was further divided into an assessment district, with district assessors chosen to get lists of taxable property from taxpayers.[21] To give one example, the carriage tax act required "that every person having or keeping a carriage or carriages . . . shall yearly . . . make and subscribe a true and exact entry . . . with the collector appointed by virtue of the act" a list of carriages owned and the tax due on each. The tax amounted to twenty dollars a year on coaches and seventeen dollars a year for chariots. The government tax collectors were as intrusive as anything the Federalists had imagined in the 1790s. Collection was slow initially, as it took time to rebuild the tax administrative system nullified by Jeffersonian policy, as Gallatin later admitted. Collection costs ran 7.8% in the first year, before declining to 4.8% later.[22]

In 1814, Secretary of the Treasury George W. Campbell, named to replace Gallatin in February, advocated extending the wartime tax system to enable continued borrowing. In support of this proposal, he pointed out, "The very expenditures which render necessary the imposition of additional taxes, will themselves have increased in the community the ability to pay them." The idea that government spending enhanced the income of the country, making tax collections easier, was not often appreciated in the nineteenth century; Campbell's advocacy was very modern. Not modern at all was his second point: "The promptness and cheerfulness with which the present taxes are paid afford the best pledges of the spirit with which the people will meet such demands as the interest and safety of the nation may require."[23] No one in the twentieth century would talk about taxes being paid with cheerfulness.

The next secretary of the treasury, Alexander J. Dallas, repeated the warning that a decline of public credit was taking place due to inadequate taxation. As he saw it, "[T]he wealth of the nation . . . remains almost untouched by the hand of government." He urged continuation and increase of the direct and internal taxes to "re-animate the confidence of the citizens" who could lend money to the government.[24] The citizens Dallas had in mind may have been in New England. When banks in that region had subscribed to only half a million dollars of a $16 million loan, Gallatin had secured the funds elsewhere but had discounted the bonds heavily. Federalists were criticizing "the war loans as a devious means of prosecuting a wicked war."[25]

The imposition of these taxes took time, and collections lagged. The internal taxes brought in $2 million in 1814 and $5 million in 1815. The direct tax brought in $2.2 million in 1814 and a like amount in 1815. Total tax collections for 1812–15 were $51 million, compared to total spending of $120 million. The public debt rose from $56 million to $127 during the war.[26]

Jefferson, home in Monticello, thought the whole system would collapse and "a tax of 3[00] or 400 millions will be levied on our citizens who had found it a work of so much time and labor to pay off a debt of 80 millions." Jefferson recommended the emission of paper money instead. Madison, however, understood that such a plan would create inflation comparable to "the career of the old Continental currency."[27]

The wartime taxing system of the Madison administration took the lessons of the Revolutionary War to heart and repeated the Federalist program of the 1790s.

In fact, they were willing to go further, for in January 1815, secretary of the treasury Dallas proposed that Congress enact an income tax and an inheritance tax. By then the war was over, and these novel taxes had to await another day.[28]

In terms of Gallatin's principles of wartime finance, the fiscal policy of the war of 1812 was a success. In 1813 the nonmilitary spending of the government was $5.6 million, including $3.6 million for interest, while revenues were $14.3 million; in 1814 that spending amount was $7 million, including $4.6 million for interest, compared to $11.2 million in revenues. In both years the government was able to cover the costs of its normal operations and the increased interest payments. The rest it was able to borrow.

The borrowing program was not a total success. Many issues of government securities had to be sold at a discount, which meant that of $55 million in face value issued, only $48 million was brought in. Part of the problem was the refusal of New England banks, especially in Boston, to purchase any of the debt. Smuggling activities in that region, especially illegal trade with British forces in Canada, had bolstered the gold holdings in that area, but little of it went to the government in loans or taxes. Many of the government bonds had to be sold for state banknotes, which were of less value than gold. As a result, the proceeds in specie of the securities sold amounted to only $28 million.

Some of this failure can be attributed to the demise of the Bank of the United States, which might have kept currency values higher in relation to gold and could have bought substantial bonds with its own notes. Instead, the government had to keep special accounts in a variety of banknotes that had no national circulation, and many state banks that had been opened eventually had to suspend payment of their notes with gold. This suspension of gold as the monetary unit made tax collections difficult.[29] A national bank could have managed the money supply with greater effectiveness.

While the record of wartime finance was thus not perfect, it was better than the experience of the Revolutionary War. Jefferson's suggestion to Madison to issue paper money was not followed.[30] Despite the fears of many members of Congress, the monetary disasters of the Revolutionary War were not repeated. The move to a new form of government under the Constitution proved its value. Armed with taxing powers that the Continental Congress lacked, the federal government was able to establish its credit sufficiently to borrow what it needed and raise enough taxes to keep its notes from depreciating. The next challenge was to complete the second part of Gallatin's plan, paying off the debt in the postwar period.

POSTWAR FINANCE

The quick and sudden ending to the War of 1812 proved a boon for the government's finances, especially due to time lags in changing policy. Madison recognized that a change of policy was in order, and, along with the peace treaty he submitted to the Senate in February 1815, he included a suggested plan for improving the military establishment and retaining direct taxes.[31] Although military spending remained well above prewar levels, it did fall from $27.7 million in 1814 to $23.5 million in 1815 and $20 million in 1816; by 1818 it was back in the normal range of $8 million.

Meanwhile, tax receipts began climbing. The internal taxes were bringing in $4.7 million a year in 1815 and $5.3 million in 1816. The collections of the direct tax still dribbled in, so even though the last levy for 1816 was reduced to $3 million, $4.4 was collected in that year, and $1.8 million in the following year, when the tax had expired. Of $12 million in direct taxes imposed on homes, land, and slaves during the war, nearly $11 million was collected, certainly a better record than the direct tax of the Federalists.[32]

Even more important, as the wartime restriction on trade ended, imports soared from $13 million in 1814 to $147 million in 1816, and with them customs receipts reached $36 million in 1816. Tax collections totaled $48 million in that year, a surplus of $17 million. The government's finances revitalized, which allowed for tinkering with taxes.

In his treaty message of 1815, Madison pointed out how much domestic manufacturing had grown during the war and reminded members of Congress that it might not be a bad idea to protect it with higher tariffs.[33] Protection of U.S. industry, the third pillar of Hamilton's system, was now actively on the agenda. The American Society for the Encouragement of Manufactures argued that England was glutting U.S. markets with manufactured goods and that protection was needed.[34]

With talk of military spending financed by internal taxes, a bank, and protectionism, Federalists had a chance to gloat. In 1816 Gouverneur Morris, for example, wrote to Rufus King that "the Party now in Power seems disposed to do all that federal men ever wished." Henry Clay even proposed reintroduction of the whiskey tax. This sentiment was not yet widely shared in Congress, however. Madison still saw a difference between the parties, even if he and his party had "become reconciled to certain measures which were prematurely urged upon us by the Federalists."[35]

In his own "Report on Finances," secretary Dallas expressed regret that it had taken so long to bring the internal taxes to bear on the government's finances and suggested that some of them not be allowed to expire. At this time Congress still followed the procedure of placing a time limit on certain, specific taxes, forcing them to be renewed. Such was the case of the doubling of the tariff rates, and Dallas urged that the higher rates be extended. He also wanted a few increases in some tariffs to offset the elimination of some internal taxes. Because the public debt had grown considerably, Dallas asked that the annual debt appropriation be increased to $10 million.[36]

The Committee of Ways and Means followed Dallas' suggestions on revising the tax system. The Congress as a whole, however, toned down the internal taxes. In the House of Representatives, Charles H. Atherton (Federalist of New Hampshire) spoke against direct taxes, calling them "the most offensive of any on the long catalogue of taxation."[37] Robert Wright (Republican of Maryland) asked for a return to the successful Jefferson policy of 1801. As for debt repayment, he went

Jefferson one better, arguing that in Washington's administration debt repayment had been planned for twenty-eight years. The speedy repayment plan of Dallas was not crucial, and taxes could be reduced. Randolph contended that the treasury proposal was a sure sign that Madison had abandoned true Republican principles. The wartime tariffs were extended to June 30, 1816.[38]

In March 1816 Congress considered again revisions to the tariff. A new attitude surfaced in opening remarks by Samuel Ingham (Republican of Pennsylvania) that the issue with respect to the changes was not revenue, which had already been provided for, but protection for manufacturing, commerce, and agriculture. Nearly $100 million had been invested in manufacturing during the embargo and war, and Congress should not let it go to waste. Thomas Telfair (Republican of Georgia) disagreed, not with protection, but with the priority. Revenue should come first, as it was in the general interest, whereas protection was for the good of special segments. Not so, countered Samuel Gold (Federalist of New York), who indicated that all manufacturers were seeking protection and read excerpts from Hamilton's *Report on Manufactures* into the record, calling him "one of the brightest stars of our political hemisphere." Protection of manufacturing was in the national interest.[39]

John C. Calhoun gave the best presentation of this national interest. In time of war the country would need manufactured goods, so their growth should be encouraged. Moreover, while agricultural productivity in the United States grew, events in Europe continued to shrink the overseas market for that output. Encouragement of manufacturing would create a domestic market for food and foster a balanced growth of agriculture and manufacturing.[40] Although he mentioned no names, Calhoun had read his Hamilton. He might also have heard from Jefferson, who, from the experience of the war, thought that U.S. independence required a stronger manufacturing sector.[41]

The preponderance of the debate focused on the merits of duties on specific items, and two examples must suffice to demonstrate the contrast in intent from earlier tariff legislation. In the first tariff of 1789 cotton manufactures were duty-free; in 1804 they carried a 17.5% duty, which was doubled to 35% during the war. The 1816 act reduced the rate to 25%. Rolled or hammered iron imports were taxed at 7.5% in 1789; that was raised to 17.5% in 1804, to 35% in 1812, and cut to 30% in 1816. Tariffs averaged 20% overall, and the law also put in a minimum tariff on cotton goods that rounded off the value of items to the highest whole number and placed a minimum value of twenty-five cents on them no matter what their cost. As a result, there was a minimum tax on cotton goods imports no matter how cheap they were.[42] The purpose of the minimum was to exclude cheap cotton goods from India, which the East India Company was using to flood world markets even to the detriment of British cotton manufactures.[43]

The Tariff Act of 1816 marked a shift in the debate over tariffs. There had always been protectionists in Congress, but they had muted their pleas due to the pressing needs of the government for revenue. The contraction in foreign trade brought about by the embargo and the war had permitted a number of industries to spring up in the United States. The return to peace brought a flood of British goods to compete with them, and budding manufacturers wanted something done by the government to help them. In response, Congress reduced the wartime rates but kept them well above their previous levels. There was more of a spirit of protection in this tariff schedule than ever before. Eventually, protectionism would help to precipitate constitutional conflict of a very serious nature between North and South.

At first glance, however, the tariff of 1816 hardly protected much. After all, imports soared in 1816, and, as noted earlier, so did customs receipts. Did not this increase in collections indicate that not much protection was being given? The tariff was enacted in April 1816, so its full effect was not felt until later. In addition, much of the importation of 1816 had to be due to pent-up demand from wartime restrictions on trade with Europe. In any event, tariff collections fell to $26 million in 1817 and $17 million in 1818, which indicates, allowing for other events, that some protection took place. Afterward they leveled off to about $20 million a year for the decade of the 1820s.[44] Revenue improved, but the tariff afforded the protection for manufacturing so near to Hamilton's heart.

Another feature of Hamilton's system was revived by the Second Bank of the United States. Secretary of the treasury Dallas had proposed the chartering of a new bank during the war to lend to the government, and in 1815 Congress had passed a bank bill. Madison, however, vetoed the bill because Congress had departed too much from the administration's recommendation.[45]

Madison accepted the constitutionality of the Bank of the United States partly because it had worked well and had been found acceptable by the country. A bill to charter the new bank that met with his approval was passed in 1816, and he signed it. The constitutionality of the Second Bank of the United States was eventually upheld by the Supreme Court in the 1819 case of *McCulloch v. Maryland*, with Chief Justice John Marshall delivering a decision that echoed Hamilton's original defense of the bank. Madison left office having resurrected many of the ideas of his old friend and enemy.

Another of Hamilton's conceptions, the sinking fund, came under scrutiny in 1817. Payment of the debt still involved the use of the sinking fund. Annual payments into the fund of $9 million had been appropriated as soon as postwar finance permitted. Now Congress had to consider Dallas' urging of an increase to $10 million. The debate in Congress expressed concern that such a high annual appropriation might require that the internal taxes be retained indefinitely,[46] much as Hamilton desired.

In its next session the members of the House of Representatives deliberated a motion to repeal all of the internal taxes. The report of the Ways and Means Committee noted that with customs receipts booming, the internal taxes had become superfluous. Opponents reminded how difficult it had been to raise the internal taxes in a timely fashion during the recent war and urged that some internal taxes be kept in place to make financing another war easier. Some of the more oppressive taxes might be repealed, but others should be kept on a standby basis. Proponents responded by pointing out that the treasury was quite filled with money and that if the taxes were kept in force, there would be a temptation to find things to spend it on. Otherwise, money would lie idle in the treasury. The bill to eliminate the internal taxes passed overwhelmingly.[47]

In assessing these arguments, both sides had valid points. The idea that taxes would be spent on wasteful projects has evolved into the modern epithet of "tax and spend," so it is fascinating that members of Congress worried about it in 1817. In terms of the need for standby taxes in the event of a war, it would be thirty years before that necessity turned up. Concern that money would lie idle in the treasury, however, was unfounded. Instead, that money would be deposited at the Second Bank of the United States, where it could be lent. Members of Congress still did not understand banks as well as Hamilton had.

While the reductions in revenue from higher tariffs and the elimination of all other taxes took place, government spending did not fall as quickly. Annual interest payments were $6–7 million in the postwar years, and Congress began providing generous military pensions. Gallatin's program of internal improvements was revived. Here again, Hamilton was being outdone, but by a new generation that included Henry Clay, John C. Calhoun, and Daniel Webster. The surplus in the budget fell to the $2–3 million per year range for the rest of the decade. Nonetheless, the public debt was reduced from $123.5 million in 1816 to $90 million by 1820.

CONCLUSION

The Jeffersonians had eliminated much of the Hamiltonian tax system. In the face of a possible war, Gallatin had proposed a plan that compromised with Hamilton's, but it had gone nowhere. Political leadership would have been necessary to accomplish it. When war came, however, resort was made to Hamiltonian policies. Internal taxes were levied, and efforts to charter the Second Bank of the United States eventually succeeded. It was perhaps not coincidental that Hamilton had whetted his political teeth during a war period. His system evolved in response to the financial stresses of the Revolutionary War and its aftermath, and he wanted it kept intact to support the military spending he felt needed to keep the United States secure in a hostile world. Only after the early disasters of the War of 1812 had Madison admitted that a low-cost government was a high-risk one when war came.[48]

With their agrarian notions of government, debt, and taxes, the Jeffersonians had dealt Hamilton's system a heavy blow, but it was not a death blow. Instead, Hamiltonianism revived and seemed to be carrying the day. It would do so for another decade, until a different form of agrarianism held sway.

NOTES

1. James Madison to Thomas Jefferson, Orange, July 19, 1786, in Banning, *Jefferson and Madison*, p. 164. See also pp. 43–44, 186–89.

2. James Madison to Thomas Jefferson, New York, February 4, 1790, in Banning, *Jefferson and Madison*, p. 173.

3. Sloan, *Principle and Interest*, p. 86.

4. Stabile and Cantor, *The Public Debt*, pp. 31–32.

5. Studenski and Kroos, *Financial History*, pp. 72–73.

6. Cited in Ibid., p. 70.

7. Dewey, *Financial History*, pp. 124–25; Studenski and Kroos, *Financial History*, pp. 70–71.

8. Albert Gallatin, *Report from the Secretary of the Treasury on the Subject of Manufactures, April 19, 1810* (Boston: Farrand, Mallory, 1810), pp. 4–26, 27.

9. Ibid., p. 29.

10. Sloan, *Principle and Interest*, p. 204.

11. "Report on the Finances, for 1811," in *Reports of the Secretary of the Treasury*, pp. 448–49.

12. Dewey, *Financial History*, pp. 128–30; Studenski and Kroos, *Financial History*, pp. 75–76.

13. Dewey, *Financial History*, pp. 122, 124–25, 141.

14. Rutland, *The Presidency of James Madison*, pp. 105–8.

15. Cited in Ibid. p. 101.

16. "Direct Taxes! Loans! Fruits of Commercial Restrictions!" Worcester, MA: Isaac Sturtevant, printer, 1812, 1-page broadside, copy in the collection of the American Antiquarian Society.

17. Dewey, *Financial History*, pp. 135–37; Studenski and Kroos, *Financial History*, pp. 76–77.

18. *History of Congress*, 12th Congress, Appendix, 1812, pp. 1280–81.

19. "Report on the Finances, for 1813," in *Reports of the Secretary of the Treasury*, p. 491.

20. Dewey, *Financial History*, pp. 131–41.

21. *Acts of Congress Relating to the Direct Tax and the Duty on Furniture and Watches*, Washington: 1815, pp. 11–12, 16–17.

22. *The System of the Laws of the United States, in Relation to Direct Taxes and Internal Duties* (Philadelphia: Jane Aitken, 1813), p. 6; Douglas B. Ball, *Financial Failure and Confederate Defeat* (Urbana: University of Illinois Press, 1991), p. 44.

23. "Report on the Finances, for 1814," in *Reports of the Secretary of the Treasury*, p. 531.

24. *Letter from the Chairman of the Ways and Means Committee to the Secretary of the Treasury on the Subject of a System of Revenue to Maintain Unimpaired the Public Credit*, Washington, DC: A. and G. Way Printers, 1814, p. 10.

25. Rutland, *The Presidency of James Madison*, p. 127.

26. Dewey, *Financial History*, pp. 131–42; Studenski and Kroos, *Financial History*, pp. 77–79.

27. Cited in Rutland, *The Presidency of James Madison*, Jefferson on p. 146 and Madison on p. 179.

28. Ratner, *Taxation and Democracy*, p. 34.

29. Studenski and Kroos, *Financial History*, pp. 77–80.

30. Rutland, *The Presidency of James Madison*, p. 146.

31. Shaw Livermore, Jr., *The Twilight of Federalism* (Princeton: Princeton University Press, 1962), p. 14.

32. Dewey, *Financial History*, pp. 140, 168–69; Studenski and Kroos, *Financial History*, p. 77.

33. Irving Brant, *James Madison: Commander in Chief, 1812–1836* (Indianapolis: Bobbs-Merrill, 1961), p. 399.

34. *Memorial of the American Society for the Encouragement of Domestic Manufactures*, January 19, 1817, copy at American Antiquarian Society.

35. Livermore, *Twilight of Federalism*, pp. 16, 56, 104.

36. "Report on the Finances, for 1815," in *History of Congress*, 13th Congress, Appendix, 1816, pp. 1602–45.

37. "Speech of Mr. Atherton in Favor of a Repeal of the Direct Tax," Washington, DC: 1816, 1-page broadside, copy in the collection of the American Antiquarian Society.

38. *History of Congress*, 14th Congress, 1st Session, 1816, pp. 517–21, 683–87, 694.

39. Ibid., pp. 1240, 1316, 1326.

40. Ibid., pp. 1330–36.

41. Thomas Jefferson, Letter dated January 9, 1816, in Frederich List, *Outlines of American Political Economy, in a Series of Letters* (Philadelphia: Samuel Parker, 1827), pp. 37–38.

42. Dewey, *Financial History*, pp. 161–65; Studenski and Kroos, *Financial History*, pp. 90–91.

43. *History of Congress*, 14th Congress, 1st Session, 1816, p. 1323.

44. Figures derived from table in Studenski and Kroos, *Financial History*, p. 92.

45. Ibid., p. 81.

46. *History of Congress*, 14th Congress, 2nd Session, 1817, p. 1032.

47. *History of Congress*, 15th Congress, 1st Session, 1817, pp. 426–43.

48. Rutland, *The Presidency of James Madison*, p. 138.

Chapter 10

AN UNPRECEDENTED SPECTACLE

In the period following the War of 1812, there was a resurgence in the elements of Hamilton's plan of economic development. Hamilton had sought to restore public credit with taxation, to maintain a sound currency through the Bank of the United States, and to support the development of manufacturing in the new nation. Regarding his espousal of banking, in the 1820s the Second Bank of the United States began operating just as he had wanted. His plan had employed tariffs both to raise revenue and to protect certain industries. His successors in the 1820s proposed a set of tariffs that were tilted more toward protectionism than had been the case in the past. They were just trying to stay within the framework for taxes and economic development that the Constitution had left them.

This agreement over Hamilton's system was sufficiently widespread that the administration of President James Monroe has become known as "the Era of Good Feelings." An editorial in the *Baltimore Federal Republican* in 1819 summed up this spirit, "The nearer the Democratic administration and party come up to the old federal principles and measures, the better they act and the more we prosper—that is the reason that everybody is contented with President Monroe's administration."[1] Monroe indicated that his support for the national bank aimed to "attach the commercial part of the community in a much greater degree to the government."[2]

This spirit was not to last, however. In a growing country dependent on foreign trade for many manufactured items, any changes in taxes would hurt some persons and regions and help others. Dispute was inevitable, as is the case with any tax policy, and the constitutional basis for protective tariffs would threaten the nation. Moreover, as the U.S. economy became more developed and complex, it soon became apparent that tax rates were not the only factor in determining how much revenue the federal government would collect. Economic conditions in general became more important as a component of public finance.

THE FIRST RECESSION

One of the costs of industrial society is the periodic recurrence of the ups and downs in economic activity known as the business cycle. In an agrarian society, changes in output usually result from climatic conditions external to the economy or from wars. Industrial economies, however, develop internal forces that lead to a downturn. For a government trying to plan a budget, the business cycle can be as troublesome as a war.

The downturn that began in 1819 demonstrates this problem quite well. As the economy went into a slump, total spending in the economy declined, and there were pockets of unemployed workers for the first time in U.S. history. The reduction in spending hit foreign trade, and the purchase of imports fell from $121 million in 1818 to $87 million in 1819 and about $60 million in 1821. As a result, customs receipts dropped from $20 million in 1819 to $15 million in 1820 and $13 million in 1821. The only other source of revenue at the time, the sale of public land, also declined from $3.3 million in 1819 to $1.6 and $1.2 million in the next two years. Budget deficits appeared in 1820 and 1821, albeit small ones of less than 10% of total spending. New loans had to be taken out, both to meet the deficit and to pay off debt that came due.[3]

This pattern of budget deficits has recurred with each recession ever since. At this time the policy to offset the deficit was to cut government spending from $21.5 million in 1819 to $15.8 million in 1820. Government spending was a small part of the total economy at that time. A good way to see this is a comparison of the government budget of about $20 million with total imports, which averaged $100 million and were a small part of the total economy. The changes in government spending would have a very small impact on the overall economy.

The spending cuts were made permanent, however. When the economy revived, tax collections increased; tariff receipts rose to $17.6 million in 1822 and $19.1 million in 1823. With government spending constantly at a lower level, budget surpluses appeared again, starting in 1822 and continuing for the rest of the decade, with the exception of 1824, which saw an extraordinary expense of $5.1 million for the purchase of Florida.[4]

THE THEORY OF PROTECTIONISM

With the government's finances back on a prudent footing, Congress embarked on a more ambitious program of protectionism with the tariffs of 1824 and 1828. While the recent economic depression had led to calls for higher tariffs to save businesses and jobs, the call for tariff revisions in 1824 was prompted by the need for additional revenue. In his "Report on Finances for 1822," Secretary of the Treasury William Crawford had suggested some tariff increases for that purpose, especially if the duties were raised on "various other articles, not in any degree connected with our domestic industry."[5] Once the discussion on tariffs was started, special interests channeled it to their own needs. Tariffs were raised on manufactured goods and raw wool. The minimum valuation on cotton was increased to thirty cents, and the practice was extended to wool. Not everyone agreed with the new course, however, and the act was weaker than its proponents wanted.[6]

The debate over the virtues of protection bred a series of conflicts that continue today. The benefits of free trade had been spelled out by Adam Smith with his perception that a person should "never attempt to make at home what it will cost him more to make than to buy."[7] In his example a tailor should not make his own shoes. This principle governed the division of labor. Suppose an individual tailor had the ability to produce shoes, but shoes take him a lot of work to make. Smith's idea was that the tailor was better off using the time spent in making shoes to produce a coat and trade it for shoes. At the same time, someone else, perhaps another tailor, would devote more time in making shoes to trade for clothes.

In this process each would specialize and become more efficient in his or her specialty. Individuals should choose the best industry to place their efforts, without government interference. Production would increase, and the price of clothes and shoes might both decline. The key was how much trade would take place, which led to Smith's maxim that the division of labor depended on the extent of the market. Before a person could specialize in shoe production, there had to be enough customers for shoes to make it worthwhile. Since restrictions on trade limited the extent of the market, they hindered specialization and the division of labor.

Smith applied this concept to trade between nations. Instead of trying to be self-sufficient, nations should also specialize. There should be a division of labor among nations, with each producing what it was best suited for. Since protectionism placed restrictions on the flow of goods, it limited this international division of labor.

The issue was not that clear-cut, however. Another English economist, David Ricardo, writing in 1818, elaborated on the theory of trade with his principle of comparative advantage. Ricardo is justly famed for his account of the theory of comparative advantage and its underpinning of international trade. Under this theory each person or country should find what it was best at, relative to all its options, and specialize.

More important, Ricardo made clear the factors that governed the choice of specialization—the resources a country had, including raw materials, labor, technology, and capital. Under this theory firms in each country put their capital into industries where it would be most effective in productivity compared to what business in other countries invested. Included in the theory was the assumption that capital and labor did not flow between countries. Ricardo thought that capital would not move across borders because capitalists would have less control over it and have to operate under unfamiliar customs. Rather, they would have "the natural disinclination which every man has to quit the country of his birth and connections." Ricardo placed great stock in the sense of community feeling of business owners and investors and called them "feelings which I should be sorry to see weakened."[8] Once England gained an edge in manufacturing, the principle of comparative advantage required that no capital, labor, or technology left England for other areas.

But this flow of resources was exactly what opponents of free trade wanted to promote. Hamilton had perceived that just because England had started out in manufacturing first, this did not mean that it would always retain an advantage in producing goods. To have believed that would have meant that the United States would have had to remain an agrarian society, and this Hamilton did not want. Besides, he recognized that England's advantage over the United States in manufacturing was partly the result of trade restrictions—the colonies had been forbidden to produce their own manufacturing industries. In fact, only after England gained superiority in manufacturing did its leaders become interested in free trade. In 1824, moreover, England did not have free trade, for there existed the Corn Laws, which were specific tariffs on the import of food items into England.

Hence, protectionists could argue, following Hamilton, that free trade would serve to make secure England's advantage in manufacturing, and England was not engaged in free trade itself. A better policy was Hamilton's protection for infant industries. Protect the growing U.S. industrial sector from English goods, and it would grow stronger and be able to gain in efficiency until it would outstrip England. A free trade policy would keep the United States in its colonial status as a producer of raw materials for English manufacturing.

This same point was made by the German economist Frederich List, whose ideas were eventually brought before the American public in a series of letters published in 1827. List maintained that in a national economy there had to be harmony among agriculture, commerce, and manufacturing. Any policy toward foreign trade had to be tempered by conditions in a particular country. The real purpose of trade was not the exchange of commodities, as Smith thought, but "to gain productive and political power" for the nation. In the case of the United States, conditions were such that, with a period of protection, within half a century, it would be able to compete with England as a power on an equal basis. A nation was only as independent as its manufacturing allowed it to be free from reliance on foreign suppliers.[9]

One obvious sticking point with this nationalist ideology was that some citizens of the United States had done well under that colonial status and were satisfied with it. The southern plantation owners had a well-established system of trade with England based on raw materials—tobacco and indigo at first, but by 1824 the all-important cotton—in return for manufactured goods, especially cheap cotton and woolen garments to clothe slaves. There were also merchants in all regions of the country who specialized in international trade, buying English goods and selling them at a profit. Protectionism would disrupt the trading system under which planters and merchants had prospered.

While the disruption that planters and merchants would face through an introduction of protection can be construed as an argument in favor of free trade, it highlights another difficulty with the theory of free trade: how well are workers and businesses able to cope with transitions in international trade? In addition to the assumption of no movement of resources, modern trade theory has indicated that a key assumption of the theory of free trade is full employment. When foreign trade disrupts domestic trade patterns, workers and businesses in industries that are undercut by foreign competitors must find something else to do. If the economy is in a condition of full employment, that transition will be easy to make—workers will readily find jobs elsewhere, and new businesses will be easy to start. When there is unemployment due to a recession, however, such transitions are less readily made. Ricardo felt that workers displaced in industries faced with competition from imports would find jobs in exporting industries. In the United States in the 1820s, the chief exporters were southern planters, hardly a source of jobs for workers in the North.

There was also the problem of revenue. As long as the tariff remained the chief source of money for the government, there were limits on protectionism. If a protective tariff worked perfectly, no items would be imported, and no tax collected. Hamilton had suggested that not everything be protected. Rather, high protective tariffs would be used to help existing industries; moderate revenue tariffs would be placed on items that were not manufactured at all in the United States. He also felt that as manufacturing in the United States grew in size and strength, it should pay its fair share by being taxed through internal taxes.

Although Ricardo's work appeared in the United States by 1819,[10] there is no evidence as to how influential he was in the tariff debates. Instead, proponents of free trade relied on Adam Smith, although they felt frustration on how readily Smith's views were ignored by their opponents. This viewpoint was expressed at the time by Condy Raguet, editor of *The Banner of the Constitution*, who wrote, "The powerful reasoning of Adam Smith . . . would have no more influence in effecting a change of the views of some we could name, than if they were the wild and silly effusions of ignorant declaimers."[11]

Despite this harsh characterization, there was a case for protection made at the time that directly challenged Adam Smith and standard economic wisdom regarding free trade. In particular, two able writers, Daniel Raymond and Mathew Carey, made a case for protectionism that indicated an implicit awareness of the crucial assumptions underlying free trade.

In 1820 Daniel Raymond wrote a primer on political economy that stated: "The doctrine, however, of buying when we can buy cheaper than we can make, as illustrated, or rather as stated without illustration, by Dr. Smith, is most erroneous and unsound." To use the individual case, Raymond said it might be better for a tailor to buy shoes instead of making them "if he can have constant employment in his own trade." If the tailor could not sell all the clothes he made, his time would be better spent in making shoes he could use than in producing clothes he could not sell. The division of labor depended on the extent of the market; unemployment limited that extent.

Raymond's argument raised the issue of how well free trade works when there was unemployment in a country, as was clearly the case when he was writing. When there was unemployment, it might be better for an employed person with a steady income to buy imported goods, but was it good for the country? Raymond thought not, asserting that "Dr. Smith's reasoning would be sound, if it was true, that national and individual interests were never opposed. Common sense, however, tells that they are often opposed." If a country had unemployment, it would be better off to put the unemployed to work making items that could be bought cheaply overseas rather than buying those items.[12] To be sure, the use of tariffs as a policy to stimulate employment can produce a round of tariff wars that totally eliminates international trade, especially if other countries also experience unemployment. Regardless, Raymond's point is well taken. When there is unemployment, the benefits of free trade are ambiguous.

The most tireless and prolific writer in favor of protection was Mathew Carey. His essays first appeared in newspapers and journals and were later published as pamphlets and collected in book form. His first aim was to fight the elimination of direct taxes that had followed the War of 1812. He considered direct taxes to be "the most equitable, economical, and beneficial mode of collecting a revenue." Since the tariff could not raise all the money for the government's needs, a direct tax was needed, and if one were placed on property, it would be heavily weighted toward the wealthy. Carey wrote, "The very rich, who now pay from 150 to 500 dollars, would have their taxes increased to from one to six thousand dollars. This would be no real evil to them."[13]

Despite his "soak the rich" rhetoric, Carey's real aim was the installation of protection. As he put it, "If there be any one truth in political economy more sacred and irrefragable than another, it is, that the prosperity of nations bears an exact proportion to the encouragement of their domestic industry." While this encouragement of industry was what Smith aimed at through his advocacy of free trade, Carey insisted, "The advocates of the system of Adam Smith ought to be satisfied with the fatal experiment we have made of it." Smith had said that workers and businesses supplanted by free trade would find other employment, but that had not happened in the United States. First of all, resources were not easily transferred from one industry to another; with the division of labor and specialization it was not easy for a tailor to suddenly become a shoemaker. Second, free trade ruined all similar industries. Manufactured imports were a general category, and if free trade ruined both the domestic shoe and tailoring industries, what was a worker to do?[14]

To support his case, Carey quoted large sections of Hamilton's *Report on Manufactures*. He also cited a letter Thomas Jefferson had written in 1816 that stated, "To be independent for the comforts of life, we must fabricate them ourselves. We must place the manufacturer by the side of the agriculturalist." This aim was so important, Carey wrote, that a good tariff was defined as one that "renders revenue subservient to the promotion of individual industry and national prosperity." According to Carey, the prosperity that had been brought by the War of 1812 was ended by the cuts in the tariff of 1816.[15]

The economic decline in the United States in the period after the War of 1812 had a lot to do with the ending of the Napoleonic Wars and the resumption of production and trade in Europe, so Carey's claim was overblown. Yet, however crude economic writers like Raymond and Carey were, they had a point. Any change in economic trade relations, such as going from free trade to protectionism or the reverse, creates winners and losers, and legislators had to balance those interests in formulating a policy.

These critiques of Adam Smith, however, overlooked his own recognition of some pitfalls of free trade and a change in any system of tariffs. Smith understood that thought had to be given as to whether or not to promote free trade "when some foreign nation restrains by high duties or prohibitions the importation of some of our manufactures into their country." When that happened, retaliatory tariffs were useful, and most countries used them.[16] He also believed that consideration must be given to the degree to which free trade should be restored when it had been disrupted for a long time. He wrote, in terms Carey should have appreciated,

Humanity may in this case require that freedom of trade should be restored only by slow gradations. . . . Were those high duties and prohibitions taken away all at once, cheaper foreign goods of the same kind might be poured so fast into the home market, as to deprive all at once many thousands of our people of their ordinary employment and means of subsistence. The disorder which this would occasion might no doubt be very considerable.

In a similar manner, the employers of those people would come under a strain. The capital they used to pay wages might employ workers in a new business, but money invested "in the instruments of trade could scarce be disposed of without considerable loss."[17] Even Smith believed that free trade had to be temporized by a concern for what happened to members of the community. The real issue was the degree to which free trade should be gradually introduced and how long it would take.

The fact that in the United States it took a long time for free trade to be instituted led Joseph Schumpeter to characterize the attitude of U.S. politicians as having "consistently supported a policy of protection" by "refusing to listen to what mere economists have to say about it."[18] As this section has indicated, there were economic arguments in support of protectionism made in the United States, and they inchoately attacked the key assumptions underlying free trade theory; they just did not follow the standard approach to free trade that Schumpeter admired. Rather, they argued, as newspaper editor Hezekiah Niles observed in 1822, that "the small advance on the duties generally proposed . . . will not be felt by the consumer, though they may sustain the producer."[19] Regardless of how widespread this argument was accepted, the economic debates over protectionism were not nearly as dramatic as the political ones.

THE POLITICS OF PROTECTIONISM

The debate over tariffs engrossed the House of Representatives for much of 1823-24. Henry Clay (Republican of Kentucky) made the development of the home market part of his "American System" and reminded that other nations protected their industries with tariffs, even England.[20] George Holcombe (of New Jersey, with no party affiliation), a proponent of protection, expanded the argument and proclaimed that the purpose of the tariff was to protect manufacturing in the United States and enable it not only to supply domestic needs, but to grab a share of the overseas market. In support of these objectives, he cited the case of England, which had followed protectionism long enough to become the most powerful nation in the world. In Spain, however, "the doctrine of the author of the Wealth of Nations, the unrestrictive system," had operated for a long time and with poor results.[21]

The economic doctrine of free trade was downplayed by proponents of the bill to raise tariffs. Rollin Carolus Mallary (of Vermont, with no party affiliation) stated quite clearly that the idea that individuals would seek their most profitable trade, considered by opponents as a natural law, was "unsound, both in theory and practice." All countries interfered in the economy to encourage certain industries.[22] Later in the debate John Tod (Democrat of Pennsylvania) would continue this refrain, asserting that "the chief effect in destroying our manufactures, and almost bringing us back into colonial bondage, was that theory of foreign speculative writers called political economy."[23]

In fact, some of them were willing to go beyond Hamilton's tenets of protection. As Holcombe pointed out, the early stages of protection aimed at protecting infant industry. Now the issue was whether or not to "sustain and extend our matured ones." The purpose of helping mature industry was to foster its ability to compete overseas. Reference was made frequently to the balance of trade and the supposition that the United States had a negative one. More was bought overseas than sold there, and this was felt to be draining the country of wealth. Protection of domestic manufacturing would reduce imports, enhance exports, and bring about a favorable balance of trade.[24]

Both sides of the debate cited Adam Smith as an authority on free trade, even as they endeavored to combat his ideas. George McDuffie (of South Carolina, with no party affiliation) argued, "I will lay down a general principle, upon the authority of Adam Smith, who, notwithstanding the terms of sweeping condemnation which have been applied to his speculations, . . . that capital and labor, if left to their direction from individual sagacity, will naturally seek, and speedily find, the most profitable employments."[25] In response to the idea that no country practiced free trade, Samuel Foot (of Connecticut, with no party affiliation) observed that England at least was "receding from the system of arbitrary dictation and restriction."[26]

In addition to the case for free trade, opponents of the tariff challenged the bill on the basis of its impact on the social fiber. Edward Tattnall (of Georgia, with no party affiliation) raised the Jeffersonian specter of a nation corrupted by manufacturing. First, he pointed out that as a nation the United States did not need to be self-sufficient. Instead, using the argument of the South, he insisted, "Let us furnish materials—let others fabricate them." There was no need for manufacturing, as those items could be traded for. Second, the spread of manufacturing meant that mill owners would become wealthy, but workers would become "more fit for the fetid atmosphere of despotism than for this free country." The outcome would be a population of wage slaves, as bad off as the real slaves of the South. Did Congress want to support a policy that produced this outcome?[27]

Opponents also broached the constitutionality of the tariff. Holcombe rested this case on the idea that the Constitution gave the federal government the power to levy taxes only to pay debt, provide defense, and promote general welfare. Nowhere did the Constitution give a power to levy taxes that would reduce revenue, which was what the protective tariff would do. John Rhea (Republican of Tennessee) added to this interpretation that if, as was stated, protection came under the power to regulate commerce, that did not imply a "power to destroy commerce with foreign nations by high duties."[28]

The idea that the high duties would eliminate foreign trade and tariff revenues was repeated by opponents. Churchill Caldom Camberleng (of New York, with no party affiliation) argued that previously the intent of tariffs was revenue, with protection only incidental. With the protective intent of this bill, "for the first time it is, with a full treasury, broadly proposed to tax the people of this country, for the said purpose of fostering a few manufactures."[29] Daniel Webster (Federalist of Massachusetts) concurred, arguing, "The power of collecting revenue by duties on imports, and the habit of the Government of collecting almost its whole revenue in that mode, will enable us, without exceeding the bounds of moderation, to give great advantages to those classes of manufacturers which we may think most useful to promote at home."[30] James Hamilton (of South Carolina, with no party affiliation) agreed with Webster and complained that proponents "had not officially consulted the Secretary of the Treasury; and a bill, either most oppressively to increase or injuriously to diminish our revenue, is about to be passed, without his public sanction."[31]

Proponents responded by pointing out that the revenue features of the bill were being retained by taxing items not produced in the United States, as Hamilton had suggested. A 10% increase was slated for silk and linens, which were not produced at all, so they would bring in more revenue. The same argument held for increases in tariffs on iron, hemp, tea, sugar, coffee, and salt. Indeed, James Buchanan (of Pennsylvania, with no party affiliation) considered the "bill as a revenue measure."[32]

Debate went on for another session of Congress, dealing primarily with the specifics of individual rates on particular items. Each section of the country had its own industry to protect, and despite the overall opposition of the South, the protective elements of the tariff were passed. Forty years later Hamilton had won another victory.

The set of policies flowing from Hamilton's *Report on Manufactures* was not easy to evaluate. Anyone could start up in a new industry and then ask for protection, and the principle could be extended to mature industry. As McDuffie pointed out, the infant industry argument was valid, but it was also the point where "the limit of the protecting system is distinctly indicated. It must be satisfactorily shown, that the protection sought is only temporary." Protected industries must eventually prove themselves by producing more cheaply than foreign ones.[33]

In addition, after the demise of Federalism, there had never been a strong sentiment for internal taxes on manufacturing to replace revenue lost from protective tariffs. The claim, instead, was that a tariff had a mix of duties, one set for revenue and one for protection. These double duties make it difficult to determine whether or not revenue was being lost. With the passage of the tariff of 1824, for example, collections fell from $19.1 million in 1823 to $17.9 million in 1824, but increased to $20.1 million in 1825 and $23.1 million in 1826.[34]

This result indicates a serious problem in economic analysis. Most economic arguments isolate a few factors for analysis by assuming that all other influences remain constant. The argument that a protective tariff will reduce tax collections thus cannot be clearly evaluated without reference to the effect that the general state of the economy might have on imports and tax collections. Imports will increase as the economy grows. This effect clouds the issue of the impact of the tariff of 1824 on tax collections. The increase of imports due to prosperity in the 1820s offset the decline that would have been anticipated from the tariff. At least that is the best educated guess economics can make, although a record of the customs receipts for each item taxed might give a clearer picture.

An effort to present such a clearer picture was provided by Hezekiah Niles, editor and publisher of *Niles' Weekly Register*, a nationally circulated newspaper. Niles estimated that the cost of protecting U.S. industry since 1790 was $120 million and that the costs of the War of 1812 should be added to that total. But Niles did not regret that cost. He wrote: "Now, though the protection of commerce has cost the people of the United States, or kept out of the treasury (according to the present wise mode of calculation), a far greater sum than I have put down,—I am prepared to say that the cost, or loss, was infinitely advantageous to the people at large."[35] Commerce had increased greatly during this period and the country had prospered.

In political terms all of the major presidential candidates running in 1824, John Quincy Adams, Henry Clay, and Andrew Jackson, were advocates of protectionism. Jackson, for example, said from his seat in the Senate, "It is my opinion therefore that a careful and judicious tariff is much wanted."[36] In the four years after the tariff of 1824, the protectionist debates intruded more forcefully into politics. The election of 1828 saw protectionism play a more important role. Again, Adams and Jackson both favored protection. Jackson, as a man of the South and dependent on holding his southern support, had to soft-pedal this protectionism among southerners without alienating voters in the Mid-Atlantic and Midwest who were protectionists. To make matters more difficult, New England was split.

These factors were understood by the partisan politicians in the Congress, as a new round of tariff legislation took place in 1828. At a later date all sides admitted that the strategy underlying the tariff of 1828 was that the Jackson forces proposed a set of tariff rates so high that they would offend New Englanders to the point that they would have to oppose them. Even President Adams might be against the bill. As Frank Taussig long ago characterized the scheme, "The Southern members openly said that they meant to make the tariff so bitter a pill that no New England member would be able to swallow it." Failure of the tariff to pass would discredit Adams without hurting Jackson.

The plan backfired, however. The bill passed in the House of Representatives, which came as no surprise. In the Senate, where the South and New England had a disproportionate number of votes, the reverse was expected. Instead, Daniel Webster, who had previously been antiprotection, switched sides and brought enough New England senators to pass the bill.[37]

As a result of these machinations, the tariff of 1828 pleased no one. It raised tariffs on a number of items, including raw materials such as molasses and certain types of hemp, for which there were no domestic substitutes. The tax on wool products was increased, but so was the minimum taxable value. Most important manufactured items saw significant new taxes. Despite this protectionist intent, customs receipts were not diminished, growing from $22.7 million in 1829 to $28.5 million in 1832. Nevertheless, the act proved so unpopular that it was referred to as "the tariff of abominations" or "the black tariff."[38]

This unpopularity notwithstanding, there was general support for tariffs. During the tariff debate, members of Congress were presented with special pleas from manufacturing groups favoring protection.[39] As one plea indicated, petitioners were "deeply impressed with the necessity of such a change in the policy of this country as shall protect the industry of its citizens . . . from the injurious interference and competition of foreign nations." Only such a change could "cause that division of labor which the welfare of the country demands."[40] Hezekiah Niles found that in the 1818 debate over tariffs, representatives from areas with a population of 5 million persons supported the tariff, while opponents represented only 3 million.[41]

Tariffs were used for revenue and protectionism in the United States for another century, and it would be hard to argue that the country was harmed by them. The United States became an industrial giant during a period of high tariffs. More germane to this book, tariff revenues were sufficient for the federal government's needs, with balanced budgets taking place in peacetime for most of the next century, when tariffs remained the most important tax.

THE JACKSONIANS

When Andrew Jackson entered office, his views on government debt and banking were so severe that even Jefferson might have found them overdone. Writing in 1824, Jackson had labeled the public debt "a national curse" and promised that if elected president, his policy would be "to pay off the national debt."[42] He also made known his opposition to the Second Bank of the United States as fiscal agent for the treasury, once—just before taking office—going so far as to tell Alexander Hamilton's son the odd notion, "Your father was not in favor of the Bank of the United States."[43] More importantly for Jackson, economic and political conditions were on his side.

The financial state of the government was in excellent condition when Jackson took over as president in 1828. The tariff of abominations of 1828 had raised the average tax rate on dutiable items to 41%. A new tariff act in 1832 reduced the rates on imports, but not by a large amount. A constitutional crisis was set off when South Carolina issued its Ordinance of Nullification, whereby it attempted to declare the tariffs of 1828 and 1832 null and void after February 1, 1833.

The constitutional issue over protective tariffs had been building throughout the 1820s. Early in the decade, the venerable John Taylor attacked a "Report of the Committee on Manufactures of the House," dated January 15, 1821, on the need for higher tariffs. He wrote, "I believe that a loss of independent internal power by our Confederate States, and an acquisition of supreme power by the Federal department . . . would finally become a tyranny." Protective tariffs were a wedge toward such a tyranny.[44]

The equally venerable James Madison, in 1828, addressed directly the constitutionality of protective tariffs, asking if the constitutional power to regulate trade included protective tariffs. In two letters that were widely circulated, Madison argued that the place to find the intent behind the Constitution was at the ratifying conventions. Since they were ambiguous on the issue of tariffs for regulating trade, Madison used legal argumentation to claim that Congress did have the power to regulate trade as long as its members were "responsible to their constituents." Free trade was a laudable ideal, but since it did not exist in the world, tariffs could regulate trade to protect infant industries and to attract foreign labor.[45]

Madison's legal theory notwithstanding, the general assembly of South Carolina in 1829 made a case that protective tariffs were not part of the intentions of the framers of the Constitution.[46] During 1832–33, the people of South Carolina held a nullification convention to state their grievances more forcefully. The members of the convention traced out the history of U.S. tariffs, indicating that they had been used primarily for revenue. After the tariff reduction of 1816, they continued, "under the pretext of imposing duties for the payment of the public debt . . . acts are passed containing provisions . . . for securing to the American manufacturers a monopoly of our own market." While the people in manufacturing gained more as producers than they lost as consumers, the reverse was true in South Carolina.[47]

More important than economic disadvantage, the tariffs represented a change in the compact among the states: "It is not merely that Congress have resorted for unwarrantable purposes to an exercise of powers granted them by the Constitution; but that they have usurped a power not granted." This usurpation would "reduce the Constitution to a dead letter." Since Congress had no power to use a tax to regulate trade, South Carolina had a right to nullify the law underpinning the tax.[48]

To make their case, members of the convention offered a direct address to the country. In it they declared that the tariffs of 1828 and 1832, by "altering and amending the several acts imposing duties on imports, are unconstitutional, and therefore, void and of no binding force within the limits of this state." They then stated their aim. Nullification would "produce a general dissolution of the union," and "the protecting system . . . would be utterly overthrown and demolished." Since the decline of the union and the elimination of the entire protective system that went with it would ruin the economy of the North, adherents of protection should think twice before acting further.[49]

Some adherents of protection did think twice, but only to make their case stronger. Mathew Carey opposed the nullifiers as revolutionaries and insisted that the tariffs had not been injurious to South Carolina, regardless of how its people felt.[50] Carey also argued that tariff reduction in 1816 had forced manufacturers into agriculture, depressing prices and incomes, and that the same would happen if tariffs were reduced at South Carolina's request. Instead, he predicted that the union would be dissolved on January 1, 1833, and wrote an appropriate epitaph.[51] Although not a friend of protectionism and an advocate of direct taxes as opposed to tariffs, John C. Calhoun pointed out to his fellow South Carolinians that protection of cotton manufacturers in the United States would increase the demand for cotton and keep prices of raw cotton higher in Europe. On this basis, the benefits of protection outweighed the costs "that have been charged to the account of the tariff."[52]

President Jackson had the better argument. He countered the nullification movement by taking a forceful stand on enforcing the Constitution as the unbreakable law of the land and threatening military action. South Carolina backed off its claims. It also helped when Congress passed a compromise tariff in 1833, reducing the existing rates.

THE DECLINE OF HAMILTON'S SYSTEM

In the 1830s there was a boom in the sale of public land. The proceeds from those sales and the revenue from the high tariffs produced large surpluses for the treasury. Annual federal revenue doubled during the Jackson administration, from $25 million to $50 million. As an opponent of Hamilton's view on government debt, Jackson had once proclaimed, "I am one of those who do not believe a national debt is a national blessing."[53] In 1835 the $17.9 million budget surplus was greater than total government expenses for the year; the next year the surplus reached $20.4 million. By January 1835, for the first and only time, all of the government's interest-bearing debt was paid off. Secretary of the treasury Levi Woodbury enthusiastically announced, "An unprecedented spectacle is thus presented to the world, of a Government . . . virtually without any debt."[54]

To diminish the surplus there needed to be a reduction in taxes, but the compromise that had been reached over the tariff in 1833 would not allow for any further tinkering with tax policy. Expenditures for internal improvements such as Hamilton or Gallatin would have favored could have been increased, but Jackson was opposed to these, as indicated by his 1830 veto of government funding of the Maysville Road. Secretary of the Treasury Levi Woodbury thought the surplus should be maintained as a fund to meet future deficits, but Congress decided to distribute the surplus to the states, many of which were heavily in debt at the time. As a result, in the early months of 1837 a total of $28 million of the surplus was lent to the states, with no repayment expected.

This movement of funds from the federal government to the states was directly opposite to what Hamilton would have wanted. Jackson took another step away from the Hamiltonianism of the 1820s when the recharter of the Second Bank of the United States had to be resolved. The debate itself took place at several levels. At a legal level, there was still some question in many minds about the constitutionality of the Second Bank of the United States. Jackson noted, for example, "Ever since I read the history of the South Sea Bubble, I have been afraid of banks. I have read the opinion of John Marshall . . . and could not agree with him."[55] Jackson's distrust of banks could have come from financial difficulties he had experienced in his youth. Here again an agrarian mistrust of commercial attitudes countered what good the Second Bank of the United States might have done for the economy.

It had done some good. In terms of economics, the Second Bank of the United States had taken on more and more of the role of a central bank. It alone through its branches had a national network of contacts with state banks; due to its large reserves, on its own account and as agent for the government, it had the wherewithal to keep a check on state banks. By presenting the circulating notes of smaller banks for payment or by holding them in its vault, the Second Bank of the United States had an influence on the supply of paper money that Hume would have found admirable. As secretary of the treasury Richard Rush noted in his annual report for 1828, the Second Bank of the United States' expansion and contraction of its notes in response to the needs of the economy made it "the instrument alone by which Congress can effectively regulate the currency of the nation."[56]

The assistance of the Second Bank of the United States in avoiding an undue influence of treasury actions on the money markets was well known. In his message to Congress in 1829, Jackson himself observed that in a recent payment of the public debt, "It was apprehended that the sudden withdrawal of so large a fund from the banks in which it was deposited, might cause much injury to the interests dependent on bank accommodations. But this evil was wholly averted by an early anticipation of it at the Treasury, aided by the judicious arrangements of the officers of the bank of the United States."[57]

In recognition of this service, the recharter application for the Second Bank of the United States was approved by both houses of Congress (by 28 to 20 in the Senate and by 107 to 85 in the House of Representatives). On July 10, 1832, however, Jackson vetoed this approval, and the Second Bank of the United States could not secure sufficient votes to override the veto.[58]

On September 18, 1833, Jackson announced a policy of withdrawing government funds from the Second Bank of the United States. Starting in October 1833, the treasury began depositing new government revenues in state banks, the so-called pet banks, while paying expenditures from funds in the Second Bank of the United States. It appeared that the government could function without the Second Bank of the United States, but appearances soon proved to be wrong.

Under provisions of the Deposit Act of 1836, on July 11, 1836, Jackson issued the executive order known as the Specie Circular, which stated that only specie would be used for buying plots of public land in excess of 320 acres. The Specie

Circular might not have caused a problem for banks, but taken in combination with the closing of the Second Bank of the United States and the flow of funds to and from state banks as part of the distribution of the surplus to the states, there were just too many shocks for the banking system to cope with. The depository banks had only $15.5 million in specie reserves compared with $45 million in government deposits.[59] International outflows of specie were also a problem at this time. Many banks had to suspend payment in specie, and the resulting panic brought about a recession in 1837.

The decline in government revenue caused by the depression of 1837 turned the recent budget surpluses back into a deficit; the last distribution of the surplus to the states had to be canceled, and the treasury issued almost $20 million in securities during 1837-39. Because state banks that had suspended specie payment were prohibited from acting as government depositories, federal revenue agents were forced to store funds in the mint or temporarily in strongboxes and vaults. By then, Jackson was in retirement, and the increase in the public debt came during the administration of his successor, Martin Van Buren.

CONCLUSION

The period after the War of 1812 saw a resurgence of Hamilton's thinking in the form of a revival of a national bank and in a subtle transition whereby tariffs were tilted toward protection and away from revenue. In the former case, the Second Bank of the United States functioned well in managing the supply of money and credit, but there was still a legitimate concern over giving a private bank that much power. Regarding tariffs, it is easy to overestimate how protective they really were. Tariff revenue did rise during this period, although the selective use of some tariffs for revenue and others for protection might have contributed to this rise. That was surely the aim of tariff policy.

The period ended with the government out of debt and with the country rid of the Second Bank of the United States, all the work of Andrew Jackson. His success in these accomplishments must be weighed against the costs. In his message vetoing the bank's rechartering, Jackson challenged the bank because of its power and questionable constitutionality. Both arguments were overdone, especially the constitutional issue. He also argued that since the public debt was being paid off, there was no longer a need for a national bank to help manage and administer it. Here Jackson was on solid logical ground. There was only one problem: what would happen if the government had to go back into debt?

Despite Jackson's optimism about the government's being able to stay out of debt, within a year of his departure it had to begin borrowing again. It then faced a problem of how to manage that debt without an institution comparable to the Second Bank of the United States. Hamiltonianism had been defeated; there were no central bank, no internal taxes, a small public debt, and a minimal amount of protectionism and internal improvements. The agrarian attitude toward banks, debt, and taxes had prevailed, and it would be nearly a century before a federal financial policy comparable to what Hamilton had envisaged would emerge again, except during a war.

NOTES

1. Harry Ammon, *James Monroe: The Quest for National Identity* (New York: McGraw-Hill, 1971), p. 378.

2. Ibid., p. 371.

3. Dewey, *Financial History*, pp. 165–67; Studenski and Kroos, *Financial History*, pp. 92–94.

4. Studenski and Kroos, *Financial History*, pp. 92–93.

5. "Report on the Finances, for 1822," *History of Congress*, 17th Congress, 2d Session, 1822, p. 456.

6. Dewey, *Financial History*, pp. 173–76.

7. Smith, *Wealth*, vol. 1, p. 478. Smith's views on free trade, summarized in this section, are presented on pp. 474–95.

8. David Ricardo, *The Principles of Political Economy and Taxation* (London: Dent (Everyman's Library), 1976), p. 83.

9. List, *Outlines of American Political Economy*, 1827, pp. 7, 10–12, 18, 33.

10. David Ricardo, *Principles of Political Economy and Taxation*, 1st American ed. (Georgetown, DC: Joseph Milligan, 1819).

11. Condy Raguet, "The Principles of Free Trade," *The Banner of the Constitution*, January 13 and February 20, 1830, excerpted in George Rogers Taylor, *The Great Tariff Debate, 1820–1830* (Boston: D.C. Heath, 1953), p. 52.

12. David Raymond, *Thoughts on Political Economy* (Baltimore: Fielding Lucas, Jr., 1820), excerpted in Taylor, *The Great Tariff Debate*, pp. 65–67.

13. Mathew Carey, *A Defence of Direct Taxes and of Protective Duties* (Philadelphia: U. Hunt, 1822).

14. Mathew Carey, *Essays on Political Economy* (Philadelphia: H. C. Carey and I. Lea, 1822), pp. 9, 14, 27–29.

15. Ibid., pp. 100–126, 277, 296–97.

16. Smith, *Wealth*, vol. 1, p. 489.

17. Ibid., pp. 491, 494.

18. Cited in Stanley Lebergott, *The Americans: An Economic Record* (New York: W. W. Norton, 1984), pp. 139–40.

19. Hezekiah Niles, "The Rights of Men and Things," from the *Niles' Weekly Register*, February 1, 1822, reprinted as a pamphlet by the *Delaware Gazette*, 1823, p. 1.

20. Henry Clay, Speech of March 31, 1824, in Taylor, *The Great Tariff Debate*, pp. 5–9.

21. *History of Congress*, 17th Congress, 1st Session, 1823, pp. 739–42.

22. Ibid., p. 772.

23. *History of Congress*, 18th Congress, 1st Session, 1824, p. 1474.

24. *History of Congress*, 17th Congress, 1st Session, 1823, pp. 744, 900.

25. George McDuffie, Speech of April 16, 1824, in Taylor, *The Great Tariff Debate*, p. 36.

26. Samuel A. Foot, Speech of April 12, 1824, in Taylor, *The Great Tariff Debate*, p. 31.

27. *History of Congress*, 17th Congress, 1st Session, 1823, pp. 751–53.

28. Ibid., pp. 759–60, 783–86.

29. Ibid., pp. 760–61.

30. Daniel Webster, Speech of April 2, 1824, in Taylor, *The Great Tariff Debate*, p. 19.

31. James Hamilton, Speech of April 6, 1824, in Taylor, *The Great Tariff Debate*, p. 24.

32. *History of Congress*, 17th Congress, 1st Session, 1823, pp. 782, 898.

33. George McDuffie, Speech of April 16, 1824, in Taylor, *The Great Tariff Debate*, p. 36.

34. Studenski and Kroos, *Financial History*, p. 92.

35. Hezekiah Niles, "The Prohibitory System," *Niles' Weekly Register*, April 19, 1823, in Taylor, *The Great Tariff Debate*, pp. 47–48.

36. Cited in D. G. Harriman, "The Benefits of Protection," in Taylor, *The Great Tariff Debate*, p. 79.

37. F. W. Taussig, *The Tariff History of the United States*, 4th ed. (New York: G. P. Putnam's Sons, 1892), pp. 84–102.

38. Dewey, *Financial History*, pp. 176–81; Studenski and Kroos, *Financial History*, p. 100.

39. *Memorial of the American Society for the Encouragement of Domestic Manufactures, January 19, 1822* (Washington, DC: Gales and Seaton, 1822). For an opposing viewpoint, see *Memorial of the Chamber of Commerce of New York, Remonstrating against the Passage of the Bill to Amend the Several Acts for Imposing Duties on Imports* (Washington, DC: Gales and Seaton, 1824).

40. *Memorial of the National Institution for the Promotion of Industry*, January 4, 1821 (Washington, DC: Gales and Seaton, 1821), p. 3.

41. Niles, "The Rights of Men and Things," p. 8.

42. Savage, *Balanced Budgets*, p. 104.

43. Robert Remini, *Andrew Jackson and the Bank War* (New York: W. W. Norton, 1967), p. 46.

44. John Taylor, *Tyranny Unmasked* (Washington, DC: Davis and Force, 1822), pp. ii–iv.

45. James Madison, *Letters on the Constitutionality of the Power in Congress to Impose a Tariff for the Protection of Manufactures* (Washington, DC: S.C. Ustrick, 1828), Letter One, September 18, 1828, p. 7, and Letter Two, October 30, 1828, p. 172.

46. *Protest of the Legislature of South Carolina, Against the System of Protecting Duties, Adopted by the Federal Government* (Washington, DC: Duff Green, 1829), pp. 1–2.

47. *The Report, Ordinance, and Addresses of the Convention of the People of South Carolina, Adopted November 24, 1832* (Columbia, SC: A. S. Johnston, 1832), pp. 3–7.

48. Ibid., pp. 8–11.

49. *Address to the People of the United States by the Convention of the People of South Carolina* (Columbia, SC: A. S. Johnston, 1832), pp. 3–4.

50. Mathew Carey, *Essay on the Dissolution of the Union* (Philadelphia: L. Johnson, 1832), pp. 23–27.

51. Mathew Carey, *Epitaph* (Philadelphia: no publisher, February 22, 1832), broadside of 4 pages.

52. John C. Calhoun, *Mr. Calhoun's Defence of the Tariff and Internal Improvement*, pamphlet (Philadelphia: no publisher, 1831 or 1832), p. 2.

53. Arthur M. Schlesinger, Jr., *The Age of Jackson* (Boston: Little, Brown, 1950), p. 36.

54. Secretary of the Treasury, *Annual Report* (1835), p. 643.

55. Hammond, *Banks and Politics*, p. 373.

56. Timberlake, *The Origins of Central Banking*, pp. 30–31.

57. Hammond, *Banks and Politics*, p. 375.

58. Schlesinger, *The Age of Jackson*, pp. 88–90.
59. Timberlake, *Origins of Central Banking*, pp. 50–58.

Epilogue: As Sure as Debt and Taxes

When the leaders of the colonies that became the United States declared their independence from England, they faced a series of challenges that had to be met to make their declaration succeed. None of those challenges were more daunting than that posed in the area of public finance. Could they do a better job than the English in getting resources from their citizenry? There were two questions involved in defining that challenge. Could they raise enough money to pay for the military services necessary for achieving independence? Could that "enough" be raised effectively?

The first question was answered in a clearly positive fashion. The patriots fought a long, hard war against a well-organized and well-funded British army and won their independence; the patriots' armies had enough resources to meet their needs, if barely. The second question, however, was more problematic. The U.S. war effort was financed by the printing of money and by debt. When it came time to levy taxes to retire that money and debt, U.S. leaders fell short. The federal government under the Articles of Confederation relied on the states for its finances, and the states did not supply the needed funds.

WAR, DEBT, AND TAXES

For over a decade, leaders in the new nation debated over what to do to put the national government's finances in order. Several plans were set forth by the Congress for raising taxes from the states in amounts sufficient to call in the paper money and take care of the debt used to pay for the War of Independence. The states would not cooperate in any of these plans; nor would they grant the federal government the minimal taxing power of a national system of tariffs on imports.

With the passage of the Constitution, the relationship between the federal government and the states changed, especially in the area of public finance. By design, the Constitution ended the practice of using paper money for public finance, at both the national and state level. Public finance would employ debt and taxes alone. There were limits placed on the taxing power of the federal government by the Constitution, but they were designed to appease slave owners—not to be in accord with principles of public finance. In the ratifying conventions of the states, Anti-Federalists tried unsuccessfully to establish additional restrictions on the power to tax.

In the first period of Federalist governance a set of tariffs was put in place, but the debt was not reduced. Nevertheless, Federalist policies did initiate a debt management program of establishing public credit. The methods of public finance used in this period were in line with the commercial attitude held by Federalist leaders such as Washington and Hamilton. When the tariff proved inadequate to balance the budget, Federalists expanded the tax base with internal taxes such as the whiskey tax, the carriage tax, and the house tax. The only problem was that the system of public finance they employed, with the aim of accustoming the citizenry to pay taxes, proved unpopular. Still, the financial system Hamilton put together, combining debt service, broad-based taxes, and a national bank, was pathbreaking.

It also raised several constitutional issues. What was a direct tax? Did the government have the power to charter a national bank? Could the law of the land be enforced throughout the land? All these questions were arguable. Resolution of them was necessary for the United States to become the commercial nation it now is. Although the Federalists won the arguments in the period under study in this book, they ultimately were voted out of office as a result. Nevertheless, they made taxation acceptable enough to put the government's finances on a sound basis. Given how far they had to come from the edge of bankruptcy on which the government remained for most of the previous decade, what they did in a short period was quite an accomplishment.

So, too, was the financing package put together by Jefferson and the agrarian approach. The Jeffersonians had a policy of reduced government spending and significant debt reduction, as befits agrarians. Had the Napoleonic Wars not spilled over into the New World, Jefferson would have succeeded in his goal of eliminating the public debt of the United States. Ultimately, under Jackson, the debt was paid. To be sure, there was more than a little luck in the form of a robust economy involved with this triumph of Jacksonian public finance, and the period of a debt-free government was very short.

The debt reduction programs of the agrarians had two important elements: tax reform that replaced the unpopular internal taxes with offsetting increases in tariffs and reduction of federal government spending. Jefferson eliminated internal taxes but increased tariff rates, with a result that the federal government collected more money in taxes during his administration than it had under the Federalists. This increase in revenue, when combined with spending cuts, made debt reduction easy.

The same program took place in the 1820s, and Jackson was astute to take advantage of it during his years in office to pay off the public debt.

One advantage available to Jefferson was that the Federalists had cleared a path for him. Before the Constitution, imposition of a tariff of only 5% had proved impossible. After a decade of whiskey taxes, carriage taxes, window taxes, and stamp taxes, the 15% average tariffs instituted under Jefferson seemed reasonable. Another advantage he had was that the area where he cut spending, national defense, was not thought to be important. Again, it helped that the Federalists had led a military buildup. The cuts in spending did not eliminate the army and navy; they only reduced them heavily.

During this period, two changes in federal finance are important to note. First, a transition took place from a system of money and debt, to a system of debt and taxes, both tariffs and internal taxes; that was the achievement of the Federalists. Second, there was a transition to a tax system based completely on tariffs and debt reduction in peacetime, as supplemented by internal taxes and debt during wars. This system was accomplished when, during the War of 1812, Jeffersonians recognized that war finance required a compromise with the Hamiltonian system.

This blending of both commercial and agrarian attitudes set a pattern that continued unabated. All that the nationalist members of Congress under the Articles of Confederation had wanted was a small tariff as a secure source of revenue. What they got was a tax system that worked well for over a century and a half. Wars would be financed on credit, and the debt reduced during peace. The pattern of war, debt, and taxes lasted until the 1980s; up to then, major increases in the public debt took place only during wars. While the methods for handling public finance would evolve, the overall system contained all three of the elements of Hamilton's original plans for money, debt and taxes, as the following brief review of the history of U.S. public finance shows.[1]

TAXES: A CENTURY OF TARIFFS

For nearly a century, the keystone of that system of public finance would be the tariff. Tariffs worked effectively as the main source of revenue, because they were a hidden tax and a voluntary tax. Consumers of imports could never be sure how much tax they were paying, and if tariffs made the prices of imports too high, consumers could purchase other items that were not taxed. Few persons objected to tariffs as a source of revenue, although there were heated debates over their use for protection. Regardless, because of the element of protection included in tariffs, there was additional support for their use. From the War of 1812 to the Civil War, tariff collections were the overwhelming source of federal government revenue. In the period after the Civil War, they remained the largest source of federal finance. Not until World War I did internal taxes replace tariffs as the primary source of government tax collections.

The first episode that tested the system of public finance after Jackson took place during the two-year Mexican War, started in 1846. To help pay for the war, taxes were raised by $15 million; treasury secretary Robert J. Walker judiciously adjusted the tariff structure to increase some rates where there was no domestic production and reduce others, and more revenue was raised. Because it was not a long, all-out war, the financing of the Mexican campaign proved easy to handle.

The real challenge came with the Civil War. A watershed in so many ways, this war brought about significant changes in public finance. Taxes contributed about half a billion dollars to the federal government's finances during the war. With tariffs unable to contribute more to government revenue than their $60 million annually of the previous decade, extensive internal taxes and an income tax were levied during the war. The income tax, passed on August 5, 1861, exempted the first $600 of income and was 3% on income between $600 and $10,000 and 5% on income above $10,000.[2] After the war, the income tax was repealed, but internal taxes remained as a supplement to tariffs. When the income tax was revived, as part of a program of tariff reduction, the Supreme Court, in a 5 to 4 vote in 1894, determined that the income tax was a direct tax under the Constitution. Since income was not distributed among the states in the same proportion as population, this decision made use of the income tax impossible. Tariffs remained the major revenue source for fifty years after the Civil War.

When World War I came, as had been the case in the past, its costs were too great for tariffs to carry the burden, especially after the tariff reductions that had taken place by the Underwood tariff of 1913. Internal taxes had been used since the Civil War, chiefly taxes on alcoholic beverages; in 1912 this later version of Hamilton's whiskey tax constituted 68% of internal tax collections. By then, however, the Sixteenth Amendment to the Constitution had been passed to make an income tax constitutional, and this new tax became a bulwark of government finance during World War I. In 1917 the federal government collected $800 million in income tax from 780,000 taxpayers. By the next year, 6 million taxpayers filed income tax returns, bringing in $3.7 billion. Taxes covered about one-third of the costs of the war. During World War II the federal government raised the income tax rates to very high levels and instituted a series of new taxes. The income tax has been the biggest contributor of federal government tax revenue ever since.

DEBT: A PATTERN OF RISE AND FALL

Despite the use of taxes, the federal government would never be out of debt after 1836. Instead, it used debt to finance its wars. As a result, there developed a pattern of a growing debt during wars and diminishment of the debt in the postwar period. Two consequences followed from this pattern, however. With every experience of war, the size of the federal government in terms of its budget was never restored to prewar levels, and while it was reduced, the public debt never returned to its prewar level.

The Mexican War, for example, added $49 million to the public debt; by 1857, the debt had been reduced to $28.7 million. In 1860, on the eve of the Civil War, the public debt of $64.8 million was barely larger than the federal government's annual budget of $63.1 million. By the end of the war, the public debt would total $2.2 billion, and interest payments alone totaled $77.4 million, more than the prewar budget. In 1899 the public debt stood at $1.9 billion, barely a reduction from the level of 1865. The public debt was being managed but not reduced. Few political leaders spoke as loudly as Jefferson and Jackson had about paying off the public debt.

Over the course of this century, the public debt has crept upward, with major increases during war and modest reductions after. In 1919, at the end of World War I, the public debt stood at $25 billion. Government budget surpluses during the 1920s, helped by increases in tariffs, reduced that debt to $17 billion. Although it does not seem as apparent, the same pattern of debt increase and then reduction held for World War II. The war was financed by borrowing about $190 billion. In the postwar years, the debt was reduced slightly, remaining at about $250 billion during the remainder of the 1940s. Although it approached $1 trillion by 1980, the public debt declined as a percentage of gross domestic product; adjusted for inflation, it remained at its 1940s level. This was a pattern not unlike that of the past.

MONEY: A TOOL OF LAST RESORT

When Andrew Jackson vetoed the bill renewing the charter of the Second Bank of the United States, his action denied the federal government an important way to finance its needs. A bank with the scale and scope of either of the Banks of the United States could marshal vast resources in terms of banknotes and use them to purchase government securities. During the Civil War, this lack of a reliable source of finance was overcome in several ways.

First, the federal government, with passage of the Legal Tender Act of 1862, resorted to the printing of money, the greenbacks, and a total of $450 million of these paper dollars was put into circulation. This issue of paper money contributed to the 80% inflation during the war, but that was not an excessive growth in prices. In the Confederate states, where paper money was the chief source of finance, prices rose by 9,000%.[3] After the war, Congress set aside tax revenues to redeem the greenbacks in gold. As president, Abraham Lincoln had fretted over the constitutionality of the issuance of paper money of his administration. In a series of close votes in several cases in the postwar era, the Supreme Court upheld Congress' authority to issue paper money and declare it legal tender.

Second, without a national bank such as the Bank of the United States to help manage the sale of government securities, the federal government initially resorted to private stockbrokers such as Jay Cooke. Then Congress gave itself the power to charter national banks under the National Bank Act of 1863; notes issued by national banks had to be backed by government securities, however, so national banks, perhaps reluctantly, purchased $300 million in government bonds. The end result was an adjunct to the system of finance comparable to, though more complex than, what the Bank of the United States might have accomplished. In the postwar era, however, the treasury often piled up reserves of gold in anticipation of the redemption of debt, with no method available to recirculate the gold into the economy.

In 1912 Congress finally solved the dilemma of how to secure the services of a national bank by creating the Federal Reserve System as an independent quasi-government agency, sealed off from congressional and presidential influence in day-to-day operations. The Federal Reserve was too new to be very helpful in financing World War I. In the 1930s, Congress tightened the seal between the federal government and the Federal Reserve by prohibiting the Federal Reserve from purchasing government securities directly. Instead, the Federal Reserve could purchase government securities from banks and individuals in what are called open market operations. In this way, federal government control over the printing of money was disconnected. During World War II the Federal Reserve very successfully kept interest rates low with open market operations, through which it purchased government securities from banks and the public. This policy meant that paper money was also used to finance the war, and it has been estimated that this method paid for about 21% of the war and caused an inflation tax of 5%.[4] Money was used as a tool of public finance, but the difference from the Revolutionary War, where paper money accounted for 80% of spending and produced an inflation tax of several hundred percent, was significant. Since World War II, the Federal Reserve has been very cautious about helping the federal government out with an obliging open market policy; money has remained a tool of last resort in public finance.

THE CURRENT ERA: DEBT WITHOUT WAR

In the period after World War II, it is important to note, another transition in taxation has taken place. The federal government has become reliant on personal and corporate income taxes for most of its revenue. A problem with the income tax, however, is that it is a direct tax in the sense that the taxpayer pays the tax directly to the federal government. Whereas the tariff had remained hidden and voluntary, the income tax being paid by an individual taxpayer was obvious and unavoidable. The transition was necessary, however, because federal government spending levels had become too high for tariffs to be a major source of revenue. Indeed, they would have to be so high that it would be a sure case of how "in the arithmetic of the customs two and two, instead of making four, make some times only one."

The income tax has proved unusually unpopular, as is evinced by how successfully Ronald Reagan attacked it in the 1980s. Reagan and his followers translated Swift's maxim into the supply-side notion that in the arithmetic of the income tax, higher rates could produce lower tax collections. If income tax rates became too high, taxpayers might refuse to work and instead accept lower incomes, resulting in slower economic growth and lagging tax collections. If income tax rates were cut, they argued, the economy would grow rapidly, and tax revenues would rise. Income tax rates were cut under this supply-side plan, but with no tax increases in other areas and no cuts in federal government spending, the public debt soared. If we were to look at a graph of the growth of the public debt since the beginning of the country, the 1980s would look like a period of war, not as large as World War II but large enough. With the Federal Reserve less willing to help fund this debt through open market operations, interest rates, adjusted for inflation, have remained at historically high levels, creating a hidden cost to taxpayers.

Three differences set this period apart from previous eras of debt increases: (1) there was not a war (only a cynic would refer to the war on high taxes); (2) budget deficits were large, and the debt grew even during periods of prosperity; and (3) the growth in debt has continued for fifteen years, longer than for any war. As a result, despite increases in taxes in the early 1990s, the public debt reached $5.5 trillion in February 1998. The question yet to be answered is whether the old pattern of debt reduction after a large buildup will be restored.

One potential solution to this debt buildup receiving a great deal of attention is an amendment to the Constitution requiring the Federal government to have balanced budgets except for emergencies. Given how difficult it would be to determine an emergency, however, this approach remains more of a gimmick than a policy. Advocates of the balanced budget have not been forthcoming in detailing how they would balance the budget once the amendment was passed.

Another approach to ending the period of federal government budget deficits would be to change to a new tax system. The most promising new system that has been put forth has been a consumption tax; instead of taxing the income that is earned, the federal government would tax that income only when it was spent. While this system would not be as hidden as the tariff, it would have the advantage of the tariff (and excise taxes) of being voluntary. Individuals who wanted to avoid paying the tax could cut back on their consumption. A consumption tax that would raise enough revenue for the federal government's needs must be fairly high, however. The tax forms whereby taxpayers calculated and justified the amount they spent on consumption (or how much they had saved) would be an added complication to an already complex tax code. Another tax system, the value added tax, would place taxes on products at each stage of production. This system would be more hidden than the income tax or a consumption tax, but it would have to be very high to replace either of them.

Regardless of the costs and benefits of any new system of taxation, there has not yet been enough pressure to foster change. As this is being written, February 1998, the government's budget for fiscal year 1998 shows a projected surplus. In addition, President Bill Clinton and the Republican Congress have put into law a program of modest tax cuts and reductions in government spending that projects a balanced federal government budget by the year 2002. Whether or not the program will be successful is a question for the future, but it would be wise to remain skeptical, as no one seems willing to tackle the really tough issues. Too much of the federal government's budget, the parts earmarked for Medicare and Social Security, are beyond the control of budget cutting efforts. Too little of the public seems willing to pay taxes for these popular programs. As a result, the plan relies heavily on the continuation of prosperity. The battle of the budget goes on, but the efforts of the leaders in the fight seem diminutive compared to those of the leaders of the constitutional era.

One of the highlights of this study has been a recognition of the courage and vision showed by Hamilton and the Federalists in building a solid tax base for the new government. They perceived that promoting the general welfare required that the new nation pay its debt and were responsible enough to want to collect taxes from a grudging citizenry to at least manage that debt. It helped that they had a leader as popular as Washington, but they were willing, whether consciously or not, to sacrifice that popularity to the greater good of having the federal government meet its financial obligations. No leader today would ride at the head of an army sent out to punish tax avoiders, as Washington and Hamilton did. Can anyone imagine a U.S. president and his secretary of the treasury working alongside of Internal Revenue Service agents in a symbolic gesture to make the point that taxes would be collected?

In the early days of the country, the individual states under the Articles of Confederation had all of the benefits of a federal government but were not willing to pay for them. As long as one or more of them indicated an unwillingness to pay taxes, it was not to be expected that the others would pay. Hamilton and Madison both understood that, and in their hands the Constitution became a device for transferring that tax liability from the states to their citizens. When those citizens are unwilling to pay their share of taxes and give vocal expressions of that unwillingness, it is not to be expected that taxes will ever be popular.

But if taxes remain unpopular, and spending programs remain popular, there is one thing for certain. Debt will remain the chosen form of public finance.

NOTES

1. The following review of the history of U.S. public finance in this Epilogue is based on Stabile and Cantor, *The Public Debt*, pp. 44–45, 51–68, 78–83, 92–100, except where otherwise noted.

2. James M. McPherson, *Battle Cry of Freedom: The Civil War Era* (New York: Ballantine Books, 1988), p. 448.

3. Ibid., p. 447. For a complete study of Confederate finance, see Ball, *Financial Failure and Confederate Defeat*.

4. Milton Friedman and Anna Schwartz, *A Monetary History of the United States* (Princeton, NJ: Princeton University Press, 1963), p. 571.

BIBLIOGRAPHY

Acts of Congress Relating to the Direct Tax and the Duty on Furniture and Watches. Washington, DC, 1815.

"Address." *Gazette of the United States,* December 1794.

Address and Recommendations to the States by the United States in Congress Assembled. Copy in collection of American Antiquarian Society. Richmond, 1783.

Address to the People of the United States by the Convention of the People of South Carolina. Columbia, SC: A. S. Johnston, 1832.

"Alexandria." *Gazette of the United States,* September 1794.

Ammon, Harry. *James Monroe: The Quest for National Identity.* New York: McGraw-Hill, 1971.

Annual Report. Secretary of the Treasury, 1835.

Ball, Douglas B. *Financial Failure and Confederate Defeat.* Urbana: University of Illinois Press, 1991.

"Baltimore." *Gazette of the United States,* October 1794.

Banning, Lance. *Jefferson and Madison: Three Conversations from the Founding.* Madison, WI: Madison House, 1995.

———. *The Sacred Fire of Liberty: James Madison and the Founding of the Federal Republic.* Ithaca, NY: Cornell University Press, 1995.

Baumann, Roland M. "Philadelphia's Manufacturers and the Excise Tax of 1794: The Forging of the Jeffersonian Coalition." In Steven R. Boyd, ed., *The Whiskey Rebellion: Past and Present Perspectives.* Westport, CT: Greenwood Press, 1985.

Beard, Charles A. *An Economic Interpretation of the Constitution of the United States.* New York: Macmillan, 1960.

Bishop, Abraham. "National Debt, from the Appendix of Mr. Abraham Bishop's celebrated Oration on Political Delusion." *The Political Magazine and Miscellaneous Repository* (Ballston, NY) 1 (November 1820).

"The Blessings of the New Government." *Philadelphia Independent Gazetteer.* In John P. Kaminski and Gaspare J. Saladino, eds., *The Documentary History of the Ratification of the Constitution.* Madison: State Historical Society of Wisconsin, 1981.

Bowers, Claude G. *Jefferson in Power.* Boston: Houghton Mifflin, 1936.

Boyd, Julian P., ed. *The Papers of Thomas Jefferson.* Princeton, NJ: Princeton University Press, 1951.

Brant, Irving. *James Madison: Commander in Chief, 1812–1936.* Indianapolis: Bobbs-Merrill, 1961.

Broadside, Continental Congress. Copy in collection of American Antiquarian Society, 1786.

Brown, Ralph Adams. *The Presidency of John Adams.* Lawrence: University Press of Kansas, 1975.

Brown, Roger H. *Redeeming the Republic: Federalists, Taxation, and the Origins of the Constitution.* Baltimore: The Johns Hopkins University Press, 1993.

"Brutus I." In John P. Kaminski and Gaspare J. Saladino, eds., *The Documentary History of the Ratification of the Constitution.* Madison: State Historical Society of Wisconsin, 1981.

"Brutus V." In Herbert J. Storing, ed., *The Complete Anti-Federalist.* Chicago: University of Chicago Press, 1981.

Buchanan, James M. *The Economics and Ethics of Constitutional Order.* Ann Arbor: University of Michigan Press, 1991.

Buchanan, James M. and Gordon Tullock. *The Calculus of Consent.* Ann Arbor: University of Michigan Press, 1965.

By the United States in Congress Assembled, February 20, 1782. Copy in collection of American Antiquarian Society, 1782.

Caldwell, Lynton K. *The Administrative Theories of Hamilton and Jefferson.* 2d ed. New York: Holmes and Meier, 1988.

Calhoun, John C. *Mr. Calhoun's Defence of the Tariff and Internal Improvement.* (Pamphlet) Philadelphia: N. p., 1831 or 1832.

Callender, James. *A Short History of the Nature and Consequences of Excise Laws.* Philadelphia, 1795.

"Cambridge." *Gazette of the United States,* September 1794.

Carey Mathew. *A Defence of Direct Taxes and of Protective Duties.* Philadelphia: U. Hunt, 1822.

———. *Epitaph.* Philadelphia: N. p., 1832.

———. *Essay on the Dissolution of the Union.* Philadelphia: L. Johnson, 1832.

———. *Essays on Political Economy.* Philadelphia: H. C. Carey and I. Lea, 1822.

Carpenter, Thomas, transcriber. *The Two Trials of John Fries.* Philadelphia: William Woodward, 1800.

"Centinel I." In John P. Kaminski and Gaspare J. Saladino, eds., *The Documentary History of the Ratification of the Constitution.* Madison: State Historical Society of Wisconsin, 1981.

"Centinel II." In John P. Kaminski and Gaspare J. Saladino, eds. *The Documentary History of the Ratification of the Constitution.* Madison: State Historical Society of Wisconsin, 1981.

Chandler, Lester V. *The Economics of Money and Banking.* 4th ed. New York: Harper and Row, 1964.

Charles, Joseph. *The Origins of the American Party System.* New York: Harper and Brothers, 1961.

"A Circular Letter from His Excellency General Washington, etc." Reprinted in *The American Museum or Repository of Ancient and Modern Fugitive Pieces.* Philadelphia, 1787.

Considerations on the Subject of Finance. Pamphlet in collection of American Antiquarian Society, 1779.

Cooke, Jacob E., ed. *The Reports of Alexander Hamilton.* New York: Harper and Row, 1964.

Cunningham, Noble E., Jr., ed. *Circular Letters of Congressmen to Their Constituents.* Chapel Hill: University of North Carolina Press, 1978.

————. *The Process of Government Under Jefferson.* Princeton, NJ: Princeton University Press, 1978.

Dallas, A. J. *Cases Argued and Decided in the Supreme Court of the United States.* Vol. 3. Rochester: Lawyers Co-operative, 1926.

Dewey, Davis R. *Financial History of the United States.* New York: Longmans, Green 1934.

"Direct Taxes! Loans! Fruits of Commercial Restrictions!" Worcester, MA: Isaac Sturtevant, printer, c. 1812.

Dorfman, Joseph. *The Economic Mind in American Civilization.* Vol. 1. New York: Viking Press, 1948.

Dumbauld, Edward. *The Bill of Rights and What It Means Today.* Norman: University of Oklahoma Press, 1957.

"Easton." *The Gazette of the United States,* September 1794.

Elliot, Jonathan. *The Debates of the Several State Conventions on the Adoption of the Federal Constitution.* Vol. 2. New York: Burt Franklin, reprint of 1888.

"Essay by A Farmer and Planter." In Herbert J. Storing, ed., *The Complete Anti-Federalist.* Chicago: University of Chicago Press, 1981.

"Essays of John Dewitt." In Herbert J. Storing, ed., *The Complete anti-Federalist.* Chicago: University of Chicago Press, 1981.

Excise. Copy in collection of American Antiquarian Society. Philadelphia, 1797 (presumed).

"Extract from the Proceedings of Congress." Report of the Board of Treasury, February 8, 1786, *Journals of the Continental Congress,* 1786, quoted in *The American Museum, or Universal Magazine.* Philadelphia, 1787.

Faulkner, Harold U. *American Economic History.* New York: Harper and Brothers, 1929.

Ferguson, E. James. *The Power of the Purse.* Chapel Hill: University of North Carolina Press, 1962.

————. "What Were the Sources of the Constitutional Convention?" In Gordon S. Wood, ed., *The Confederation and the Constitution.* Washington, DC: University Press of America, 1979.

Findlay, William. *A Review of the Revenue System.* Philadelphia: Dobson, 1794.

Fitzpatrick, John C., ed. *Journals of the Continental Congress, 1774–1789.* Washington, DC: U.S. Government Printing Office, 1934.

————. *The Writings of George Washington.* Westport, CT: Greenwood Press, 1970.

Fleming, Thomas. *The Man Who Dared Lightning.* New York: William Morrow, 1971.

Friedman, Milton, and Anna Schwartz. *A Monetary History of the United States.* Princeton, NJ: Princeton University Press, 1963.

"From the Rights of Men to the Enemies of Anarchy." *Gazette of the United States,* December 1794.

Gales, Joseph, comp. *Debates and Proceedings of the Congress of the United States.* First Congress, First Session. Washington, DC: Gales and Seaton, 1834.

Gallatin, Albert. *Report from the Secretary of the Treasury on the Subject of Manufactures, April 19, 1810*. Boston: Ferrand, Mallory and Co., 1810.

——— . *Report of the Secretary of the Treasury on the Subject of Public Roads and Canals* (1808). New York: Augustus Kelley, 1968.

——— . *Views of the Public Debt, Receipts and Expenditures of the United States*. New York: M. L. and W. A. Davis, 1800.

Goebel, Julius, Jr., and Joseph H. Smith. *The Law Practice of Alexander Hamilton*. New York: Columbia University Press, 1980.

Hamilton, Alexander. "First Report on the Further Provision Necessary for Establishing Public Credit." In Harold C. Syrett and Jacob E. Cooke, eds., *The Papers of Alexander Hamilton*. New York: Columbia University Press, 1961.

——— . "The Continentalist, Nos. I–IV." In Harold C. Syrett and Jacob E. Cooke, eds., *The Papers of Alexander Hamilton*. New York: Columbia University Press, 1961.

——— . "Report on the Difficulties in the Execution of the Act Laying Duties on Distilled Spirits." In Harold C. Syrett and Jacob E. Cooke, eds., *The Papers of Alexander Hamilton*. New York: Columbia University Press, 1961.

——— . "Report on a Plan for the Further Support of Public Credit." In Harold C. Syrett and Jacob E. Cooke, eds., *The Papers of Alexander Hamilton*. New York: Columbia University Press, 1961.

——— . "Report on the Improvement and Better Management of the Revenue of the United States." In Harold C. Syrett and Jacob E. Cooke, eds. *The Papers of Alexander Hamilton*. New York: Columbia University Press, 1961.

——— . "Report on a Plan for the Further Support of Public Credit." In Harold C. Syrett and Jacob E. Cooke, eds. *The Papers of Alexander Hamilton*. New York: Columbia University Press, 1961.

Hammond, Bray. *Banks and Politics in America*. Princeton, NJ: Princeton University Press, 1957.

Henry, Patrick. "Speeches in the Virginia Ratifying Convention." In Herbert J. Storing, ed., *The Complete Anti-Federalist*. Chicago: University of Chicago Press, 1981.

"Hints Respecting an American Excise." *The American Museum, or, Universal Magazine*. Philadelphia, September 1790.

History of Congress. 13th Congress. Appendix, 1816, 17th Congress, 1st and 2d Sessions, and 18th Congress. 1822–24.

"History of the National Debt" and "Review of the Revenue System." *The National Magazine* 2 (1799).

Hume, David. "Of Public Credit." In Eugene F. Miller, ed., *Essays: Moral, Political and Literary*. Indianapolis: Liberty Classics, 1987.

——— . "Of Taxes." In Ernest C. Mossner, ed., *An Enquiry concerning Human Understanding and Other Essays*. New York: Washington Square Press, 1963.

"Introduction" and "*Baltimore Maryland Gazette*, May 22, 1788." In John P. Kaminski and Gaspare J. Saladino, eds., *The Documentary History of the Ratification of the Constitution*. Madison: State Historical Society of Wisconsin, 1981.

Jefferson, Thomas. "Autobiography, 1743–1790." In *Thomas Jefferson: Writings*. New York: Library of America, 1984.

——— . *Public and Private Papers*. New York: Vintage Books, 1990.

Jensen, Merrill. *The New Nation: A History of the United States during the Confederation, 1781–1789*. Boston: Northeastern University Press (reprint), 1981.

Johnstone, Robert M., Jr. *Jefferson and the Presidency.* Ithaca, NY: Cornell University Press, 1978.

Kaminski, John P., and Gaspare J. Saladino, eds. *The Documentary History of the Ratification of the Constitution, Vol. XIII, Commentaries on the Constitution, Vol. 1.* Madison: State Historical Society of Wisconsin, 1981.

Keenan, Joseph T. *The Constitution of the United States.* 2d ed. Pacific Grove, CA: Brooks/Cole, 1988.

Kelly, Alfred H., and Winfred A. Harbison. *The American Constitution: Its Origins and Development.* 4th ed. New York: W. W. Norton, 1970.

Kenyon, Cecilia. "Men of Little Faith: The Anti-Federalists on the Nature of Representative Government." In Gordon S. Wood, ed., *The Confederation and the Constitution.* Washington, DC: University Press of America, 1979.

Koch, Adrienne. *Jefferson and Madison: The Great Collaboration.* New York: Oxford University Press, 1964.

Kurtz, Stephen G. *The Presidency of John Adams.* Philadelphia: University of Pennsylvania Press, 1957.

"Lancaster." *Gazette of the United States,* February 1795.

Lebergott, Stanley. *The Americans: An Economic Record.* New York: W. W. Norton, 1984.

Letter from the Chairman of the Ways and Means Committee to the Secretary of the Treasury on the Subject of a system of Revenue to Maintain Unimpaired the Public Credit. Washington, DC: A. and G. Way Printers, 1814.

"Letter of North Carolina Delegates to Governor Richard Caswell." In John P. Kaminski and Gaspare J. Saladino, eds., *The Documentary History of the Ratification of the Constitution.* Madison: State Historical Society of Wisconsin, 1981.

"Letters of Cato." In Herbert J. Storing, ed., *The Complete Anti-Federalist.* Chicago: University of Chicago Press, 1981.

List, Frederich. *Outlines of American Political Economy, in a Series of Letters.* Philadelphia: Samuel Parker, 1827.

Livermore, Shaw, Jr. *The Twilight of Federalism.* Princeton, NJ: Princeton University Press, 1962.

Logan, George. *Letters Addressed to the Yeomanry.* Philadelphia, 1791.

Madison, James. "Observations Written Posterior to the Circular Address of Congress in Sept. 1779, and Prior to their Act of March, 1780," reprinted in *Federal Reserve Bank of Minneapolis Quarterly Review* (Fall 1997), pp. 3–7.

———. *The Debates in the Federal Convention of 1787 Which Framed the Constitution of the United States of America.* Edited by Gaillard Hunt and James Brown Scott. New York: Oxford University Press, 1920.

———. *Letters on the Constitutionality of the Power in Congress to Impose a Tariff for the Protection of Manufactures.* Washington, DC: S. C. Ustrick, 1828.

Malone, Dumas. *Jefferson the President: The First Term, 1801–1805.* Boston: Little, Brown, 1970.

McClellan, James, and M. E. Bradford, eds. *Jonathon Elliot's Debates in the Several State Conventions on the Adoption of the Federal Constitution: Debates in the Federal Convention of 1787 as Reported by James Madison.* Richmond, VA: James River Press, 1989.

McDonald, Forest. *The Presidency of George Washington.* Lawrence: University of Kansas Press, 1974.

McPherson, James M. *Battle Cry of Freedom: The Civil War Era*. New York: Ballantine Books, 1988.

Memorial of the American Society for the Encouragement of Domestic Manufactures. Washington, DC : Gales and Seaton, 1822.

Memorial of the Chamber of Commerce of New York, Remonstrating against the Passage of the Bill to Amend the Several Acts for Imposing Duties on Imports. Washington, DC: Gales and Seaton, 1824.

Memorial of the National Institution for the Promotion of Industry. Washington, DC: Gales and Seaton, 1821.

Message from the President of the United States. Published by order of the House of Representatives, December 1799.

Miller, John C. *Alexander Hamilton: Portrait in Paradox*. New York: Harper and Row, 1959.

————. *The Federalist Era*. New York: Harper and Row, 1960.

Mitchell, Broadus. *Alexander Hamilton: The National Adventure, 1788–1804*. New York: Macmillan, 1962.

Monroe, James. "Some Observations on the Constitution." In Herbert J. Storing, ed., *The Complete Anti-Federalist*. Chicago: University of Chicago Press, 1981.

Morris, Richard B. *The Forging of the Union: 1781–1789*. New York: Harper and Row, 1987.

"Mr. Martin's Information to the General Assembly of the State of Maryland." In Herbert J. Storing, ed., *The Complete Anti-Federalist*. Chicago: University of Chicago Press, 1981.

Nelson, John R., Jr. *Liberty and Property*. Baltimore: Johns Hopkins University Press, 1987.

The New Haven Gazette and Connecticut Magazine. March 1786.

Niles, Hezekiah. "The Prohibitory System." *Niles' Weekly Register,* April 19, 1823.

————. "The Rights of Men and Things." *Niles' Weekly Register,* February 1, 1822; reprint in *Delaware Gazette,* 1823.

"Of Indirect Taxes." *The Weekly Museum*. Baltimore, February 1797, 33.

Paine, Thomas. *The Crisis Extraordinary*. Copy in collection of American Antiquarian Society, 1780.

Paul, Randolph E. *Taxation in the United States*. Boston: Little, Brown, 1954.

Peterson, Merrill D. *Thomas Jefferson and the New Nation*. New York: Oxford University Press, 1979.

"Philadelphia." *Gazette of the United States,* September 1794.

Proposals to Amend and Perfect the Policy of the GOVERNMENT of the United States of AMERICA. Copy in collection of the American Antiquarian Society. Philadelphia, 1782.

Protest of the Legislature of South Carolina, against the System of Protecting Duties, Adopted by the Federal Government. Washington, DC: Duff Green, 1829.

Raguet, Condy. "The Principles of Free Trade," *The Banner of the Constitution*. In George Rogers Taylor, *The Great Tariff Debate, 1820–1830*. Boston: D. C. Heath, 1953.

Rakove, Jack N. *The Beginnings of National Politics*. Baltimore: Johns Hopkins University Press, 1979.

————. *Original Meanings: Politics and Ideas in the Making of the Constitution*. New York: Alfred A. Knopf, 1996.

Ratner, Sidney. *Taxation and Democracy in America*. New York: John Wiley and Sons, 1967.

Raymond, David. *Thoughts on Political Economy*. Baltimore: Fielding Lucas, Jr., 1820.

"Remarks on the Resolves of the Inhabitants of the Western Country of Pennsylvania against the Excise Laws." *The American Museum, or, University Magazine.* Philadelphia, September 1791.

Remini, Robert. *Andrew Jackson and the Bank War.* New York: W. W. Norton, 1967.

Report of the Commissioners of the Sinking Fund. Copy in collection of American Antiquarian Society, 1796.

Report of the House Committee: Appointed to Enquire Whether Any, or What Further Revenues Are Necessary for the Support of Public Credit; and If Any Further Revenues Are Necessary, to Report the Ways and Means. Copy in collection of American Antiquarian Society, 1794.

Report of the Secretary of the Treasury, on the Act for Laying Duties on Spirits and C. Copy in collection of American Antiquarian Society, 1792.

"Report on Finances." *Reports of the Secretary of the Treasury of the United States.* Washington, DC: Duff Green, 1828.

The Report, Ordinance, and Addresses of the Convention of the People of South Carolina, Adopted November 24, 1832. Columbia, SC: A. S. Johnston, 1832.

Ricardo, David. *Principles of Political Economy and Taxation.* 1st American ed. Georgetown, DC: Joseph Milligan, 1819.

———. *Principles of Political Economy and Taxation.* London: Dent (Everyman's Library), 1976.

Riesman, Janet A. "Money, Credit and Federalist Political Economy." In Richard Beeman, Stephen Botein, and Edward C. Carter III, eds., *Beyond Confederation: Origins of the Constitution and American National Identity.* Chapel Hill: University of North Carolina Press, 1987.

Rossiter, Clinton. Introduction to *The Federalist Papers.* New York: Mentor Books, 1964.

Rutland, Allen. *The Presidency of James Madison.* Lawrence: University Press of Kansas, 1990.

Savage, James D. *Balanced Budgets and American Politics.* Ithaca, NY: Cornell University Press, 1988.

Schlesinger, Arthur M., Jr. *The Age of Jackson.* Boston: Little, Brown, 1950.

Slaughter, Thomas P. *The Whiskey Rebellion.* New York: Oxford University Press, 1986.

Sloan, Herbert E. *Principle and Interest: Thomas Jefferson and the Problem of Debt.* New York: Oxford University Press, 1995.

Smith, Adam. *An Inquiry into the Nature and Causes of the Wealth of Nations.* Chicago: University of Chicago Press, 1976.

———. *The Theory of Moral Sentiments.* Edited by D. D. Raphael and A. L. Macfie. Oxford: Clarendon Press, 1976.

"Speech in the Virginia Ratifying Convention." In Herbert J. Storing, ed., *The Complete Anti-Federalist.* Chicago: University of Chicago Press, 1981.

"Speech of Mr. Atherton in Favor of a Repeal of the Direct Tax." Washington, DC: 1816.

"Speech of George Mason, etc." In Herbert J. Storing, ed., *The Complete Anti-Federalist.* Chicago: University of Chicago Press, 1981.

Stabile, Donald R. "Adam Smith and the Natural Wage: Sympathy, Subsistence and Social Distance." In *Review of Social Economy* 55 (Fall 1997): pp. 292–311.

———. *Work and Welfare: The Social Costs of Labor in the History of Economic Thought.* Westport, CT: Greenwood Press, 1996.

Stabile, Donald R. and Jeffrey A. Cantor. *The Public Debt of the United States: An Historical Perspective, 1775–1990.* New York: Praeger, 1991.

Stewart, Donald H. *The Opposition Press of the Federalist Period.* Albany: State University of New York Press, 1969.

Storing, Herbert J., ed., *The Complete Anti-Federalist.* Chicago: University of Chicago Press, 1981.

Studenski, Paul, and Herman E. Kroos. *Financial History of the United States.* 2d ed., New York: McGraw-Hill, 1963.

Swanson, Donald F. *The Origins of Hamilton's Fiscal Policies.* Gainesville: University of Florida Monographs, 1963.

――――. "Thomas Jefferson on Establishing Public Credit: The Debt Plans of a Would-be Secretary of the Treasury?" *Presidential Studies Quarterly* 23 (Summer 1993), 499.

The System of the Laws of the United States, in Relation to Direct Taxes and Internal Duties. Philadelphia: Jane Aitken, 1813.

Taussig, F. W. *The Tariff History of the United States.* 4th ed., New York: G. P. Putnam's Sons, 1892.

Taylor, George R., ed. *Hamilton and the National Debt.* Boston: D. C. Heath, 1950.

――――. *The Great Tariff Debate, 1820–1830.* Boston, D. C. Heath, 1953.

Taylor, John. *An Argument respecting the Constitutionality of the Carriage Tax.* Richmond: Davis, 1795.

――――. *Tyranny Unmasked.* Washington, DC: Davis and Force, 1822.

――――. *An Enquiry into the Principles and Tendency of Certain Public Measures.* Philadelphia: Dobson, 1794.

Thoughts on the Five per Cent. Copy in collection of American Antiquarian Society. Providence, 1792.

Timberlake, Richard H., Jr. *The Origins of Central Banking in the United States.* Cambridge:Harvard University Press, 1976.

"To the American Farmers and Planters." *The American Museum, or, Universal Magazine.* Philadelphia, February 1790.

Walters, Raymond, Jr. *Albert Gallatin: Jeffersonian Financier and Diplomat.* New York: Macmillan, 1957.

Walton, Gary M., and Hugh Rockoff. *History of the American Economy.* 6th ed. New York: Harcourt Brace Jovanovich, 1990.

Webster, Petaliah. *Political Essays on the Nature and Operation of Money, Public Finances, and Other Subjects.* New York: Burt Franklin, 1969.

"Whiskey versus Government." *The American Museum, or, Universal Magazine.* Philadelphia, April 1791.

White, Leonard D. *The Federalists: A Study in Administrative History, 1789–1801.* New York: Free Press, 1948.

Whitten, David O. "An Inquiry into the Whiskey Rebellion of 1794." *Agricultural History* 49 (July 1975): 491–504.

Wickham, John. *The Substance of an Argument . . . in . . . The United States vs. Hylton.* Richmond: Davis, 1795.

Wood, Gordon S. *The Creation of the American Republic, 1776–1787.* Chapel Hill: University of North Carolina Press, 1969.

――――. "Interests and Disinterestedness in the Making of the Constitution." In Richard Beeman, Stephen Botein, and Edward C. Carter III, eds. *Beyond Confederation: Origins of the Constitution and American National Identity.* Chapel Hill: University of North Carolina Press, 1987.

Wood, John. *The Suppressed History of the Administration of John Adams (From 1797 to 1801), As Printed and Suppressed in 1802.* Philadelphia: Printed for the editor, 1845.

INDEX

About the Author

DONALD R. STABILE is Professor of Economics at St. Mary's College of Maryland and Associate Editor of *Business Library Review*. His recent books include *Work and Welfare: The Social Costs of Labor in the History of Economic Thought* (Greenwood, 1996) and *The Public Debt of the United States: An Historical Perspective, 1775–1990* (Praeger, 1991).

ISBN 0-313-30754-7

90000>

EAN

9 780313 307546

HARDCOVER BAR CODE